SANTA A

REPUTATIONS

NAPOLEON

R.S. Alexander

Associate Professor of History,
University of Victoria, Canada

A member of the Hodder Headline Group
LONDON
Co-published in the United States of America by
Oxford University Press Inc., New York

First published in Great Britain in 2001 by
Arnold, a member of the Hodder Headline Group,
338 Euston Road, London NW1 3BH

http://www.arnoldpublishers.com

Co-published in the United States of America by
Oxford University Press Inc.,
198 Madison Avenue, New York, NY10016

The advice and information in this book are believed to be true and
accurate at the date of going to press, but neither the author nor the publisher
can accept any legal responsibility or liability for any errors or omissions.

British Library Cataloguing in Publication Data
A catalogue record for this book is available from the British Library

Library of Congress Cataloging-in-Publication Data
A catalog record for this book is available from the Library of Congress

ISBN 0 340 71916 8

1 2 3 4 5 6 7 8 9 10

Production Editor: Wendy Rooke
Production Controller: Bryan Eccleshall
Cover Design: Terry Griffiths

Typeset in 10 on 12 pt Sabon by Phoenix Photosetting, Chatham, Kent

What do you think about this book? Or any other Arnold title?
Please send your comments to feedback.arnold@hodder.co.uk

Contents

Illustrations

General editorial preface

Hero or villain? Charlatan or true prophet? Sinner or saint? The volumes in the Reputations series examine the reputations of some of history's most conspicuous, powerful and influential individuals, considering a range of representations, some of striking incompatibility. The aim is to demonstrate not merely that history is indeed, in Pieter Geyl's phrase, 'argument without end', but that the study even of contradictory conceptions can be fruitful: that the jettisoning of one thesis or presentation leaves behind something of value.

In Iago's self-serving denunciation of it, reputation is 'an idle and most false imposition; oft got without merit, and lost without deserving', but a more generous definition would allow its use as one of the principal currencies of historical understanding. In seeking to analyse the cultivation, creation and deconstruction of reputation, we can understand better the well-springs of actions, the workings out of competing claims to power, the different purposes of rival ideologies – in short, see more clearly ways in which the past becomes History.

There is a commitment in each volume to showing how understanding of an individual develops (sometimes in uneven and divergent ways), whether in response to fresh evidence, the emergence or waning of dominant ideologies, changing attitudes and preoccupations in the age in which an author writes, or the creation of new historical paradigms. Will Hitler ever seem *quite* the same after the evidence of a recent study revealing the extent of his Jewish connections during the Vienna years? Reassessment of Lenin and Stalin has been given fresh impetus by the collapse of the Soviet Union and the opening of many of its archives; and the end of the Cold War and of its attendant assumptions must alter our views of Eisenhower and Kennedy. How will our perceptions of Elizabeth I change in the presence of a new awareness of 'gendered history'?

There is more to the series than illumination of ways in which recent discoveries or trends have refashioned identities or given actions new meaning – though that is an important part. The corresponding aim is to provide readers with a strong sense of the channels and course of debate from the outset: not a Cook's Tour of the historiography, but identification of the key interpretative issues and guidance as to how commentators of different eras and persuasions have tackled them.

Acknowledgements

I would like to thank Christopher Wheeler, Director of Academic Publishing and commissioning editor at Arnold, for suggesting this project to me in the first place, and for his patience thereafter. Thanks are also due to the anonymous readers who made such helpful suggestions concerning my initial book proposal. To my colleagues Angus McLaren, Greg Blue, Perry Biddiscombe and Tom Saunders I owe a great deal for their sparing of precious time to help with proof-reading; any remaining errors are, of course, solely my fault. To my colleague David Zimmerman I especially wish to express gratitude for his unfailing provision of expertise, encouragement and enthusiasm for history 'for its own sake'. Finally, I suspect that most of us have at least one Napoleonic figure lurking somewhere in our acquaintance or family background. In my case, there is an obvious one and this book is dedicated to Richard 'Dixie' Alexander, an Eagle who flew across the Channel to combat a twentieth-century conqueror.

Introduction

When confronted by the point that some 220,000 works had been written on Napoleon by the mid-1980s, one is inclined to reflect fondly on Morris Zapp's plan to write the definitive study of Jane Austen, so that no one need ever write about her again. Yet, Napoleon will never meet his Morris Zapp. It has become something of a convention to begin a book on the 'life' or the 'times' by apologizing for adding yet another title to the lists, but Martyn Lyons, Charles Esdaille and David Gates surely will not be the last authors to argue that there are lacunae in our knowledge, new studies to be synthesized, imbalances in previous assessments, or new perspectives to be considered. Moreover, how could any author gain sufficient mastery over all the available source material to write something truly definitive?[1]

This book, however, is not a biography or study of the era. Nor is it an attempt to identify the 'real' Napoleon. Very short perusal of Napoleonic historiography reveals that authors have seen in him very different and often contradictory things. Diversity becomes even more apparent if we take into account representation of Napoleon in the graphic arts, music, poetry, fiction and film. It would be inaccurate to describe the result of so many interpretations as a cacophony; certain themes or motifs are repeated and provide a degree of unity. All the same, Napoleon's reputation is a very complex work, and the purpose of this study is to analyse how it has come about.

Napoleon's reputation is composed of images and associations which are interrelated, but which can be detached and viewed in isolation. What is most striking is that there are so many of them:

Napoleon as demon, as conqueror, as *condottiere*, as Mafia god-father, as tyrant, as proto-fascist dictator, as charlatan, as inveterate gambler, as 'Man on Horseback', as embodiment of the 'little man' complex, as destroyer of the Revolution, as heir of the Revolution, as agent of the Revolutionary bourgeoisie, as French patriot, as 'outsider', as European visionary and unifier, as state builder, as modern Prometheus, as exemplar of careers open to talent, as embodiment of the human will, as superman, as the 'Little Corporal' of the people, or as modern Alexander, Caesar, Justinian, Attila, Charlemagne, Mehemet or Christ. This list is by no means exhaustive, but the extraordinary range of what has come to mind when people ponder Napoleon is obvious.

The images and associations tend to compete for predominance. Some are relatively strong, more enduring, and hence more familiar. Others are relatively weak; they might flourish under certain conditions, but they might also fall by the wayside. Some are closely related and potentially complementary: the conqueror and tyrant can walk hand-in-hand and at times have been joined by the modern dictator. But some are antagonistic and have long done battle: the destroyer versus the heir of the Revolution, the egoist versus the visionary, or the superman versus the Little Corporal. At different points in time, some of the images have gained ascendancy, but, perhaps ironically, all are truly Napoleonic in being unable to subdue their rivals permanently. There is no single image that encapsulates Napoleon's reputation.

It is the dynamic of this process that most concerns me. Why is it that certain images and associations dominate perception for a time, subsequently give way to others, and then, perhaps, rise again? In pondering this, I have concluded that there are three main factors which determine the strength of a particular image or association. The first consists of historical evidence. To remain strong within Napoleon's reputation, images and associations need to have sufficient grounding in empirical evidence to be at least plausible. One cannot speak with absolute certainty concerning the future, but for now it can be said that Napoleon as bisexual emperor has not proved a lasting image. On the other hand, 'the facts' alone are seldom sufficient to explain the potency of the leading images and associations.

The second factor lies in what can be termed 'intentional construction', be it by writers, graphic artists, musicians, or whoever seeks to give an impression of Napoleon. Such impressions inevitably entail a certain interpretation of the evidence, or subjective choice as to what should be remembered. An image or association can also be enhanced by sheer artistic ability. Yet, Pieter Geyl's survey of different interpretations in *Napoleon: For and Against* serves as a reminder that not all views are equally credible, and the same holds for images. In the case of Napoleon, debate and contrast place limits on the subjective power of artistic licence, without eliminating it entirely. During the Restoration, an author facetiously argued that Napoleon was, literally, a Sun God; this interpretation enjoyed a certain vogue and was taken seriously by some of the more smitten Napoleonists. But Napoleon as Apollo is now a historical curiosity; it tells us something about Bonapartism, but few authors currently argue that Napoleon was a God.[2]

The third determinant lies in historical context. That contemporary preoccupations often colour interpretation of the past is a fairly conventional observation, and we will find many examples of it. Perhaps less obvious is that Napoleon's reputation has also been affected by the methods employed to examine the past. In the twentieth century, the rise of history 'from the bottom up', structuralism, and cultural history all posed certain challenges to a reputation largely formulated by the 'Great Man' school of the nineteenth century. Moreover, there is a third component of context: historical events or the force of circumstance also shape reputation by focusing attention on certain images. Perception has altered especially due to the advent of subsequent leaders who provided a reminder of certain aspects of Napoleon's reputation. For the nineteenth century, figures such as the Emperor Soulouque of Haiti and General Santa Anna of Mexico shone a particular light on Napoleon, revealing the 'Man on Horseback'. For the twentieth century, the rise of Mussolini and Hitler encouraged perception of Napoleon as the first of modern dictators. But events, rather than individuals, have also shaped the reputation: the mass carnage of World War One was anything but favourable to the 'Little Corporal' image.

As an undergraduate student, I attended a course which featured Wilson Bryan Key, author of a book entitled *Subliminal Seduction: Ad Media's Manipulation of a Not So Very Innocent America*. By the end of the course I could see subliminal messages imbedded in walls and ceilings where others could see only flaking paint. Writing this book has at times been a similar experience, in that colleagues have taken to posting advertisements featuring Napoleon on my office door, or slipping internet news items into my pigeon hole. Idle times in front of the television have been jolted by reminders of Napoleon, reading newspapers has been much the same, and even passing buses have informed me that the streets are no safe haven. This has left me wondering why advertising agents find reference to Napoleon so useful in, say, 'pitching' a certain alcohol, automobile or, my favourite, barbecue.[3]

The names Napoleon and Bonaparte obviously hold strong connotations, but the key lies in how readily recognizable the name, image and associations are. Napoleon is so imbedded in our culture that we immediately recognize certain visual symbols, especially those of the 'Little Corporal': the *bicorne* (cocked hat), grey frock-coat and black boots. Certain poses are 'Napoleonic': the hands folded behind the back, or the right hand tucked inside the vest or waistcoat. These images are so strong that another face can be superimposed upon Napoleon's body and we still know to whom the figure is alluding, and what he connotes. In North America, at least, Napoleon has long been an icon of consumer culture; for over a century he has stood for what one can acquire provided one works hard enough.

Among historical figures there are very few who can rival Napoleon as an icon in contemporary western media. A number of reasons can be put forward for this. For one thing, he was the most prominent person in a period which is still considered as marking the advent of modern history. Partly for this reason, he has been associated with forces (changes in social structure and new forms of polity) which continue to affect the contemporary world. Similarly, he has often been viewed as a prototype for some phenomenon which, while it may be discernible in earlier times, took a more familiar appearance in him. Napoleon as the first modern dictator is a familiar example, but a similar line of thought lay behind citing him as the quintessential example of careers open to talent.

Not all of the associations are modern; a theme in portrayal has been to view Napoleon as a 'throwback' to the times of Attila, Genghis Khan or Tamerlane. Yet, such analogies have declined over time, perhaps reflecting contemporary media's preference for history as seen through film footage or photographs. Moreover, association with figures such as Caesar or

Attila usually refers to a very general phenomenon, that of conquering, and one can cite many more recent examples of this sadly familiar historical theme. At base, fascination lies in the acquisition of power, at home or abroad, and Napoleon continues to loom large in computer and board games. He was certainly a keen competitor and, as we are often reminded, he cheated at cards.

What distinguishes Napoleon from other leading modern figures who wielded extraordinary power is that his reputation is composed of such diverse images and associations. The difference is perhaps more one of degree than kind, but it seems fair to say that while the connotations evoked by, say, reference to Hitler or Stalin are preponderantly negative, those of Napoleon are a mixture of positive and negative. While other 'greats' such as Churchill or Kennedy might have a more positive connotative balance sheet, they do not have the fascinating attributes of conquering and possession of seemingly absolute power. At the end of the day, there is little doubt that Napoleon acquired great power, but whether this was for better or worse for suffering humanity remains very much subject to dispute.

At varying points, Napoleon has been linked to almost all of the leading 'isms' of our age: liberalism, conservatism, fascism, totalitarianism, republicanism, royalism, individualism, egoism, socialism, patriotism, nationalism, chauvinism, militarism, cosmopolitanism, sexism, neo-classicism and Romanticism. That such divergent associations have been made points to the protean character of the reputation, but it also suggests a certain hollowness at the core. How can any individual be seen as representative of so many opposed forces?

The protean nature of the reputation results partly from the simple fact that so much is known, and has been said, about Napoleon. Like most individuals, he progressed through various stages, and if one wants, one can identify any of these stages as being definitive. But the ambiguity surrounding Napoleon's reputation also derives directly from the 'ism' that his life most consistently illustrated – opportunism. Perhaps the most appropriate image of Napoleon is that of chameleon, a creature which alters its appearance according to its surroundings. Even the famous change of name illustrates his willingness to alter identity in terms of where opportunity lay.

Napoleon was the opposite of a 'conviction politician'. His

often expressed dislike of *idéologues* and the emphasis he placed
on pragmatism spoke clearly of his subordination of principles to
what was useful in the immediate context. This is not to say that
he was completely unprincipled, or that principles are necessarily
an unmitigated virtue. At least in domestic politics, Napoleon
was very skilled when it came to necessary compromise, and he
never let principles blind him to such factors as public opinion.
But Napoleon was a creature of circumstance, which meant that
he and the principles he espoused altered dramatically over the
passage of time.

Most important was that Napoleon had the consummate
political skill of allowing others to see in him what they wanted
to see. He had learned a great lesson from the execution of Louis
XVI, and he was determined to shape his public image through
propaganda. Yet, beyond consistent association with greatness,
what is most striking about Napoleon's self-portrayal is his willingness to attach himself to anything that might be considered
positive at the time. Napoleon referred to his own life as a novel,
suggesting that it was something to be crafted for public appeal,
and it is this malleable aspect of his character that is his most
beguiling feature.

He certainly succeeded in his pursuit of lasting fame. Partly
this is a product of the significance of what he did. But he has also
continued to hold attention due to what Geyl termed 'the debate
without end' over his claims to greatness. Each age provides its
own answer to the question of whether he was great. More
interesting is that successive generations see him in such differing
ways. Changing times do, of course, offer new perspectives, but
it is also true that the ambiguity at the core of his life offers
endless opportunity for new interpretations to arise.

How does one approach such an elusive subject? It is obvious
that not all of the works in which Napoleon is portrayed or
considered can be taken into account. Moreover, a contention of
this book is that the reputation has been shaped by developments
subsequent to Napoleon's death, and the broad sweep of history
also lies largely beyond our grasp. Given this, I have settled for a
thematic approach which concentrates in individual chapters on
some of the more powerful images and associations, but which
continuously analyses the process by which the reputation has
evolved. The reputation will continue to evolve, but one can seek
to identify how the three factors cited above have shaped it.

In the first chapter I have provided a basic account of Napoleon's life and times, assuming that not every reader will be familiar with the materials upon which the reputation is partly founded. In this chapter, I have also included discussion of how Napoleon sought to set the terms for subsequent interpretation, even as he went about making his mark on history. As an aid to memory, I have also provided a chronology at the end of the book.

Decisions as to how to define Chapters 2–8 have not been easy, but I have tried to shape the work with three basic points in mind. First, the process of change in the reputation is the primary consideration. I do not think it necessary to consider all Napoleonic images and associations to identify this process, although I have sought to include a broad sampling. Given that my focus is upon change, I have paid more attention to volatile images and associations – those which are sometimes prominent, but are significantly less conspicuous at other points in time. Certain images, however, tend to be relatively stable within the reputation. Academics do, of course, frequently assess whether Napoleon was a 'Great Commander', and conclusions vary. Yet, the 'Great Commander', rightly or wrongly, is largely fixed in Napoleon's public reputation. For this reason, I have not devoted an entire chapter to the 'Great Commander' image, but I have included it as an integral part of the more volatile image of 'Man on Horseback' discussed in Chapter 3.[4]

As a second principle, I have sought to provide ample consideration of the evolution of Napoleon's reputation in both the nineteenth and twentieth centuries, although the volume and intensity of debate over his 'meaning' were greater in the nineteenth. This has led to some chapter formulations which may initially seem odd. It would have been interesting to have extended consideration of Napoleon and the Left beyond the Great War, but I think the basic elements of the relationship emerge clearly enough within the more narrow definition. The same line of thought lay behind restricting discussion of the 'Man on Horseback' to the nineteenth century, but here there were other considerations affecting definition. Most studies of the 'Man on Horseback' focus on the twentieth century, and concentrating on the nineteenth century struck me as a means of complementing, rather than duplicating, available literature. This meant forgoing several fascinating examples, including General De Gaulle and Emperor Boukassa, but the possibilities are limitless and one cannot entirely please everyone, including oneself. Moreover, there is an obvious relation between Chapters 3 and 4, and the latter primarily concerns the twentieth century. De Gaulle could also have been included in Chapter 7 as a Napoleonic state builder, but this ground has already been instructively travelled by Philip Thody, and I chose to emphasize the more global dimension of the image, particularly through reference to Mehemet Ali and Kemal Atatürk.[5] Other decisions also were necessitated by confining myself to the realm of the possible. Discussion of cinema in Chapter 6 could have been greatly extended, but my purpose was simply to make a basic point concerning the decline of the 'Little Corporal'. Many volumes could have been written on Napoleon and Europe, but given the availability of Geyl's *Napoleon* and the complement Geoffrey Ellis has recently provided in his *Napoleon*, there seemed no pressing need to reconsider older sources in Chapter 8. It is difficult to say anything unfamiliar concerning Napoleon, but one can at least try.

The third guiding point is that I have sought to investigate Napoleon's reputation as a global phenomenon. Most historical figures remain largely within national confines and only a few imbed themselves in a broader culture; Napoleon is one of the latter. Thus I have not restricted myself to how French artists and writers have depicted Napoleon, although they have played a pre-eminent part in the construction of his reputation. As a means towards assessing the global nature of the reputation, I have at various points considered figures who gained the appellation 'the Napoleon of'. The frequency with which this term is still used, I think, tells us a great deal about several of the essential characteristics of the reputation.

It also says something about Napoleon's reputation that a certain vocabulary has developed in discussion of it. The subject of memory construction is very much in vogue in academic circles at present, but I have sought to eschew the more arcane elements of academic discourse, preferring to employ language that is readily familiar to non-specialists. Nevertheless, I should explain my usage of certain terms. First, it helps to distinguish between the cult of Napoleon and the Legend. In this work, the cult of Napoleon will refer to admiration, bordering on worship, of Napoleon as an individual. I will use the 'Legend' to refer to interpretation of the Napoleonic period as a 'golden age'. Most often authors use this term to refer to the Empire, but the basic idea holds for the Consulate as well. A third term, the 'Black Legend', refers to reaction against both the cult and the Legend, and consists of deprecating Napoleon and his period of rule. Terms such as legend and myth often crop up in Napoleonic literature, but at times their usage can be problematic. In his *Reflections on the Napoleonic Legend*, Albert Guérard essentially defined the Legend and cult as all that was falsely alleged about Napoleon and his period of rule. He had a point, but I find his formula too confining. The cult, Legend and Black Legend were not entirely based on fiction or entirely mythical. At least in part, they all derived from facts which can be verified empirically. On the other hand, they often included great exaggeration and some of their components were entirely based on deliberate falsehood. The mixing of truth and lies does not, of course, render them any less meaningful or significant as historical phenomena. But when I use the terms I will be referring to beliefs which contained a mixture of fact and fiction. In the latter regard, they were akin to the central images of the Napoleonic reputation.[6]

Notes

1 The rather Napoleonic Morris Zapp appears in David Lodge's *Changing Places* (London, 1975). See also M. Lyons, *Napoleon Bonaparte and the Legacy of the French Revolution* (London, 1994), pp. 1–4, C. Esdaille, *The Wars of Napoleon* (London, 1995), pp. ix–xi, D. Gates, *The Napoleonic Wars 1803–1815* (London, 1997), pp. xvi–xix. F. McLynn makes the point about voluminous source material in the preface to his *Napoleon* (London, 1998).
2 See A. Sonnenfeld, 'Napoleon as Sun myth', *Yale French Studies*, 26 (Fall–Winter 1960–61), pp. 32–6.
3 W.B. Key, *Subliminal Seduction: Ad Media's Manipulation of a Not So Very Innocent America* (Englewood Cliffs, N.J., 1972).
4 Readers who would like to investigate Napoleon's current status as 'Great Commander' can turn to P.J. Haythornthwaite *et al.*, *Napoleon: The Final Verdict* (London, 1996), noting David Chandler's opening comment.
5 Several twentieth-century 'Men on Horseback' can be found in A.R. Willner, *The Spellbinders: Charismatic Political Leadership* (New Haven, 1984). See also P. Thody, *French Caesarism* (Basingstoke, 1989).
6 A. Guérard, *Reflections on the Napoleonic Legend* (London, 1924).

1

The life and times

Before considering Napoleon's reputation, it makes sense to consider the materials that artists and writers have drawn upon in seeking to interpret or portray him. Roughly speaking, these materials fall into three broad categories: biographical information, the events in which Napoleon participated, and Napoleon's relation to the salient developments of his era. Representation of Napoleon inevitably involves subjective selection of which materials should be considered. This observation certainly holds for the summary of the 'life and times' that follows, but the latter has been written with the objective of simply introducing the main areas of discussion, while keeping interpretation to a minimum. First in the queue of those who sought to reveal the 'true' Napoleon, however, was Bonaparte himself. To follow the development of his reputation, we need to take this component into account from the very start, and hence it will provide a central theme in this chapter.[1]

Corsican patriot

Napoleon has often been described as an 'outsider': he was born in Corsica, spoke French with a Corsican accent, and for much of his early life identified with the cause of Corsican independence. Having purchased the island from the Republic of Genoa in 1768, the French had commenced their rule by repressing a revolt led by the patriot Pasquale Paoli. Defeat at Ponte Novo on 8 May 1769 had commenced twenty years of exile in England for Paoli, and left the Buonaparte family with decisions to make.

Born at Ajaccio on 15 August 1769, Napoleone Buonaparte was the second son of Carlo and Letizia. Preceded by Joseph in 1768, he would be followed by (taking only those who survived into adult years into account) Lucien in 1775, Elisa in 1777, Louis in 1778, Pauline in 1780, Caroline in 1782 and Jerome in 1784. Potentially compromised by his part in Corsican resistance, Carlo entered into collaboration. By doing so he acquired recognition of family claims to nobility, and was also able to pursue his legal career while gaining election to the Corsican Estates as a deputy of the nobility. All of these improvements were facilitated by Count de Marbeuf, military governor of the island. Whether Marbeuf's patronage stemmed from more than friendly relations with Letizia is a matter of debate, but sure it is that Marbeuf's favours were crucial to the opportunities grasped by young Napoleone.

No individual entirely escapes familial and social origins. Evaluating the import of such influences is by nature imprecise, but it is clear that Napoleone's most important early ties were to his mother and Joseph. Carlo was often absent, pursuing career interests and adulterous liaisons, and Letizia ran the household. She was thrifty and resourceful, and this was important because, while the household was never truly impoverished, there were points when family fortunes were low. Relations between Letizia and Napoleone were tempestuous; the mother was a disciplinarian, while her second son was determined to be the centre of attention. The initial target of much of young Napoleone's assertiveness was Joseph, and when push came to shove, the elder brother yielded.

Social conditions have provided much grist for interpretive mills. Corsica did not possess a dominant landowning nobility and extremes of wealth were not a feature of social relations. Moreover the influence of the state was negligible, giving the island a frontier ethos in which family honour and vendetta provided an informal and essentially lawless code for relations. One can see in such conditions a breeding ground for meritocracy – mediocrity of fortunes encouraging struggle for success based on achievement. On the other hand, one can also link Corsica's lawless nature to Napoleon's penchant for imposing order.

Equally seminal to character formation was Napoleone's education in the army. He entered the military school of Brienne (in Champagne) in April 1779, and passed on to Paris in October

1784, graduating as a sub-lieutenant in September 1785. His initial posting was at Valence, where he was commissioned as a lieutenant, prior to entering the artillery school at Auxonne in June 1788. Napoleone created opportunities for himself through excellence in mathematics, and this, in combination with engineering skills, made his entry into the artillery a wise choice. Prospects for promotion based on merit were higher in the artillery due to the importance of technical expertise. One should not overstate matters however; entry into Brienne had been due to Marbeuf's patronage.

These early stages can readily be accommodated to the image of 'outsider'. Relative poverty, inferior social status and awkwardness in personal relations assured that Napoleone spent long hours alone, honing his work ethic. Yet, if he ran up against *ancien régime* prejudice, the lax professionalism of the old order also allowed him to pursue interests close to his heart. He was well read in the classics, fascinated by accounts of distant lands, and fond of history. He also read widely in Enlightenment literature and was influenced by Rousseau. The latter enthusiasm was shared by an entire generation, but in Napoleone's case Rousseau was particularly appealing because the author showered praise on 'nobly savage' Corsica. Napoleone took to writing a potted history of his native isle.

A striking aspect of Napoleone's early career was how little time he spent in France. Between September 1786 and June 1788, with the exception of three months of lobbying in Paris for family financial interests, Napoleone was on leave in Corsica, asserting his primacy as head of the family (Carlo had died in 1785), and seeking contact with old Paolists. Between September 1789 and February 1791 he was again in his *patrie*, throwing himself into local politics. The Buonapartes identified themselves with the Left, and Napoleone was a founder of the Ajaccio Jacobin club. Among connections forged at this time was one with Christophe Antoine Saliceti, a deputy of the Constituent Assembly who played a leading role in gaining amnesty for Paoli in February 1790. The triumphant Paoli was then named governor of Corsica in July 1790. Prior to returning to France, Napoleone was commissioned to write a polemic attacking Paoli's Corsican rivals. Return to the mainland did not, however, last long; Buonaparte served at Auxonne and Valence until October 1791, but then journeyed back to Ajaccio. To avoid recall to the regular army, in March 1792 he secured election as a lieutenant-colonel in the National Guard. While support from Paoli was secured, rough handling of Pozzo di Borgo during speeches confirmed a dangerous personal rivalry. The key to immediate prospects lay in relations with Paoli. Suspicion in the Paolist camp ran deep due to previous Buonaparte collaboration with the French, and this was exacerbated by fragmentation in the Paolist movement. While the Buonapartes were part of a radical wing, Paoli moved steadily to the right, drawing closer to the likes of Pozzo. Complicating matters was that prolonged leave jeopardized Napoleone's place in the army, so that he had to pass much of the summer of 1792 in Paris, lobbying for reinstatement. Relations with the Paolists unravelled further when in October 1792 Napoleone's request that Lucien be made Paoli's *aide-de-camp* was rejected. Thus prospects in the Paolist camp looked poor when the Paolists rebelled against increasingly radical French rule in 1793. A brief attempt to repress the revolt, involving Saliceti and the Buonapartes, failed and the Buonaparte clan had to take flight, arriving at Toulon in early June.

For the virtually destitute Buonapartes, the future lay in France; that they recognized this could be seen in their change in spelling of the family name. Napoleone Buonaparte became Napoleon Bonaparte thereafter. Whether the future lay with the Revolution was, however, less clear. To the extent that Napoleon had seen the French Revolution, as an officer subduing grain riots close to Auxonne, or as witness to the massacre of Swiss Guards in Paris in August 1792, he had drawn conclusions that fit uncomfortably with Revolutionary idealism. Indeed, his main observation concerning the crowd in August was how easily it could have been repressed.

Officer of the Republic

According to some, Bonaparte was the quintessential example of how the Revolution of 1789 opened careers to talent. In the *ancien régime* army, opportunities were severely limited by prejudice in favour of social status; while Napoleon could claim nobility, he was hardly an aristocrat. But with its assault on absolutism (beginning with the assertion of sovereignty that transformed the Estates General into the National Assembly in June–July 1789) and destruction of formal social hierarchy (begun on the night of 4 August 1789), the Revolution alienated many nobles. By limiting the powers of the throne, and through a programme of secularization which greatly reduced the authority of the Catholic Church, the National (June 1789 – September 1791) and Legislative (October 1791 – September 1792) Assemblies furthered noble alienation. Resultant counter-revolution was by no means simply a noble affair, but the number of noble officers who went into exile or retired from service greatly enhanced the prospects of those who remained. Meanwhile war against the First Coalition, commenced in April 1792, brought vast expansion of the army; by August 1794 France had roughly 800,000 men in the field.

Invasion by Austrian and Prussian forces radicalized politics in the summer of 1792, giving rise to the storming of the Tuileries on 10 August, and the prison massacres of 2–7 September. Elections then produced the Convention (September 1792 – October 1795), in which two Jacobin factions, the relatively moderate Girondins and extremist Montagnards, vied for control. The first act of the Convention was to declare France a republic on 21 September 1792; Louis XVI was executed for treason on 21 January 1793. Power was centralized for prosecution of the war effort by creation of the Committees of Public Safety and General Security in March and April, and another Parisian insurrection in early June purged Girondins from the Convention. This left government largely in the hands of extremists such as Maximilien Robespierre, and Terror became state policy for uniting France through repression of dissent.

The repercussions of this radicalization were vast. In the course of combatting, at one point or another, most of the other European Powers, France took a major step towards total war. While initial expansion resulted partly from an infusion of 100,000 volunteers in 1792, recourse had to be made to con-scription, which contributed to the outbreak of royalist civil war in the Vendée in March 1793. The growing influence of Parisian radicals also provoked the federalist revolt of 1793–94. Federalism was largely republican in character, but it amounted to civil war against Montagnard extremism. For part of 1793 cities such as Bordeaux, Marseilles, Toulon and Lyons were in open defiance of the central government.

War also contributed to dramatic growth of the state. In part this was attributable to economic mobilization. But it was also true that, to secure popular rallying, the Jacobins began a host of social reforms, ranging from replacing Catholic hospitals and charities with government institutions, to expansion of a secular education system. Most such initiatives failed due to the draining of resources by the war effort and the replacement of Montagnard rule by more conservative regimes during Thermidor (August 1794 – October 1795) and the Directory (November 1795 – November 1799). Yet, an important precedent had been set.

What did all of this mean for Napoleon? It certainly improved prospects for promotion; by early 1793 roughly three-quarters of the *ancien régime* officer corps had departed. Expansion increased the number of senior offices, although it also meant that Bonaparte would have to compete for the public spotlight with a growing number of rivals. But at a more profound level, Napoleon's opportunities were enhanced by the political and social impact of the Revolution. From the declaration of war onwards, the fate of Revolutionary France became directly linked to battle, and the status of the army rose accordingly. Moreover, the role of the army in repressing dissent steadily grew, increasing both the politicization of military command and the militarization of politics.

Political positioning was crucial to Napoleon's fortunes. When they arrived at Toulon, just prior to federalist revolt in July 1793, the Bonapartes were aligned with Montagnard Jacobinism. Napoleon strengthened such ties with *Le Souper de Beaucaire*, a pamphlet arguing that Montagnard and Girondin conflict played into the hands of the real enemy – royalism in the Vendée. This was music to the ears of Saliceti, who had been appointed Representative on Mission to the army at Toulon by the Committee of Public Safety. Saliceti gave a copy to Augustin Robespierre and arranged a meeting between Napoleon and General Carteaux, in charge of the siege of Toulon.

Toulon marked Bonaparte's entry onto the public stage. His part in driving the British from France's principal naval port, in turn, illustrated the importance of both influence in high places and martial ability. Napoleon's plan was to take Fort Eguillette, which would make the position of the British fleet untenable. Execution of the plan, however, necessitated overcoming Carteaux's objections, which would not have occurred without the intervention of Saliceti. Success in December 1793 brought promotion in February 1794 to the rank of brigadier-general, and appointment as commander-in-chief of artillery of the Army of Italy.

If political 'pull' had advantages, it also carried liabilities. The latter became apparent after the fall of the Robespierrists, when Thermidor commenced a period wherein power shifted to the right. Saliceti, to save his own skin, denounced Bonaparte as an agent of the Robespierre brothers and both Napoleon and Lucien were incarcerated for most of August 1794. Subsequently, when he realized his position was safe, Saliceti had the Bonapartes released and Napoleon reinstated in the army. Thereafter Napoleon found a more centrist position in the patronage of Paul Barras. However, when in May 1795 the Committee of Public Safety ordered him to transfer to the Army of the West, Bonaparte refused; he considered it below his professional dignity to fight Vendéan peasants.

Fortune sometimes favours the bold. When the Convention proclaimed a new constitution with a proviso that a new parliament would be composed largely of members of the outgoing one, anger in Paris led to a royalist uprising on 5 October 1795. Barras, in charge of the Convention's troops, put Napoleon in command of the artillery. Although his role in repressing revolt has been exaggerated, Bonaparte's 'whiff of grapeshot' did restore government favour. By 26 October he had been named commander of the Army of the Interior, and in March 1796 he was appointed commander of the Army of Italy and promoted to the rank of general. Attachment to Barras proved shrewd in that he had been elected to the governing executive directory. It was also Barras who pointed his former mistress, Josephine de Beauharnais, towards Napoleon. A Creole and mother of two (Eugène and Hortense), she had been fortunate not to share the fate of her husband, executed during the Terror. It would be unfair to label Josephine a 'gold-digger', given the limited options for women in her position. Nevertheless, her attachment to Napoleon, six years her junior, was anything but an affair of the heart; her adultery became notorious. Bonaparte was, however, truly smitten.

Continued warfare was both a curse and blessing for the Thermidorean and Directorial regimes. From the defeat of the Austrians at Fleurus in June 1794 onwards, France was largely on the offensive; fortunes fluctuated, but most fighting was conducted elsewhere. Gradually perseverance gained reward; in March 1795 peace was negotiated with Prussia, and in June Spain came to terms. Conquest in Belgium and Luxembourg (annexed to France in September 1795), and the east bank of the

German Rhine (placed under military occupation), and reduction of Holland to satellite status as the Batavian Republic (in May 1795), brought compensation in the form of taxes, requisitions, forced tributes and brute plunder. Supply contracting and war profiteering created new fortunes and, in combination with purchase of nationalized lands confiscated from the Catholic Church and French *émigrés*, contributed to massive redistribution of wealth.

Yet war also took a huge toll. Poor harvests, exacerbated by military requisitioning, meant that famine stalked the land in the mid-1790s. Conflict with Britain, entailing the loss of overseas trade, shattered the economies of maritime cities. Although the Jourdan Law of September 1798 put conscription on a more equitable basis, high rates of desertion and draft-dodging produced huge bands of brigands who could be put to the purposes of counter-revolution. By the end of the Directory, the majority of departments had been placed under state of siege, and an increasing number of the French had sought solace in return to the Catholic faith. Religious and grain riots illustrated deteriorating civil order. If war provided the means by which Napoleon gained recognition, it also contributed to the conditions that favoured his appeal as a man of order.

The first of the Italian campaigns (April 1796 – April 1797) revealed several key features of Napoleon's rise. Italy was not intended by the government to be the main theatre of operations; it was Bonaparte's victories that made it so. Victory also played a decisive role in galvanizing an army expected to live off the land. Among the leading profiteers were the generals; while Napoleon did little to rein in their predatory instincts, he did assert his authority over potential rivals such as Sérurier, Augereau and Masséna. His performance on the field was not uniformly brilliant; he was fortunate at Arcola (15–17 November 1796) when the Austrians failed to exploit vulnerable French positioning. Yet, most of the famous skills and tactics were on display – rapid movement, concentration of forces at decisive moments, ability to innovate, and steadiness of nerve. Bonaparte exploited his victories with army bulletins and newspaper reports proclaiming him 'Saviour' of France.

Italy also gave Napoleon his first taste of rule. He encouraged collaboration with hints of future Italian unification; creation of the Cispadane Republic (comprising Modena and the Legations) and then the Cisalpine Republic (adding

Lombardy and Bergamo to the Cispadane) fostered such illusions. The Cisalpine gained a constitution modelled on that of
France, and French laws were introduced, including civil
marriage and nationalization of Church lands. Such reforms
fired the hopes of Italian Jacobins, but Bonaparte was more
interested in the support of elements attracted by civil order
rather than democratization. Yet, Napoleon was also ruthless
when it came to looting, especially of art treasures. Victory also
enabled Bonaparte to direct foreign policy. He conducted negotiations with Austria according to his own lights, but the
Directory was in a poor position to complain when the Treaty
of Campo Formio (signed on 17 October 1797) forced Austria
to accept creation of the Cisalpine Republic. As a sweetener,
Bonaparte conquered the Republic of Venice and handed it
over to the Habsburgs. For the moment the First Coalition was
broken, but it was highly improbable that Britain or Austria
would accept the *status quo*, and meanwhile conflict in German
lands had yet to be resolved.

For Napoleon, peace was a mixed blessing. Having returned to
Paris in December 1797, he established relations with Charles
Maurice de Talleyrand-Périgord, a wily Revolutionary veteran
currently serving as Foreign Minister. Although Bonaparte had
helped Barras in the coup of Fructidor against royalists in
September, suspicions between Napoleon and the directors were
mutual. Bonaparte avoided obvious alignment and cultivated an
image of disinterested *savant*; entry into the Institut enabled him
to rub shoulders with the French intelligentsia. After months of
futile preparation for an invasion of Britain, Napoleon took up
an alternative scheme for troubling France's remaining adversary.
The Ottoman Empire was already viewed as the 'sick man of
Europe', and thus suitable for depredation, but at a strategic level
possession of Egypt might pose problems for British naval power
in the Mediterranean. Better yet, it could perhaps provide a
means to harass the British in India by linking up with Tipoo
Sahib, Sultan of Mysore. The expedition also appealed to
Napoleon's 'oriental complex', a fascination with the Middle
East. The scientific expedition that accompanied the military
campaign was not a cause for the enterprise, but it did fuel public
interest.

The campaign began well. After taking Malta, the French
landed in Egypt in late June 1798. Alexandria and Cairo had
fallen by late July, and French military and technological

superiority enabled them to inflict massive defeats on Mameluke forces. But invasion of Syria went awry and Napoleon suffered his first major defeat when the French failed in the siege of Acre in April–May 1799. By then Nelson's destruction of the French fleet at Aboukir Bay on 1 August 1798 had ended any hope of reinforcements. Revolt in Egypt necessitated brutal repression, while plague took a harsh toll on the troops in Syria. Meanwhile the expedition had encouraged formation of the Second Coalition (Britain, Austria, Russia, Naples and Turkey), and news of French losses in the European theatre had given Bonaparte a pretext for abandoning a lost cause. In August 1799 he departed.

The Egyptian campaign was a defeat, but it became a classic example of Napoleon's ability to shape his own reputation. Bulletins despatched to France depicted episodes such as the battle of the Pyramids (July 1798) in terms calculated to thrill a generation raised on readings of classical antiquity. No mention was made of the execution of several thousand prisoners at Jaffa, nor of euthanasia of wounded French soldiers unable to join in retreat. More enduring was the impact of the scientific expedition, as some 167 scholars studied the pyramids, charted the land, and stumbled upon the Rosetta stone. His association with the founding of Egyptology gave Napoleon the image of visionary. On the other hand, there was something less exalted in his commencement of serial adultery when forced to acknowledge the truth about Josephine's infidelity.

Republican consul

At the start of the Consulate (November 1799 – May 1804), Bonaparte declared that the Revolution was over. Yet, did the Consulate constitute consolidation or reversal? When Bonaparte returned to France in August 1799 he was certainly guided by ambition, but whether he had plans for dictatorship is by no means clear. The *coup d'état* of Brumaire (18–19 November 1799) was in fact conceived by others – principally the abbé Sieyès and Roger Ducos, directors, Talleyrand and Joseph Fouché, the Minister of Police. Lucien would play a part as president of the lower house of parliament, but Napoleon was at best third on a list of generals whom the *brumariens* initially considered as the means to assure acceptance by the army.

Napoleon did not perform well during the seizure of power. His task was to assure that the Councils of Five Hundred and Ancients accepted allegations of Jacobin conspiracy and followed directions to reassemble at Saint Cloud, distancing them from any support Paris might offer. But resistance surfaced when the two Councils gathered at Saint Cloud, and Napoleon's hectoring of the parliamentarians only worsened matters. The turning point occurred when Lucien harangued the troops, alleging that the deputies had attacked his brother. Led by Murat, Napoleon's brother-in-law, the troops rapidly cleared the assembly. Afterwards a rump of parliamentarians was rounded up to pass laws dissolving the Directory and creating a new regime.

Among the *brumariens* it was only Bonaparte who had a significant power base, essentially in the army, but also in public popularity. Sieyès and Ducos could hardly appeal to Jacobin or royalist elements; Talleyrand and Fouché were trimmers with no broad following; and supporting members of the intelligentsia known as the *idéologues* appealed only to a small band of liberals like themselves. Bonaparte did not, however, have a constitution to put forward, and thus he had to work with one presented by Sieyès. The key lay in Bonaparte's ability to block plans for division of powers. The executive consisted of three consuls, but Bonaparte insisted that he would be First Consul and the other two would simply advise. Theoretically, the consuls were to be elected by a Senate, yet Napoleon secured an initial period of office for ten years. Thus he gained control of administrative and military appointments and could choose his own ministers, who were responsible solely to him. The First Consul could also initiate laws through the Council of State, a body, appointed by the executive, which gathered information for proposed bills and watched over the administration and judiciary.

Among three houses of parliament, control over the Senate was crucial. The Legislative Chamber and Tribunate were composed of members chosen by the Senate from a list of 6000 notables determined by a plutocratic system of indirect elections. Moreover, the Senate could issue decrees called *senatus consulta*, a mechanism for bypassing the legislature altogether. The Senate was appointive, mostly by the executive. One should not over-state matters; dictatorship progressed gradually. But when a liberal opposition began to coalesce in the Legislative Chamber and Tribunate, influence over the Senate enabled Bonaparte to have critics purged in early 1802. By August 1807 the Tribunate had been abolished altogether, and from 1802 onwards the Legislative Chamber never once rejected a proposed bill. For their part, the senators cooperated with the executive, encouraged by the creation of senatories (land grants yielding substantial revenues) in 1803.

Subversion of parliamentary independence was facilitated by inept opposition. Royalists initially hoped that Bonaparte might orchestrate a Bourbon Restoration, but he soon disabused them of such notions. Thus they renewed counter-revolution. A bomb placed on Bonaparte's route to the opera on 24 December 1800 missed its target, but left dozens of victims strewn on the road. Although Fouché knew the origins of the attempt, Bonaparte preferred to round up and deport some 129 Jacobins. It was expedient to do so, given the Left was opposing the regime's use of military tribunals for imposition of law and order.

Tactics were similar in early 1804, when another plot was uncovered. Arrest of Generals Pichegru and Moreau removed two of Napoleon's personal rivals; the former perhaps committed suicide while in prison, and the latter was banished. Because the conspiracy included plans for a leading Bourbon to raise revolt in France, Bonaparte made an example of the Duke of Enghien, ordering his abduction from Baden and summary execution in Paris on 20 March. Enghien in fact had played no part in the conspiracy, but assassination attempts declined precipitously thereafter. Better yet, the argument that only Bonaparte stood between France and Restoration provided the pretext for making him hereditary Emperor in May.

Illustrative though these examples were, they would not have yielded such high returns had Bonaparte not triumphed where it most counted. Even before the coup of Brumaire, the Second Coalition had begun to unravel as Czar Paul withdrew support after Russo-British forces had been forced to retreat from the Netherlands. Allied fortunes in Italy, however, had been much better, enabling them to reverse Campo-Formio. To secure the Consulate, in the early months of 1800 Bonaparte took steps to stamp out internal rebellion. General Brune was directed to strike into the heartland of revolt in the Vendée and Brittany, shooting captured rebels and burning villages. In the event, British failure to supply sufficient gunpowder forced rebel leaders to seek terms, and by 21 April republican troops could be transferred to the east.

That Napoleon's position remained tenuous could be seen in

Moreau's refusal to make Germany the main theatre of operations; hence Italy again became crucial. The Second Italian campaign in fact started badly, as Bonaparte committed several blunders capped off by dividing his forces immediately prior to the battle of Marengo on 14 June. It was only the timely return of troops under Desaix that prevented defeat. Desaix, however, died in the fighting, enabling Bonaparte to monopolize glory as the French reoccupied Lombardy and Piedmont. Peace negotiations came to little until Moreau dealt the Austrians a decisive blow at Hohenlinden on 3 December. With the door open to Vienna, the Austrians conceded defeat. By the terms of the Peace of Lunéville of 8 February 1801, French domination of northern Italy and the left bank of the Rhine was again recognized.

Only Britain remained intransigent, but here too there were promising developments. True, the British did retake Malta in September 1800, but Czar Paul's claims to it led him to form the League of Armed Neutrality, by which Russia, Sweden, Denmark and Prussia sought to block British trade from the Baltic. Assassination of Paul in March 1801, however, brought Alexander I to the throne, signalling another policy shift. When Nelson shelled Copenhagen and commandeered Danish ships, the Russians offered little aid and the League sank. Moreover, British and Turkish troops defeated the remaining French forces in Egypt in August. Yet, the latter fostered peace by removing a central British concern. In the end, the Peace of Amiens of 25 March 1802 resulted from mutual exhaustion and desire for a 'breathing space' on both sides. Britain recognized France's continental acquisitions, but not the 'sister' republics, and yielded most of the maritime conquests taken since 1792.

Lunéville and Amiens enabled Bonaparte to make the new regime his own, as skyrocketing popularity allowed him to advance claims to represent the nation personally. Plebiscites told the story. In February 1800, 1,550,000 Frenchmen voted in favour of the already inaugurated new constitution. This was not an impressive figure, and hence Lucien massaged the returns so that they were announced as 3,011,007 in favour. By August 1802, when it was time to endorse Bonaparte as First Consul for life, no such manipulation was required to produce a vote of 3,653,600 in favour. A similar level of approval, 3,572,329 votes, was given to his proclamation as hereditary Emperor in May 1804.

Peace with victory also gave Bonaparte the opportunity to

undertake a fundamental restructuring of state and society. The Revolutionary 'watchwords' of liberty, equality and fraternity were replaced by those of order and unity, and the latter were pursued by applying military forms of organization. Chain of command, with power emanating from the top and filtering downwards through delegation, was pervasive. Complementing the corrosion of parliamentary independence were the Fundamental Laws of February 1800. These transferred local government from elected bodies to state-appointed agents, led by a prefect in each department. Local and departmental councils did remain, but their function was simply to advise. Similarly, members of the judiciary would be appointed rather than elected.

Political liberty was not, however, the sole guiding objective of the Revolution. Rationalization of government administration had been part of the work of the Constituent Assembly, and from the standpoint of efficiency the record of the Consulate was impressive. Fiscal order was rapidly achieved, partly through creation of the Bank of France, and partly through more effective tax collection. Improved revenues enabled the state to expand public works, and the regime gained a reputation for drawing talented personnel who would implement its policies. All such initiatives, however, rested upon ability to impose the rule of law. Napoleonic unity through repression of factionalism amounted to obedience to one man and his state, but it did mean that the vast majority could pursue their day-to-day lives with increasing security.

Effective government came at a cost. From very early on, the rule of law was eroded when it came to holding the state accountable. Substitution of military tribunals for regular courts of law was probably necessary to reduce brigandage, yet it was part of a package in which expansion of the activities of the *gendarmerie* and the police under Fouché took on the character of a police state. Freedom of association, either political or social, could hardly prosper, given Bonaparte's antipathy towards any organization that might contest state authority. Freedom of expression was also sharply curtailed. Criticism of the state was driven underground by publication restrictions, beginning with a Consular order of January 1800 reducing the number of Parisian newspapers from seventy-three to thirteen. By 1811 there were but four and they had become government organs, a clearing house for official opinions which were then retailed to a greatly reduced departmental press. Similar controls were applied to the arts, and state patronage was directed solely towards those who sang praises to the regime.

State control of society also lay behind the Concordat negotiated with the Papacy. Signed on 16 July 1801, the Concordat was not published until April 1802, by which time Bonaparte had appended a series of organic articles unapproved by Pope Pius VII. Catholicism would be recognized as the religion of the majority of French citizens, but there would be no backsliding in terms of religious toleration and similar arrangements would be made with the Protestant and Jewish minorities. Previous sales of nationalized Church properties were declared irrevocable. Election of clergymen would end; bishops would appoint lower clergymen, subject to government approval, while the First Consul would nominate bishops and archbishops, whom the Pope would invest. Clergymen would swear an oath of allegiance to the regime, while the state would provide salaries. Ultimately the Concordat helped to pacify troublesome regions, cutting ground out from under royalism. Problems remained, but for the most part the clergy served as an effective instrument of the state, preaching the virtues of submission to authority.

Equally momentous was proclamation of the Civil Code on 21 March 1804, although this was but part of a package designed to include criminal, commercial, rural and civil procedure codes. While lending Bonaparte the image of modern Justinian, the Civil Code sought to accommodate liberal Revolutionary legislation to the more conservative character of emergent Napoleonic society. The code confirmed equality before the law, completed the extinction of feudalism and strengthened the rights of private property. It also reinforced patriarchy. While equal division of inheritance among all heirs was largely maintained, provisions were introduced for granting a greater share to the eldest male. Similarly, divorce was retained, but grounds were restricted and laws concerning adultery were frankly bigoted.

Beginning with the law of 1 May 1802, the state also embarked on expanding and regimenting educational institutions. *Lycées*, state-run secondary schools, were to be set up in roughly every second department. Entry would be based on competition for 6400 scholarships, but 2400 were set aside for the sons of government officials and military men. That service to the state was the ultimate value could also be seen in the Legion of Honour, founded on 19 May. The Legion conferred status and gave pecuniary award, but members did not gain fiscal or legal privilege. No one was excluded on the basis of social origin or religion, but the first large distribution of decorations at Boulogne in 1804 pointed to a very narrow conception of merit. Of the 2000 decorated, only a dozen were civilians. The lavish Imperial coronation of 2 December 1804 symbolized the transformation of France when Napoleon I crowned himself and Josephine. Power had been personalized by one of history's most startling examples of the 'self-made' man. Even Josephine had been subdued; while she could indulge in conspicuous consumption, males were no longer on the menu. It would be false to assert that France had been dragged kicking from Republic to Empire, but it was true that no one knew where the Emperor would take the nation that had placed its fate in his hands.

Emperor

Had the Empire meant peace, would there have been so much ado about Napoleon? Prior to renewal of war with Britain in May 1803, France had achieved her 'natural frontiers' (the Atlantic coastline, the Pyrenees, the Mediterranean coastline, the Alps and the Rhine River). Annexation of the Austrian Netherlands (Belgium) could be considered part of this objective, but addition of Piedmont suggested that more than defence of territorial integrity was at play. Moreover, the French sphere of influence had been greatly extended. The Batavian Republic (Holland), Helvetic Confederation (Switzerland), Republic of the Valais, Ligurian Republic, Italian Republic and Kingdom of Etruria (north-west of the Papal States) were satellites, while the north German states of Hanover and Oldenburg, and Neuchâtel, Parma and Lucca were occupied by the French.

Defeat of Austria in late 1805 enabled further penetration into central and south Europe. By September 1806 France had grown again, through annexation of the Ligurian Republic. The Holy Roman Empire was terminated and replaced by the Confederation of the Rhine (a satellite). Northern Italy saw creation of the Kingdom of Italy (with Napoleon as monarch), a combination of the former Italian Republic with Venetia, while in the south the Kingdom of Naples also became a satellite. Evidence of Napoleon's 'oriental complex' could perhaps be seen in occupation of lands on the east coast of the Adriatic Sea – Istria, Dalmatia and Ragusa.

Humiliation of Prussia in October 1806, forcing Prussia and Russia to sign the Treaties of Tilsit in July 1807, and another victory over Austria in July 1809 enabled more expansion. By the end of 1810 Holland, part of Hanover, the Hanse towns, the Grand Duchy of Oldenburg, the Illyrian Provinces (wherein the Adriatic possessions were extended northwards by the addition of former Habsburg lands), the Kingdom of Etruria, the Papal States and Rome itself had been added to the Empire. Much of north Germany had been reconstituted as the satellite Kingdom of Westphalia, and the Grand Duchy of Warsaw had been carved out between Prussia and Russia. Moreover, with the occupation of Lisbon in November 1807 Napoleon had begun intrusion into the Iberian peninsula.

On paper, the Empire looked overwhelming in early 1812. It had been massively expanded, was surrounded by puppet states, and Norway, Denmark, Prussia and Austria had been forced into alliance. The Third Coalition (formed by Britain, Austria and Russia in August 1805), Fourth Coalition (formed by Britain, Russia, Prussia and several smaller states in July 1806), and Fifth Coalition (formed by Britain, Austria and Spanish insurgents in April 1809) had all been despatched. Yet the greater Empire (including the satellites) lacked unity and stability; it had been patched together with lightning speed and incessant warfare prevented consolidation.

The fate of the Empire always depended on Napoleon's martial skills. There is room for debate over the latter, although only a small minority argue that Napoleon was not an inspired commander. Nevertheless, it does appear that Napoleon's skills diminished after the triumphs of Austerlitz (2 December 1805) and Jena (14 October 1806). Failure to subdue Spain had more to do with personal neglect and absence than his performance when in the field, but his record was abysmal during the Russian campaign of 1812. He was better at Lützen and Bautzen (2 and 21 May 1813), but the 'Battle of Nations' at Leipzig (16–19 October 1813) was another catastrophe. Some of his best fighting occurred during the campaign of France in 1814, yet the bottom line was that he failed to break Allied unity.

What lay behind the rise and fall of the Empire? Some authors locate causality in Napoleon's dynastic and familial agenda, and indeed there is something reminiscent of a Mafia godfather in

Napoleon's placement of relatives on European thrones. Joseph became King of Naples in March 1806 and was then 'promoted' to the Spanish throne in October 1808; Joachim Murat was made Grand Duke of Berg in March 1806 and he and wife Caroline (Bonaparte) were then transferred to rule Naples in July 1808. Louis was appointed King of Holland in June 1806 and Jerome became King of Westphalia in July 1807. Was all of this based on an assumption that his relatives would prove loyal agents? Or were such arrangements merely provisional? After all, Holland was annexed to France in July 1810 and similar plans were afoot for Westphalia.

Who would benefit by creation of a unified empire? With one vital exception, none of the Bonapartes held the Empress in much regard. Few of the Emperor's liaisons were dangerous for Josephine, although his affair with the Polish Marie Walewska did combine affection with rutting. More problematic was Josephine's inability to produce an heir. Ultimately the search for a son led to marriage on 2 April 1810 to Marie-Louise, daughter of the Austrian Emperor Francis I. The way had been paved by divorce of Josephine at the end of 1809, though not with papal approval. Austrian willingness to ignore Pius VII, who had excommunicated Napoleon in June 1809, illustrated the supremacy of power politics. By 20 March 1811 the King of Rome had been sired.

Napoleon always claimed that his wars were necessitated by the aggression of other rulers. When victories were gained, changes had to be made to secure France through creation of friendly regimes. As part of the process, European peoples would be liberated from decadent dynasties, and they would benefit by reforms modelled on French state and society. Some analysts dismiss this 'spin doctoring' entirely, seeing the Imperial episode as evidence of the dangers of appeasement. Others argue that Napoleon was an exponent of *réal politique*; he was not the only warmonger, and his ambition was neither insane nor completely unbridled. Assessment of foreign policy involves so much information that we cannot even begin to address the basic materials within the confines of this chapter, but we can at least point to some of the main lines of debate among historians. There were in fact two propositions in Napoleon's argument: one concerning why the Empire expanded, and the second concerning the nature of the Empire. We can take these in turn, starting with the causes and costs of the Napoleonic wars.

Historians find much evidence of provocation on both sides prior to the rupture of Amiens. Franco-British rivalry then provided a thread that tied all of the subsequent wars. Partly this was a matter of Britain's financing of the various Coalitions, but it also resulted from Bonaparte's continuation of Revolutionary attempts to drive British influence out of the continent. The most notorious of Napoleon's initiatives was the Continental Blockade, begun in November 1806; it was designed to exclude British commerce from Europe, partly in retaliation for British crippling of French overseas trade. Enforcement of the Blockade then provided Napoleon with at least a pretext for subsequent aggressive actions, including intervention in the Iberian peninsula and the Russian campaign of 1812.

Franco-British rivalry was, however, just one piece in a giant puzzle of inter-state relations. The continental Powers had their own reasons for combatting French expansion and their priorities were often very different from those of the British. Napoleon's creation of satellites deeply wounded the interests of the other Powers and could be viewed (by both sides) as a step towards further French expansion. Moreover, the treaties that Napoleon imposed after victory were often so draconian as to invite further conflict. On the other hand, all of the Powers had long demonstrated pronounced predatory instincts, and each of them played at least some part in provoking the wars in which they were involved. Prussia was bent on war after Napoleon's creation of the Confederation of the Rhine in July 1806, and Czar Alexander was spoiling for a fight in 1812. Similarly, why should the French accept that Italy was an Austrian 'sphere of influence', or that British interests dictated a friendly regime in the Netherlands? Thus the question arises as to whether Napoleon was more sinned against than sinning. There is, however, little sign that debate over the matter is at an end.

The costs were enormous. In the Napoleonic Wars, France appears to have lost roughly 916,000 men, including 38 per cent of the cohort born between 1790 and 1795. Figures for the satellite states were also appalling. Of 52,000 Westphalian troops who entered the Grand Army, 18,000 survived. The Kingdom of Italy contributed 30,000 men to the war in Spain, of whom 9000 lived to tell tales of horror; for the Russian campaign the figures were 27,000 souls and 20,000 corpses. For Europe as a whole, a recent estimate places mortalities at three million for military men, and another million for civilians.[2]

Towards what end? Two sorts of evidence can be presented in determining the nature of the Empire. The first consists essentially of French plundering abroad. Part of the price of Empire lay in the fiscal burdens Napoleon imposed on satellites and the tributes he extracted from defeated opponents. The Grand Duchy of Warsaw and the Kingdoms of Italy, Holland, Westphalia and Spain were driven into bankruptcy; war indemnities cost Saxony 25,375,000 *francs* in 1806, Austria a combined total of 125,000,000 *francs* in 1805 and 1809, and Prussia 112,000,000 *francs* in 1808. To this was added the burden of occupation by troops who lived off the land. Enforcement of the trade embargo against Britain caused enormous commercial dislocation everywhere, and this was exacerbated by Napoleon's Continental System. Based on tariff regulations, the Continental System was designed to reduce satellites such as the Kingdom of Italy to agricultural colonies so that France might become the industrial centre of the continent.

The Empire also included a spoils system which Napoleon used to foster elite allegiance, primarily in France. Large land endowments abroad were given to leading (especially military) officials, or used to provide revenues for pensions. This gave the elite a vested interest in defending the outer reaches of the Empire, but such policies could also encourage endless appetite for further conquering. Moreover, the spoils system was tied to reintroduction of social hierarchy in France. The granting of formal honours by the state began in early 1800 and progressed gradually through creation of institutions such as the Legion of Honour in May 1802, the senatories in January 1803, and appointment of ten 'grand dignitaries' and ten 'grand civil officers' at the time of the proclamation of the Empire in May 1804. In March 1808 Napoleon created a full Imperial nobility, with titles such as prince, count, baron and *chevalier*.

Plunder and recreation of social hierarchy raise basic questions about Napoleon's assertion that he was rescuing European peoples from reactionary dynasties. Yet, there is also evidence that Napoleon's conquering did spread core elements of the French Revolution. First of all, reintroduction of social hierarchy did not constitute a return to the *ancien régime*. Titles did not bring fiscal or legal privileges, and it would appear that only roughly 200 titles were hereditary. More importantly, Napoleon instituted the same model of state and society that had been established in France during the Consulate. Thus alongside plunder, one finds a second characteristic of the Empire: profound attack upon the *ancien régime*.

The French introduced their highly activist and highly centralized state apparatus. A consequence was heightened emphasis on building roads and bridges, draining swamps, improving postal systems, and spreading use of vaccines. In search of collaboration, the Empire targeted elites and hence imposition of civil order was paramount. The Emperor did not always insist upon immediate implementation of the Napoleonic Code (so named from 1807 onwards), with its formal abolition of feudalism, but policy decisions persistently pointed in the direction of uniform and complete application. There was a sinister side to this: imposition of egalitarian French inheritance laws was designed to erode the independence of powerful (mostly noble) families and reduce them to dependence on state favour. On the other hand, some of the more positive elements of reform provoked the most antagonism: secularizing marriage, legalizing divorce, or granting full civil rights to minorities ran smack up against popular attachment to what Voltaire labelled *l'infâme*. One can see indigenous bigotry as resistance, and blithe dismissal of it as French chauvinism. One way or another, even limited application of the French model looked Revolutionary to most Europeans. Was this, however, for the people, or to organize them better for further, global conquest? Debate over the purpose and character of the Empire continues.

Authors once portrayed the wars of liberation of 1813–14 as a manifestation of emergent mass nationalism, allegedly the main offspring of the Empire. As evidence they pointed to the civil war in Spain, and massive rebellions in the Tyrol and various parts of Italy. On the whole, however, the Empire does not appear to have been much threatened by internal rebellion, and recently historians have cast doubt on whether mass nationalism was much in evidence. Popular resistance is now more frequently attributed to defence of particular interests and local customs from state intervention. Attention thus shifts from nationalism to the extent to which European regimes subsequently adopted the Napoleonic model. From this perspective, modernization of state and society emerges as the main consequence of the Empire.

Ultimately, the Empire fell because Napoleon failed to extricate himself from Spain prior to taking the Grand Army deep into Russia. The Imperial edifice then rapidly collapsed because it had been hastily cobbled together, but the key to liberation lay in Coalition regular armies. Britain's doggedness counted for much,

although her ambitions were apparent to all, making the
'vampire of the seas' as much a source of Allied discord as unity.
Although the Sixth Coalition (composed, progressively, of
Russia, Sweden, Britain, Prussia, Austria and various smaller
states) expanded through 1813 and held in 1814, this was largely
due to Napoleon's unwillingness to settle for anything less than
victory. What that victory was meant to bring, however, remains
very much subject to debate.

Phoenix

When he was forced to abdicate on 6 April 1814, the odds
against Napoleon salvaging his rule were very long indeed. Yet,
because treachery entered into the final act, it was possible to
maintain that defeat was due to betrayal. The marshals lied when
they told Bonaparte that their troops would no longer fight.
Could Paris have been made the equivalent of Moscow and the
war continued? Talleyrand's riposte was that it was Bonaparte
who had betrayed France by jeopardizing the Revolution with
warmongering. Similar sentiments were perhaps to be seen in
administrative irresolution in the hour of crisis, the call of the
Legislature for peace in December 1813, and the Senate's collaboration with the Allied Powers in proposing a new constitution in
April 1814.

Napoleon's best advocate was always the Bourbon monarchy.
The Allies granted lenient terms in the First Treaty of Paris of 30
May 1814; France would return to her 1792 boundaries, but
there would be no reparations. By the Treaty of Fontainebleau,
Napoleon was exiled to Elba, over which he would rule, replete
with a miniature army. France would provide a stipend of two
million *francs*, although Francis I would hold Marie-Louise and
Napoleon's son as surety for good behaviour. The Allies also
leaned on the restored Louis XVIII until he granted France a
constitution, known as the Charter. The First Restoration was,
however, undermined by poor judgement. Measures in favour of
the first two Estates appeared to herald the return of privilege,
expiatory ceremonies in honour of Louis XVI, Marie-Antoinette
and Enghien raised doubts about promises in the Charter to
forget past divisions, and promotion of former rebel leaders to
plum military positions spoke very little of careers open to talent.
By the end of 1814 plotting against the regime was already afoot.

Napoleon was apprised of much of this and opportunity seemed to beckon.

Napoleon's escape and return to Paris in March 1815, the Flight of the Eagle, carried a remarkable example of image alteration. In proclamations issued upon first landing, close to Antibes, General Bonaparte charged that the Bourbons had 'learned nothing and forgotten nothing' during their exile; subsequently he thundered that he would hang priests and nobles 'from the lamp-posts' if they did not desist in attacking the rights of the nation. Meanwhile he and perhaps a thousand followers marched their way through the Alps towards Grenoble. Troops sent to confront him at Laffrey instead fell in line behind the 'Saviour'. All along the route numbers were swelled by peasants; at Grenoble civilians tore down the city gate. Reception at Lyons was similarly rapturous. Louis XVIII departed for Ghent on the night of 19 March.[3]

France during the Hundred Days presented a complicated picture. Napoleon only partially fulfilled the Revolutionary expectations he had encouraged. He called in Benjamin Constant to help in a revision of the Imperial constitution called the Acte Additionnel. Slightly more liberal than the Charter, the Acte disappointed democratic elements and secured only 1,552,942 favourable votes in a plebiscite. There were, however, strong reasons for fence-sitting; despite Napoleon's avowal that he would respect the First Treaty of Paris, the Allied Powers made clear their intention to have done with him once and for all.

While government did not bring a return of Jacobinism, there were enough reminders of the Revolution to give Napoleon's new image a certain credibility. If inclusion of Fouché in the cabinet counted for little, Carnot, organizer of victory in 1793, was another matter. To a surprising extent, the press was left to write what it pleased and the government encouraged development of a federative movement. Partly paramilitary in nature, the federations were formed by a combination of old Jacobins, liberals and partisans of the Empire. They were a response to Napoleon's claim that he ruled on the basis of national sovereignty, but especially they indicated opposition to Bourbon rule in a bipolar world.

Napoleon fell for a second time due to defeat at Waterloo on 18 June. He had managed to put a sizeable army in the field, but it was poorly equipped and badly led. Unlike in 1813–14, this time the Allies made no pretence of waging war only against a tyrant, and not France itself. The nation was, however, by no means uniform in support of the Imperial regime. The vast majority made no choice at all, and royalism did have significant strongholds in the West and the Midi. Yet when all was said and done, royalist revolt in the Vendée was but a faint echo of the 1790s, and attempts by the King's nephew Angoulême to organize resistance in the Midi had yielded derisory results. Once again there was material for subsequent claims of betrayal. Among the parliamentarians, some wanted to continue the fight as a republic, others hoped for a regency under Napoleon II, and some remained loyal to Napoleon I. Amidst the cacophony, Fouché organized capitulation, forcing Napoleon to abdicate again on 22 June, and preparing the way for a Second Restoration. The former Emperor threw himself upon the mercy of the British, who duly transported him to the remote island of Saint Helena. He would be kept under lock and key from October 1815 onwards.

For his part, Napoleon evinced great respect for liberty after power had been stripped from him. In a sense, he had become a media 'superstar', and he used this to appeal to public opinion. The element of tragedy was strong, whether he was viewed as fallen hero or false idol, and pathos was added by isolation from his wife and son. The modern Prometheus put his long hours of reflection to effect, placing his stamp on interpretation of his life and times. He assembled an extensive library so that reference to the past could be given factual verisimilitude. To keep abreast of evolving opinion, he read newspapers such as the *Morning Chronicle* and *Journal du Commerce*, journals and pamphlets of the day. This enabled him to respond to critics directly, while flattering liberals with a message attuned to their ears.

Two main types of work resulted. The first consisted of short memoirs, pamphlets and the occasional newspaper article on topical matters. The second was composed of diaries kept by his aides and subsequently published. In terms of the reputation, the diaries were the most influential. Three presented the Emperor as he wanted: Dr O'Meara's *Napoleon in Exile* (1822), Emmanuel de Las Cases's *Memorial de Sainte-Hélène* (1823) and the Comte de Montholon's *History of the Captivity of Napoleon at St Helena* (1846). A fourth, General Gourgaud's *Sainte-Hélène, Journal Inédit (1815–1818)*, was more sceptical but was not published until 1899.[4]

The *Memorial de Sainte-Hélène* has had the most impact. Covering the first eighteen months of Napoleon's exile, the work presents a journal of Napoleon's daily life and records conversations with him. The *Memorial* thus provides Napoleon with a platform to interpret the past in a way which subtly verifies his previous propaganda. It is, however, Las Cases who directly attacks anti-Napoleonic propaganda, which serves to deflect some of the polemical nature of the work from Napoleon himself. Moreover, Las Cases presents Napoleon as speaking frankly, with no calculation and convinced that history will verify his words. This impression is reinforced by occasional Napoleonic recognition of error, sometimes concerning major decisions such as intervention in Spain, but also regarding regrettable treatment of worthy individuals. But the work is no *mea culpa*: Napoleon's motives are always good and, after all, who would not have lost their temper occasionally amidst so many vexations and while undertaking so much hard labour?

Sympathy for the subject is elicited through several dramatic artifices. The *Memorial* constantly alternates between scenes of past glory and depictions of to what the 'Great Man' has been reduced at Saint Helena. Although the Emperor remains vigorous, hopping off his horse to plough a furrow in a field, dark clouds are gathering. Reports on his health and the growing gloominess of his reflections on the fate of his son are repeated themes. Napoleon shows fortitude and a great deal of humour; he is a deep thinker who enjoys reading and analysis of 'great works', and he can invigorate others through organizing activities – games, jaunts in the countryside, or gardening. But he is a man of action harmed by the persecution of the British authorities; the Eagle chafes against the tightening fetters placed on his every movement. Relations with Hudson Lowe quickly become a test of will in which all the advantages are on the side of a cruel and boorish 'gaoler'.

In his conversations Napoleon emerges as a son of the Revolution who has sought to curb its excesses. He had sought to reconcile the *ancien régime* to the Revolution without sacrificing the latter's essential principles. He was a dictator, but concentration of power was essential to stop Europe from becoming two mutually destructive armed camps. Order was a means to save liberty from the clutches of anarchy, but sage liberty was always the objective. Indeed liberty and national sovereignty are the inevitable way of the future and Napoleon has been their greatest champion. Already Europe is coming to regret the loss of the Empire, which had not been defeated, but betrayed.

The *Memorial* concludes with Las Cases finding confirmation of Napoleon's predictions in response to news of the Emperor's death in 1821. He reflects upon the words of the messiah: 'I shall gain ground every day on the minds of the people. My name will become the star of their rights; it will be the expression of their regrets.' He then quotes a speech by Lord Holland in the British parliament: 'the very persons who detested this great man have acknowledged that for ten centuries there had not appeared upon earth a more extraordinary character'. Here we have the essence of Bonapartism: the 'Great Man' who was the representative of the people. Nothing could have been a more fitting ending for the bible of Napoleonists, but the wars over Napoleon's reputation had just begun.[5]

Notes

1 As the following consists mostly of narrative, I will refrain from detailed notation. For readers who wish to pursue 'the life and times' in more detail, the following are particularly recommended. Among recent scholarly works, see D.M.G. Sutherland, *France 1789–1815* (London, 1985), W. Doyle, *The Oxford History of the French Revolution* (Oxford, 1989), I. Woloch, *The New Regime* (New York, 1994), M. Lyons, *Napoleon Bonaparte and the Legacy of the French Revolution* (London, 1994), G. Ellis, *Napoleon* (London, 1997), P. Schroeder, *The Transformation of European Politics 1763–1848* (Oxford, 1994), and M. Broers, *Europe under Napoleon 1799–1815* (London, 1996). For a lively popular biography, see F. McLynn, *Napoleon* (London, 1998).

2 See C.J. Esdaille, *The Wars of Napoleon* (London, 1995), pp. 110 and 300.

3 See R.S. Alexander, *Bonapartism and Revolutionary Tradition in France* (Cambridge, 1991), pp. 1–2.

4 See P. Gonnard, *The Exile of St Helena* (London, 1909). When an English edition of a work exists, it will be the source cited; otherwise, the French title will be cited in the text and notes.

5 See E. de Las Cases, *Memorial de Sainte-Hélène. Journal of the private life and conversations of the Emperor Napoleon at Saint Helena* (London, 1823); the quotes are from volume IV, part VIII, p. 315.

|2|

Heir of the Revolution? Napoleon and the French Left prior to World War One

Upon first glance, the Napoleonic legacy appears irreconcilable with the principal elements of the Left – liberalism, republicanism and socialism. As political traditions, all three located their origins in phases or aspects of the Revolution which Napoleon had terminated or repressed. Yet from 1814 to 1914, each of the three sought accommodation with Napoleon's reputation when circumstance warranted. In pondering why, it helps to keep in mind that many of France's leading political writers were also practising politicians.

In 1814 and 1815 France was twice invaded, and in the latter case defeat was followed by occupation until late 1818. Napoleon had fought the 'barbarian hordes' tooth and nail, until he was forced to step aside. He then shared in humiliation, exiled on a distant, barren rock. He had returned during the Hundred Days proclaiming himself once again as the 'Saviour' of the Revolution. He had held yet another plebiscite to demonstrate that he was the choice of the people, unlike the Bourbons, who were twice restored by foreign intervention but never willing to base their rule on the sovereignty of the nation. In the eyes of many Frenchmen, Napoleon had become indelibly linked to defence of the *patrie*.

Napoleon's image of arch-patriot would not have been so troubling for politicians and writers had Bonapartism not emerged as a rival political movement. Each of the three other traditions found ways to grant Napoleon limited approval as an heir of the Revolution when it suited them. Until roughly 1840 Bonapartism was not in fact perceived as an immediate threat because it consisted mostly of sentiment, lacking doctrinal clarity and political organization. Because it was ambiguous, Bonapartism intermixed with other political movements that shared opposition to counter-revolution. Thus Napoleon's reputation derived vitality partly from perceptions of shared heritage with other political traditions.[1]

Matters changed with the advent of Louis-Napoleon, who set himself up as the chief interpreter of his uncle. Worse still, he seized power and established what he termed Napoleonic government in 1851–52. Differences with liberalism and republicanism rose to the fore. In the 1860s Napoleon III sought accommodation with the Left, but this process was shattered by military defeat at Sedan in 1870.

In the long term, the fall of the Second Empire released Napoleon's reputation by diminishing association with his nephew. Bonapartism contracted in doctrinal terms, becoming fixed on the political Right, and it also declined as a political movement. While Bonapartism still remained a threat, the Left attacked Napoleon's reputation fiercely, but by the 1890s there was a perceptible softening. In a period of constant international tension, the Left again began to find a certain shared heritage with the great symbol of patriotism. He did have a place, albeit a qualified one, within the Revolution of the Great Nation.

As we will see in subsequent chapters, the battle over Napoleon's relation to the Revolution was not confined to France. In Restoration Europe, many writers used a certain version of Napoleon as a club against political reaction. That Napoleon, from exile, claimed to have been an agent of liberalism and nationalism enhanced his appeal. The latter diminished, however, when Napoleon III founded a second French Empire. Despite Louis-Napoleon's posturing as advocate of national self-determination, his policies bore the hallmarks of 'France first', triggering unfavourable memories of the conquering Napoleon I. In an age of growing mass nationalism, the French could more readily view Napoleon as their champion, and it was only in France that the cult of Napoleon gave birth to a distinct political movement.

There were several reasons for the Left to accommodate the Napoleonic heritage. Personal interest might point towards compromise, or pragmatism might lead to combination with Bonapartists against common enemies. Confronted by such advantages, the obvious strategy was to accentuate palatable elements, while playing down the less desirable aspects. Thus the Left became engaged in defining the 'true' Napoleon.

One might expect such accommodation to have been most difficult for Napoleon's contemporaries, yet one can find many examples of it. Certain republicans did remain entirely hostile while Napoleon ruled. The abbé Grégoire and Charles Lambrechts retained their positions in the Imperial Senate, but they used them to lead a tiny opposition to the Emperor. Unlike other senators, they were not rats scuttling off a sinking ship in calling for the first abdication and devising a new proposed constitution in 1814. Neither of them rallied in 1815.[2]

On the other hand, many republicans eventually made their peace with Napoleon. Lazare Carnot opposed creation of the Empire and cultivated political obscurity during most of it. The prospect of invasion in 1813, however, brought Carnot out of retirement; he distinguished himself in the defence of Antwerp in 1814 and served as Napoleon's Minister of the Interior during the Hundred Days. Behaviour was similar among the intellectuals known as the *idéologues*. To some extent, desire to have their ideas published justified compromise. Thus P.-C.-F. Daunou, purged from the Tribunate but compensated with the post of Imperial archivist, mixed his writings against clerical despotism with panegyrics to Bonaparte. A.-L.-C. Destutt de Tracy praised the Imperial regime's efforts to improve the material welfare of the masses, although he also published his liberal *Commentaire sur l'esprit des lois*, anonymously and beyond the reach of Imperial censorship, in Washington in 1811. If this was not complete subservience, neither was it utter intransigence.

More striking were the paths of the era's two leading liberals – Germaine de Staël and Benjamin Constant. Neither had much cause to admire Bonaparte. De Staël exercised considerable influence in the 1790s, due partly to her literary ability, and partly to her networking activities in Parisian salon politics. She was initially attracted to the republican general, but she encouraged Constant to organize resistance to Bonaparte's destruction of parliamentary government in the early years of the Consulate. During the sessions of 1800 and 1801, such opposition did gain some victories, but Bonaparte's growing power soon enabled him to silence critics. For Constant, this meant removal from the Tribunate; for de Staël, it meant exile from Paris.[3]

Divorce from the regime encouraged both to write bitter diatribes. De Staël's *De la littérature considérée dans ses rapports avec les institutions sociales* launched her onslaught on military despotism in April 1800 and this was followed in December 1802 by the hostile novel *Delphine*. Thereafter both liberals were essentially writers in exile; de Staël's *On Germany* was banned from the Empire in 1810, and Constant's *On the Spirit of Conquest and Usurpation* was published in Hanover and London in early 1814. In the latter, Napoleon was portrayed as an anachronistic warlord, fundamentally at odds with the pacific trends of modern society's commercial orientation.

By the fall of the Empire, both authors had become closely tied to the cause of 'European liberation', but in the spring of 1814 a certain shift could be noted. Encouraged by de Staël, Constant wrote in the preface to the third edition of *On the Spirit*: 'The reader . . . will not fail to see that, if I had written this work in France or at the present moment, I would have expressed myself differently on more than one subject'. Frustrated by the way in which France had borne the yoke of Bonaparte's government, the author had allowed himself inappropriate 'expressions of bitterness' against the Great Nation.

Allied occupation and re-familiarization with Bourbon rule then encouraged *rapprochement* directly with Napoleon in 1815. Constant's volte-face in co-writing the Acte Additionnel and entering the Council of State has often been attributed solely to opportunism; yet the revised Imperial constitution did grant parliament significant powers. In the foreword to his *Principles of Politics Applicable to all Representative Governments*, published in May 1815, Constant sought to explain the choice he had made. The *Principles* was written as a commentary on the Acte, suggesting that the latter provided for constitutional revision and further liberalization. More to the point, in working with Bonaparte, Constant was following the lead of France. The author rounded on the Allied Powers: 'Today it is no longer their own country that these peoples are defending: they are attacking

a nation . . . which claims simply her independence, and the
right to choose her own government'. Foreign despots should
take guard: 'Twenty-three years ago the language to which they
now returned shattered their thrones. Then, like now, they
attacked us because we wanted our own government, because
we had liberated the peasant from the tithe, the protestant from
intolerance, thought from censorship, the citizen from arbitrary
detention and exile, the plebian from the insults of the privileged.'
In the light of 1815, Napoleon had regained his image as safeguard against counter-revolution.[4]

Nor was Constant the only one who wavered. De Staël
supported the Acte, and combined with Lafayette in a fruitless
attempt to convince Britain not to renew war on France. Whether
this amounted to anything more than a truce with Bonaparte can
be questioned, but clearly circumstance could temper antagonism.

Thereafter de Staël fought the impact of the Hundred Days
with her *Considerations on the Principal Events of the French
Revolution*, published posthumously in 1818. Here the image of
tyrant returned in force; the essence of Napoleonic rule lay in
enslavement of independence by ruthless ambition. Bonaparte
succeeded by substituting military glory and material self-
interest for 'true' patriotism, based on love of liberty. For those
confused over his relation to patriotism, de Staël pointed to the
difference between French borders at the time of the coup of
Brumaire and following the Second Treaty of Paris. Yet here lay
the rub. The third volume of *Considerations* constituted a plea
against what was already well under way: 'Whether Napoleon
live or die, one single motive still leads me to speak of him; it is
the ardent desire that the friends of liberty should separate
entirely their cause from his, and that they should be careful not
to confound the principles of the Revolution with those of the
imperial government'. The regime of the Hundred Days had
been founded on hypocrisy, and Napoleon would have
destroyed the Acte Additionnel after his first victory.[5]

In the long term, *Considerations* was an opening salvo in a
battle to define the 'true' nature of the Revolution. De Staël's
contribution pivoted on dividing the Revolution into phases,
some of which were 'true' in that they furthered the progress of
liberty. In essence, the latter were to be found prior to the
September massacres of 1792, and to some extent the early years
of the Directory. The Terror and Napoleonic rule were regressive,
steps back to despotism.

Considerations has justly gained the status of a 'classic'; yet it failed as a piece of contemporary polemic, and some of the reasons can be found in the work itself. Certain passages reflect the context of the White Terror of 1815–16, wherein royalists took their revenge on Bonapartists, liberals and Jacobins who had rallied during the Hundred Days. Thus we find de Staël lambasting ultraroyalist government for persecution, and blasting the British cabinet for failing to intervene. Although the author has become associated with Anglophilia and German Romanticism, in *Considerations* she defends the French army and nation. Royalists liked to pretend that Napoleon's return in 1815 was entirely the work of a small band of conspirators, but de Staël could not take this route. She recognized that Napoleon's popularity had recovered because he had fought France's traditional enemies. She did remain consistent in arguing that he had misled the nation, but the tide was running against attempts to distinguish among royalism's opponents, partly because royalists themselves made few such distinctions.[6]

The paths of de Staël and Constant diverged radically from 1815 onwards. De Staël's message was taken to heart by a small group, known as the *doctrinaires*, whose advocacy of constitutional monarchy rested on confining national representation to a very narrow electorate. This was not so much out of line with Constant's political theory; he shared their fear that democracy could lead straight back to despotism. But Constant as a politician was a different, and more typical, creature in that his politics became increasingly shaped by his need to appeal to voters particularly, and the public generally.

Immediately following the Second Restoration, Constant wrote a memoir explaining his conduct to Louis XVIII; this saved him from official banishment, but he still thought it wise to depart France in October. Thereafter he remained in 'self-imposed' exile in Brussels and London for close to a year, developing his *Memoirs on the Hundred Days* through discussions with John Cam Hobhouse, friend of Byron. It was not until September 1816, after Louis XVIII had signalled a turning away from reaction through parliamentary dissolution, that Constant returned to Paris. Matters had improved in that domestic policies were directed by Elie Decazes. Gradually Decazes led King and government towards the political centre, partly relying on support from *doctrinaires* such as François Guizot. Yet what was crucial for Constant was that he found himself shut out from *doctrinaire* circles; he was given a cold shoulder in salons where previously he had been a darling.

Constant threw himself into political journalism, producing articles for newspapers such as the *Mercure de France* and the *Minerve française*. He became a member of a group of deputies and journalists who styled themselves the Independents, thus denoting opposition both to ultraroyalism and to Decazes's efforts to control elections by means both fair and foul. The new circles in which Constant moved were very much what de Staël warned against. In the capital, the character of emergent opposition could be seen at the Davilliers salon, where former republicans and Bonapartists shared their grievances against royalism. Had Independent aspirations been restricted to Paris, they would not have amounted to much more than the *doctrinaires* – a tiny elite with virtually no public following. But the Independents became the heirs of the fusion of Revolutionary tradition and Bonapartism that had marked the Hundred Days.[7]

At heart, Constant retained doubts about Napoleon, but he enjoyed the Opposition's flattering comparison of the Acte to the Charter, and the special place accorded by the Opposition to members of the Hundred Days parliament augured well for his prospects. Thus in his review of *Considerations*, commentary on de Staël's association of Bonaparte with tyranny was conspicuously absent. Constant's introduction to his 1829 edition of the *Memoirs* was only marginally more forthright. The text itself demonstrated that the success of the Flight of the Eagle was not a product of conspiracy; it resulted from the nation's rejection of the First Restoration. Nevertheless, Constant and 'the friends of liberty' had erred in thinking they could end dictatorship by rallying to the Empire. Napoleon could not repair past harm by new 'good works' in 1815; the French nation had underlined this contradiction by not preventing his second fall from power.

Such a position was ambiguous. It rested on the presumption that the Great Nation, if sufficiently determined, could not have been defeated; thus the second abdication must have resulted from a national rejection of a tyrant. Yet, much of the text of the *Memoirs* ran against this conclusion. What were readers to make of Napoleon telling Constant: 'Free elections, public discussions, responsible ministers, all that I want. Especially freedom of the press: to stifle it is absurd'? As O. Pozzo di Borgo noted in his preface to the 1961 edition of the *Memoirs*, Constant never fully believed that Napoleon and liberty were irreconcilable.

Moreover, tentative as it was, Constant's argument concerning divorce of Bonaparte from the nation could only be advanced by ignoring the army and the 'people' who rallied. Herein lay the central dilemma for a liberal politician: too clear an attempt to separate Napoleon from the nation could prove a severe liability at election time.[8]

As the Independents registered major electoral gains from 1817 onwards, they increasingly shaped their appeal to suit the public, especially the roughly 90,000 leading taxpayers who held the franchise. Effectively, this meant emphasizing unity among anti-royalist elements. Because the Independents subsequently evolved into a group known as the Liberal Opposition, there has been a tendency to presume that they were liberal. However, the Liberal Opposition was a coalition based on shared opposition to royalism and a great deal of doctrinal ambiguity. Not only were deputies such as General Foy closely associated with Imperial glory, the Liberal press trod very softly where Bonapartist sentiments were concerned. Liberals were keen to position themselves as champions of the army, and they made a point of defending the victims of White Terror – republican regicides and Imperial officers alike.[9]

Constant emerged as a star in the Liberal firmament because he was willing to compromise. Disunity in Paris blocked his first attempts to gain election, but in late November 1818 he was contacted by Charles Goyet, whose grass-roots organization had already secured the election of Lafayette in the western department of the Sarthe. Goyet was a former Jacobin who had evolved along liberal lines similar to those of Constant. His successful campaigns on behalf of Liberals caused a stir because they were conducted in what was thought to be the heartland of ultraroyalism. Yet within the electorate, Opposition could triumph as long as the government tolerated even a limited measure of independence.

Victory could not, however, be gained by angering voters who fondly recalled Napoleon's subduing of counter-revolution. Goyet warned Constant against alienation of 'patriots' through reference to Napoleonic tyranny and Constant accepted this, securing election in 1819. Thereafter he continued to woo admirers of Napoleon, and this became central to the electoral politics that would enable him to succeed in Paris in 1824 and at Strasbourg from 1827 onwards. Nor was his path untypical. Only a minority of liberal writers criticized Imperial tyranny amidst the deluge of Bonapartist tracts triggered by news of Napoleon's death. A sound assessment of public relations lay behind the republican Lafayette joining Constant in petitioning the government for return of the Emperor's ashes to France in 1821.[10]

Where Constant differed from other elements of the Left lay more in methods than ideals. Confronted by the possibility of a future Liberal majority, Restoration governments resorted to reaction from late 1819 onwards. Angered by the return of preliminary censorship and laws revamping the electoral regime, some Liberals, Lafayette among them, took to conspiracy based on the hope that the army would revolt. Wooing the army partly explains why the secret societies known as the *Carbonari* appealed to fond memories of Napoleon, but it was also true that Bonapartism had a strong base among the civilian components of the secret societies.[11]

On the whole, Liberals were stronger on what they did not want than what they did. As the Restoration progressed along counter-revolutionary lines, links between Napoleon and the Revolution were facilitated. The ultimate exile of the 'Saviour' in May 1821 made acceptance of his liberal credentials safer for the odd doubting Thomas, and publication of the *Memorial* in 1823 furthered the cause. The latter was however but one of many such tracts; for every brochure in Liberal reading rooms on the Revolution, there was one on the Empire, and in the contributions of Benoît and Cauchois-Lemaire to the *Bibliothèque historique* Bonapartism went hand-in-hand with revolutionary tradition. The Napoleon of the Restoration Opposition was first and foremost a patriot, but he was also a champion of careers open to talent, defender of Revolutionary land redistribution, and opponent of clerical or noble privilege.[12]

In the short term, Constant suffered by association with Lafayette as the electorate delivered a thumping rejection of insurrection in the early 1820s. However, from 1824 onwards his position strengthened as the Opposition returned to legal means. At the grass-roots level, Constant showed signs of reconciling himself to democracy, revealing a surprising 'common touch'. Authors occasionally refer to Constant's pleasure at speaking before crowds in the thousands at Strasbourg as 'demagoguery', and even Constant's Alsatian version of Goyet, J.-J. Coulmann, was bemused that Constant's nose was not put out of joint by peasants who crowded round the new 'Saviour'. We shall have more to say on Popular Bonapartism in Chapter 6, but for now we can note simply that attacks on Napoleon in Alsace would have destroyed Constant's popularity. Perhaps bowing to public wishes constituted opportunism, but it was good politics.

It is something of a convention to interpret the July Monarchy (1830–48) as Bonapartism without Bonaparte. Yet the Revolution of July 1830 began a process of division among Restoration Liberals, and the parliamentarians who raced to legitimize a new Orleanist dynasty did so to cut out republicanism and Bonapartism. In July and August, neither of the latter had much by way of distinct organization, and in the case of Bonapartism, the obvious leader, the Duke of Reichstadt (Napoleon's son), was removed from France by Habsburg control. Thus many former Imperial officials happily rallied to a regime which drew on them for much of its personnel. Figures such as Marshal Soult occupied key cabinet positions; they were often no more than political ciphers, but they were included to suggest continuity with Napoleonic glory. Orleanist governments also appealed to Bonapartist sentiment through completion of projects such as the Arc de Triomphe.

Yet Bonapartism was a double-edged sword for Orleanism. Directed principally by King Louis-Philippe, July Monarchy foreign policy was essentially pacific, based on friendly relations with Britain. Notions of France leading a crusade of liberation for the 'oppressed peoples' of Europe were thus consigned to the Left. Republicans such as Lafayette, General Lamarque and Etienne Cabet took the lead in demanding intervention against repression meted out by the eastern autocracies in Italy and Poland, but this also played to Bonapartism of the Left. Indeed, judging by the sentiments of the Parisian crowd that had fought at the barricades in July, it was Popular Bonapartism that posed the main potential threat to an increasingly conservative regime.[13]

The complexities of Bonapartism were apparent in the career of Adolphe Thiers. Thiers began as a Liberal journalist under the Restoration and played a major role in the founding of the July Monarchy. After several intervals inside Orleanist governments, he became primarily associated with the dynastic, or loyal, opposition. He was associated with calls for limited franchise reform, but it was mostly in the realm of foreign policy that he specialized. Nothing qualified him better in the latter regard than his *History of the Consulate and the Empire*, published in twenty volumes from 1845 to 1862. For Thiers, Napoleon was a genius, 'the greatest human being since Caesar and Charlemagne'. He was immortal for his state building and the inspiration he gave to patriotism. Nevertheless, Thiers depicted Napoleon as corrupted by absolute power, concluding that 'the country must never be handed over to one man, no matter who the man'.[14]

As the politics of the *status quo* in the domestic realm became increasingly unpopular during the July Monarchy, Thiers concluded that nothing could better promote unity than an aggressive foreign policy. Yet in each of his brief stints as *premier ministre* in the late 1830s, he managed only to convince Louis-Philippe to force Thiers's resignation over actions that threatened to reunite the other Powers against France. The ultimate consequence was to damage the regime; fostering illusions was one thing, acting was another.[15]

The Orleanist dynasty had benefited in 1830 from the absence of a viable Bonapartist leader, but when the Duke of Reichstadt died in 1832, the mantle of pretender fell to Louis-Napoleon Bonaparte, son of Napoleon's brother Louis and Josephine's daughter Hortense. Beyond genealogical lines, Louis-Napoleon had other claims to left-wing Bonapartism: in the early 1830s he dabbled in the Italian Carbonari, taking part in an uprising in the Romagna. Thereafter he twice attempted to seize power in France by *putsch*, at Strasbourg in 1836 and Boulogne in 1840. Both episodes had an element of buffoonery; Louis-Napoleon's substituting a buzzard for an eagle neatly symbolized the distance between uncle and nephew. The regime dealt with the first attempt with derision, but the second effort netted Louis-Napoleon six years of imprisonment at Ham, until 1846.[16]

During his years of exile and imprisonment, Louis-Napoleon wrote diverse tracts designed to make himself the heir of his uncle. *Political Reflections* was published in May 1832 and bore the impress of Restoration Opposition: liberal division of powers combined with a strong executive led by an Emperor who would implement the will of the people. More important was his *Napoleonic Ideas*, published in July 1839. In this work, Louis-Napoleon gave Bonapartism a doctrinal basis which retained elements of liberalism and republicanism, but provided a distinct alternative. In historical terms, Louis-Napoleon's Bonapartism derived most clearly from the regime of the Hundred Days, but *Napoleonic Ideas* also illustrated how much could be accomplished through extension of half truths. One finds, for example, little recognition that 1815 was based on renouncing old

Imperial practices. For the author, the Napoleonic epic was all of a piece, given unity by Napoleon's intentions, which remained consistent throughout.

The author's technique in the *Ideas* was to build an image of perfection, both for Napoleon and the system he created. Napoleonic government, according to the pretender, possessed elements of liberalism in that liberty, civil and political, was Napoleon's ultimate objective, pursued by steering a middle course between revolutionary Jacobinism and the *ancien régime*. Republican elements were also present in the form of the plebiscites, and the 'fact' that Napoleon had ruled in the interests of all the people, not just an elite.

Notable in the *Ideas* is an eschewing of militarism. True, France needs a strong army because she is surrounded by jealous neighbours, but the author takes pain to emphasize how little part the military plays in Napoleonic government. Moreover, Napoleon's wars are interpreted as defensive in nature; his foreign policy was based on pursuit of peace with honour. In the Emperor's grand design, victory was not a means to exploitation; conquest would lead to a confederation of monarchs who would serve the interests of their nations. Peace would, in turn, enable consolidation of liberty in France; thus foreign and domestic policies were intrinsically linked. After all, France has always been 'the fountain of progress for Western Europe'.

Somewhat understated is a final ingredient: according to the author, government is not 'a necessary ulcer; it is rather the beneficent motive power of all social organization'. In the 1840s Louis-Napoleon would heighten the role of state economic *dirigisme* with writings such as *Analysis of the Sugar Question* and *On the Extinction of Pauperism*. Louis-Napoleon was adjusting Bonapartism in answer to the 'social question' – growing alarm over the impact of the Industrial Revolution. Such 'Napoleonic ideas' jarred with the liberalism of the July Monarchy, but they were well calculated to appeal to groups alienated by the elitism associated with Orleanism. In the eyes of Louis-Napoleon, his uncle remained the great unifier, a leader who attended to all social interests.[17]

Left-wing Bonapartism was, however, but one of two keys that enabled renewal of Empire. The democratic aspirations to which Louis-Napoleon appealed were in fact more closely associated with republicanism, and when the July Monarchy fell in February 1848 it gave way to the Second Republic (1848–51).

Led by Guizot, the Orleanist regime unwisely ignored discontent
with its pacific foreign policies and apparent elitism, and when
middle-class elements of the National Guard joined, rather than
repressed, insurrection, the July Monarchy collapsed. Republican
success was attributable to public preoccupation with liberty
rather than order, but thereafter, as revolution brought increasing
civil disorder, priorities changed. In April, Radical republicans
tarnished their democratic credentials with an insurrection
against unfavourable elections, and the violence of the revolt of
the June Days made alarm over social order ascendant.

Order was a hallmark of authoritarian Bonapartism and it
provided Louis-Napoleon with his opportunity, yet he had based
his Bonapartism on the Left. The latter undoubtedly played a
part in his Imperial progress in that, as republicanism rapidly
alienated the majority, male democracy found an alternative in
Bonapartism. All levels of society contributed to the landslide
electoral victory that made him President of the Republic in
December 1848. Similarly, while there was substantial revolt
against his *coup d'état* of 2 December 1851, Louis-Napoleon
again garnered broad-based support in the plebiscite that
consecrated the Empire in 1852. Nevertheless, authoritarian
Bonapartism was crucial to Louis-Napoleon's success.

From February 1848 Louis-Napoleon positioned himself as a
man of order. Napoleonic opportunism was replicated in Louis-
Napoleon's relations with the conservative 'Party of Order', as he
played upon fears of the 'red menace' to property allegedly
represented by democratic socialists. Although he claimed to be
'above parties', his position as President provided Louis-
Napoleon with the means to give Bonapartism the rudiments of
party apparatus – an extensive propaganda machine, a growing
personal entourage, and support within the military and civil
administration. His seizure of power was in fact directed primarily against the Party of Order in parliament. The real issue lay in
its refusal to revise the constitution in favour of a second presidential term of office, but previous parliamentary revision of the
franchise so as to exclude about one-third of the poorest voters
provided Louis-Napoleon with a democratic pretext. Many
workers and peasants were in fact pleased by the coup, although
a republican backlash drove elite liberals and conservatives into
the Bonapartist camp, infusing the Second Empire with its initial
authoritarian character. Thereafter state patronage could be
deployed to secure Bonapartist domination of parliament.[18]

use it was shorn of the state patronage upon which it had
viously relied. Yet, after 1870 it was progressively weakened
division. Fragmentation partly resulted from family rivalries
r pretender status, but more debilitating was splintering
ween Bonapartists of the Left and Right. Conservatives
owed the line of Paul de Cassagnac, emphasizing dynasty and
holicism. Some Bonapartists of the Left turned to anti-
liamentarianism, basing authoritarianism on the democratic
ment of plebiscite. Both routes, however, consigned
apartism to the Right.[22]

Louis-Napoleon had managed to keep both the left-wing and
ht-wing traditions of Bonapartism in harness during the
pire, but this was made increasingly difficult during the Third
public by emergence of the extreme 'New Right'. Upon first
ance, the fierce patriotism of the New Right would seem
tirely in line with Bonapartism. Certainly General Boulanger
d his movement in the 1880s played to Bonapartism with
ilitarism. But as the New Right evolved, its patriotism became
at of 'France only' – exclusive and xenophobic. This ran
unter to the cosmopolitan strain in both republican and left-
ing Bonapartist patriotism. For the Left, France was privileged,
ut her mission was to bring progress to less fortunate peoples.
loreover, in rooting its notions of citizenship in race and
urity', the New Right took the opposite of Napoleon's
pproach. The Corsican had welcomed all to follow loyally in his
vake. Ultimately, the 'New Right' weakened Bonapartism not
ust by siphoning off some of its authoritarian elements, but also
y driving its left wing towards the Republic.

To a certain extent, the Third Republic defined itself in oppo-
ition to its immediate predecessor. Republicanism, as inspired by
Thiers and Léon Gambetta, was fused with a strong dose of
Orleanist liberalism. While this meant consolidation of political
male democracy, the Third Republic was conservative when it
came to social policy. Moreover the Republic became, by French
standards, liberal when it came to decentralization of power. All
of this constituted rejection of Louis-Napoleon's interpretation
of Bonapartism. Napoleon could be construed as the symbol of
the talented 'little man', but the little man of republican rural
France did not want grandeur of vision as interpreted by big
government.

There was, however, an element of left-wing Bonapartism
which the Third Republic carried forward – subordination of the

For some republicans, the *coup d'état* of 1851 brought a definitive rupture with Bonapartism; yet in their shrill denunciations
of the regime, there was more than a hint of guilty conscience.
The most famous of broadsides was Victor Hugo's *The
Chastisements*, wherein Napoleon I, by way of expiation for
betraying the First Republic after the *coup d'état* of Brumaire,
must bear witness to the ultimate humiliation for him – the
appalling Louis-Napoleon, or Napoleon the Little. Published in
November 1852, the poem, however, also indicated lingering
desire to claim the greatness of Bonaparte, while rejecting the
tyranny of Napoleon. Thus emerged the true Napoleon of
the Left: he was 'great' in so much as he had defended the
Revolution, but he had also betrayed France through destruction
of the First Republic.

Perhaps it was the author himself who felt chastened? As
leader of the Romantic movement, Hugo had elevated Napoleon
to the status of demi-god. 'Bored' with the pacifism and materialism of the Orleanist regime, Hugo had celebrated Imperial
glory, linking militarism to grandeur of vision and self-sacrifice.
It was not that French Romantics created Popular Bonapartism;
the latter pre-existed their conversion to the cult of Napoleon.
But the Romantics had fostered illusions. Ultimately their chief
contribution was to encourage aggression which had little to do
with defence of sovereignty, making successful foreign policy
impossible for the July Monarchy and, in turn, the Second
Republic.[19]

As Foreign Minister from June to October 1849, Alexis de
Tocqueville gained first-hand knowledge of the problems posed
by public longing for past glory. Tocqueville was perhaps the
greatest of French political theorists and he has become
renowned for his insight into the threat that democracy could
pose to pluralism. Especially perceptive were his warnings that
national sovereignty could be as tyrannical as royal despotism if
constitutional powers were not divided and the authority of the
state left unlimited. From this perspective, one would expect
hostility towards Napoleon. Moreover, Louis-Napoleon's *coup
d'état* effectively put an end to Tocqueville's political career.

Yet in Tocqueville we find an ambivalence towards Napoleon
more reminiscent of Constant than de Staël. In April 1842
Tocqueville described what he would say about the First Empire
in a speech to the French Academy: 'I reproach it for the non-
liberal side of its institutions, but at the same time I do full justice

to the personal grandeur of Napoleon, the most extraordinary being, I say, who has appeared in the world for many centuries'. Perhaps this was a matter of expediency. Amidst the Eastern Crisis of 1840, in which Thiers had provoked the possibility of the other Powers combining against France, Tocqueville wrote: 'the European nation which has all the others against it . . . must succumb in the long run; that is what one must never tell the nation, but never forget'.

Confronted by the triumph of Bonapartism, Tocqueville then wrote *The Old Regime and the French Revolution*. He had initially conceived this masterpiece as a history of the Empire, which threw 'a vivid light on the period that preceded it and on that which follows it. It is certainly one of the acts of the French Revolution that enables one to say the most on the ensemble.' Sadly, he did not live to write the second volume. Certainly the work would have differed greatly from that of Thiers, which Tocqueville intended to revise. Yet one should not jump to the conclusion that criticism of the Napoleonic state would entail utter rejection of the Napoleonic legacy. Even as he deplored France's willingness to be enslaved by despotism in the 1850s, Tocqueville likened the new regime to the July Monarchy rather than the First Empire: 'It seems to me that what he [Louis-Napoleon] had of life, of boldness, and even of a certain grandeur . . . is little by little being extinguished and enervated in the more material and more bourgeois enjoyments'. Louis-Napoleon 'seems . . . to be reduced to the basic principle of Louis Philippe; powerlessness and modesty outside, industrial politics inside'. At base, there was more to Tocqueville's ambivalence to Napoleon than expediency. For Tocqueville, as for Hugo and Thiers, Napoleon's greatness lay in his ability to inspire patriotism and self-sacrifice, a noble contrast to the petty materialism of mundane nineteenth-century life.[20]

Like the regimes before it, the Second Empire (1852–70) was destroyed by desire for grandeur. In domestic politics, Louis-Napoleon's transformation of an authoritarian Empire in the 1850s to a liberal Empire in the 1860s was remarkable. Whether it was the result of a preconceived plan, or the consequence of concessions made by a weak regime, has long been disputed. One way or another, the evolution could easily be presented by Louis-Napoleon as the completion of what his uncle had intended. Freedom of expression and association, social and political, increased dramatically in the 1860s, and, with the aid of a

younger generation of liberal republicans led by 1870 Louis-Napoleon had recast the Emp both male democracy and a genuine parliame Had the fate of the Second Empire depended politics, Louis-Napoleon's projection of Napo would have been very persuasive.

Foreign relations were, however, crucial donned Napoleon's mantle. Louis-Napoleon ha on the dangers of European coalition, and h uncle's divide and rule strategies would have to b discreetly. Hence foreign policy was formulated France as an advocate of national self-determi element of 'France first' was never absent. In th unification, France gained by acquisition of Sav offering Bismarck neutrality in the looming Aust of 1866, Louis-Napoleon was angling for annexa or perhaps part of the left bank of the Rhine. In in Louis-Napoleon doubtless believed he was doing a favour by supplying a European monarchy, but no provision for consulting the Mexican people.

There thus was a fair measure of tradition underlying claims to disinterested intervention, a dangerously like sacrifice of countless lives in the man's ambition. Louis-Napoleon's limited warm not, however, a great cause for dissatisfaction in destroyed the regime was defeat, by the Prussian September 1870. War with Prussia could certainly as in France's interests, based on sound appra threatening a united Germany could be. But there is the overweening nationalist pride that forced war b was prepared.

Why worry when the Grand Nation is led by t demi-god? Such illusions were, however, more p imagination than on the battlefield. Louis-Napole knew this; his attempt to have himself killed rather th indicated a solid understanding of mythology. Bonap been elevated to a level where it could not survive nightmare of 1814–15 was again played out, re occupation, territorial losses and reparations.[21]

Sedan damaged but did not destroy Bonapartism. F opposition, Bonapartism initially advanced as a polit

Catholic Church to the state. Because anticlericalism ultimately culminated in abolition of the Napoleonic Concordat, it is easy to mistake form for spirit, but separation of Church and state in 1905 was aimed at weakening Church influence. A great nightmare for the Left from the Restoration onwards had been theocracy. Napoleon had facilitated a Catholic revival, but within his system the Church was an instrument of the state, and not the reverse. Anticlericalism, so important to combatting the Right in the Dreyfus Affair at the turn of the century, fit comfortably with left-wing Bonapartism and provided republicanism with its one consistent theme prior to World War One.[23]

More important than such continuing elements of shared heritage was that as Bonapartism retracted in doctrinal terms, opportunities arose for other traditions to reclaim parts of the Napoleonic legacy. Reclamation unfolded in two stages. First it was necessary to clarify differences from Bonapartism, often blackening Napoleon's reputation in the process. But as Bonapartism declined as a political rival, it became tempting to express admiration for certain aspects of Napoleon's historical role. The means, as before, lay in distinguishing between the 'good' and 'bad' Bonaparte.

Some republicans began attacking Napoleon's reputation during the Second Empire, and this became predominant for roughly fifteen years after 1870. In the war of symbols, Paris Communards toppled Napoleon I from the Vendôme Column. Although the army would have the final word where the radicals of the 1870s were concerned, the Left was characterized by deep suspicion of any potential Caesar figure. Thiers's opus gave way to Lanfrey's disparaging *History of Napoleon I*, and Erckmann and Chatrian revived the image of the Ogre in their folkloric novels. At the village level, organizations such as the 'Society for Republican Education' pumped out propaganda reminding peasants of the costs of Imperial tyranny and warmongering.

Yet, republicans did have to tread softly in an era marked by longing to recover Alsace and Lorraine. Here Pierre Larousse, in a dictionary which ended reference to Bonaparte at 18 Brumaire, had cleared a path. The Revolutionary wars and Revolutionary Bonaparte were legitimate, but success lay in the *élan* of the citizen-soldier, not the professionalism of the officer. Thereafter, the incessant prospect of international conflict in the decades prior to World War One fostered further accommodation. The most representative histories were written by Henry Houssaye,

who depicted the Napoleon of 1814 and 1815, thereby accom-
modating him to left-wing patriotism. When Edmond Rostand's
play *L'Aiglon* opened in 1900, among the audience were Imperial
notables such as the Prince and Princess Murat, but they were
joined by republican stalwarts such René Waldeck-Rousseau,
Léon Bourgeois and Louis Barthou. As war with Germany
loomed, republican anti-militarism went into remission,
symbolized by President Poincaré's revival of military parades
from 1912 onwards. This was highly propitious for works such
as Maurice Barrès's *Les Déracinés*, which idolized Napoleon as
the ultimate example, and source, of patriotic devotion.[24]

Republican reclamation of Napoleon as part of their heritage
was always qualified, and, generally, socialist reluctance to
embrace the reputation was even more pronounced. Still, French
socialists did have to take patriotism into account. They did so
with a familiar line of argument: France was the seed bed of
progress and, as such, must be protected.

There was a second aspect of Napoleonic rule which could also
attract socialists: his use of the state as a mechanism for social
change. The Saint-Simonian variant of early French socialism
shared a great deal with the technocratic aspirations of the First
Empire. They had a fundamental common denominator in provision of material welfare through state-orchestrated economic
development, even if the Saint-Simonians were more concerned
by equitable distribution of production. Thus there was a certain
logic to Michel Chevalier entering the government of the Second
Empire. Moreover, Louis-Napoleon's description of himself as a
'socialist' did not subsequently appear all smoke and mirrors in
the light of the conservative social policies of the Third Republic.
Had Louis-Napoleon not followed his uncle's lead in encouraging formation of worker mutual-aid societies? Was it not a
logical progression when the Second Empire became the first
French regime at least to tolerate the organization of worker
unions, and pushed banks to provide cheap credit for smallholders and cooperatives? Was this not in line with what Louis
Blanc had called for in his *The Organization of Labour* (1839),
the most influential socialist tract of the period?[25]

Early versions of socialism came under attack at mid-century
by Karl Marx, whose ripping broadside, 'The Eighteenth
Brumaire of Louis Bonaparte', published in 1852, constituted a
complete disavowal of Bonapartism. Yet Marx's impact on

nineteenth-century French socialism should not be overestimated. Marx dismissed groups such as the Saint-Simonians as 'utopian' because they had failed to recognize the necessity of class warfare. His own 'scientific' version, however, fell well short of becoming orthodoxy, as France produced a bewildering variety of indigenous socialist strains. All the same, Marxism did become an important wing of French socialism and thus it is instructive to consider where Napoleon fit into Marx's scheme of things.

According to Marx, war could be declared on the Second Empire because history had advanced to the stage when the proletariat should rise against its oppressors. Such had not been the case, however, in the early 1800s, when it was still necessary for the bourgeoisie to finish their work of breaking the chains of feudalism. Only after the bourgeois revolution had triumphed could capitalism fulfil its mission of goading workers into recognition of their common interests. Without such class consciousness, proletarian revolt would be crushed.

Marx did not share liberal alarm over Napoleon's development of the state; after all, the state might currently be a tool of bourgeois domination, but ultimately it would serve to unlock the door to communism. It is true that, especially in his early writings, Marx recognized that Napoleon had seized power from the liberal bourgeoisie. In doing so, he had restored the autonomy of the state in order to pursue his own agenda, foreign conquest. After the fall of the Empire, however, the bourgeoisie had regained control and benefited by Napoleon's turning the state into such an effective instrument. Napoleon had thus played a role in a process which was historically inevitable. Viewed from the perspective of long-term developments, he was a true heir of the Revolution in that he had fostered, however unintentionally, the triumph of the bourgeoisie. But by the Second Empire, it was time to wrest this instrument away from capitalist oppression.[26]

Marx's view that the state could be used to liberate the oppressed was not shared by anarchists. Whether one should interpret anarchism as a type of socialism or as a distinct doctrine is not an easy question; the answer pivots on what one defines as essential to anarchism, and there is much room for disagreement in this regard. As historical phenomena, however, they developed in parallel and both were presented as means by which labour should be organized. Pierre-Joseph Proudhon, the leading French anarchist, considered himself both an anarchist and socialist, and many analysts have followed him in interpreting anarchism as a version of socialism. But for our purposes, it is helpful to view anarchism as separate from socialism, and to use Proudhon's writing as a means to gain perspective on socialism's mixed attitude to Napoleon. Anarchism was profoundly mistrustful of the state, and hence it is no great surprise that Proudhon described Napoleon as 'a man who neither represented nor served any principle, who understood nothing and built nothing by himself, and who pushed France towards an irreparable physical and moral decadence'.[27]

Yet in Proudhon's writing, Napoleon did represent a principle, even if it was the 'wrong' one. Proudhon's plan for reorganization of society, the federative system, pivoted on a notion of contract wherein power flowed from the bottom up. The citizen who contracted with any authority would receive and retain more rights than he yielded. Society would consist of small, self-governing groups. They would need to establish relations among themselves, but they would yield less power than they retained in setting up bodies to govern relations, and power would diminish with each extension to a larger entity. This was, of course, the very opposite of the Napoleonic state, in which authority was concentrated in the central government and flowed downwards.

Proudhon's attacks were, however, directed primarily at the Jacobin unitary state, and hence Rousseau and Robespierre received more of his invective than Napoleon. On the other hand, Bonaparte was the heir of this tradition through Caesarism. While the people would inevitably become the 'army of liberty', ignorance and material necessity inclined them towards authoritarianism. They placed their faith in human will, not principles, and surrendered their liberty to a leader whom they trusted. Thus the fellow-travellers of Napoleon I had issued from the Jacobin clubs. However, the more authority extended itself, through conquest, the more intolerable it became and eventually this would prove its downfall. Even Napoleon had been forced to modify the Imperial system in 1815 and swear to the principles of 1789. His compromise was, however, only with the bourgeoisie; the parliamentary system represented only their interests. Worse still, the bourgeoisie itself was committed to administrative centralization for imposition of order.

Many of Proudhon's observations echoed those of Marx, and the two shared the same objective of a classless society. Yet the means they proposed were radically different. At base, anarchism viewed government as inherently contradictory to liberty and an inappropriate instrument for worker liberation. Proudhon's rejection of governmental promotion of material or moral welfare led him to argue that Saint-Simon had been misinterpreted by his followers; he thus rejected the state socialism shared to a varying extent by Marx, Chevalier and Louis-Napoleon.[28]

French anarchism's chief influence was to be found in the trades union movement, which tended to concentrate on industrial relations and eschew politics. This made sense, given Proudhonian antipathy to government. Anarchists could, of course, put all their eggs in the basket of revolution through a general strike by which workers would paralyse government. Socialists could also place their faith in violent proletarian revolt. Marxists, for example, condemned socialist rivals as 'possibilists' when they strayed into working for social reform in combination with the 'enemy' – bourgeois radical republicans and the state. Such 'class collaboration' forestalled ultimate liberation because it mitigated the exploitation by which the bourgeoisie provoked proletarian class consciousness. But the riposte of rivals was telling – Marxists were 'impossibilists' and truly utopian in thinking the bourgeois Republic was ripe for collapse.

In time, even Marxist leaders such as Jules Guesde came to recognize that the proletarian revolution was not immediately forthcoming. Hence by the 1890s they had joined other socialists in seeking to overcome the bourgeois Republic by democratic means, seeking election to all levels of government. But here they ran up against the problem of appealing to voters. This necessitated countenancing patriotism. By the outbreak of World War One, the previously intransigent Guesde was ready to join with the rest of the political spectrum in a Republican *union sacrée* in which the strangest of bedfellows coupled in defence of the *patrie*. He had little choice, given the sentiments of the rank-and-file party membership.[29]

The figure most associated with pre-war internationalism, Jean Jaurès, also provides an example of why French socialism needed to tread carefully concerning Napoleon's legacy. Well before Guesde, Jaurès pursued social transformation through democratic means, and his willingness to 'collaborate' was apparent in his rallying to the defence of the Republic from the Right amidst the Dreyfus Affair. Defence of the Republic was also apparent in Jaurès's writing. In his five-volume history of the French

Revolution, Jaurès depicted Robespierre not as an ideologue, but as a pragmatic politician seeking to overcome the divisions produced by factional rivalry during the Terror. Robespierre was a patriot striving to save France by curbing the excesses of extremists, much as Jaurès was seeking to unite the Left by moderating the violence of Guesdists and anarchists.[30]

Jaurès's study of the Revolution was part of a series of works, entitled *Histoire Socialiste (1789–1900)*, under his general direction. The following volume covering the Consulate and Empire was written by Paul Brousse (also a major Socialist politician) and Henri Turot. Published in 1906, the work strongly bore the impress of the divisions provoked by the Dreyfus Affair. In this context, Bonaparte emerges very much along the lines of the Black Legend – he is an egocentric outsider who equates his personal grandeur with that of France. He dupes the 'people' into believing he wants peace, when in truth he is a warmonger. National glory is the appeal by which he poisons and conquers the French so that he can pursue his dreams of world conquest, and like many ambitious men (an allusion to General Boulanger), he shamelessly claims to be 'national' when he represents no one but himself.[31]

Anti-militarism was running very strong in socialist circles in 1906, and Jaurès was certainly a determined opponent of militarism. No one worked harder to prevent war through international worker solidarity. But as the aftermath of the Dreyfus Affair settled down, and the prospect of conflict with Germany became increasingly prominent, France experienced a revival of nationalism. To have surrendered patriotism entirely to the Right under these circumstances would have been disastrous for the socialists, and their opponents were not shy about branding them as pacifists and traitors. Back in 1893 Jaurès had sought to counter such charges by stating, 'we will defend to our last breath the patch of land where republican liberty was born'. Such patriotism would, however, be entirely defensive. To safeguard against the aggressive potential of a professional army, in his *L'Armée nouvelle*, published in 1911, Jaurès proposed a version of the traditional republican image of the 'citizen army' of 1792, composed of militia which would elect their own officers and fight with the unclouded enthusiasm of men who knew they were only defending their homeland. While this now appears naive, Jaurès had managed to strike a balance between anti-militarism and the seeming anti-patriotism of radical elements calling, in the event of war, for strikes, disruption of mobilization and desertion.[32] Most Socialist leaders fell in line with Jaurès's position, and the overwhelming majority of workers responded to mobilization orders, even after Jaurès had been assassinated by a nationalist fanatic. At the burial on 4 August 1914, Léon Jouhaux spoke on behalf of the CGT, the leading French trades union. His words, to a certain extent, echoed those of the Socialist martyr: 'The working class . . . remembers the soldiers of the Year II going out to carry liberty to the world. . . . We will be the soldiers of liberty . . .'. Despite Proudhon's original influence, patriotism had led the trades union movement to support the state. Moreover, carrying liberty abroad was not quite the same thing as staying at home to defend hearth and home. Both the republicans of Year II and Bonaparte had made the same claims; for the Left patriotism remained intrinsically tied to notions of French grandeur, and it was very hard not to see Napoleon as part of this tradition when it came time to fight for it.[33]

If left-wing accommodation of Napoleon's heritage was often opportunistic, it was not necessarily cynical. In his more optimistic moments, Constant did believe that Napoleon could have accepted compromise with liberalism; Hugo, Thiers and Tocqueville were genuinely impressed by Napoleon's ability to inspire something other than selfish materialism; Saint-Simonians such as Chevalier were not wrong in seeing a certain affinity with the technocratic Napoleonic state; and Jaurès did believe that defending France was tantamount to defending progress. Seeing something positive in Napoleon's legacy was not simply a matter of expediency; it was also a product of the way in which altering circumstance could place Napoleon in a different light. In the context of Restoration reaction, or looming international conflict with the forces of autocracy, Napoleon's historical role looked much more positive than when confronted by Bonapartism as a dangerous political rival.

At base, underlining assessments of Napoleon's relation to the Revolution was a common theme which preoccupation with liberty or equality could obscure but not remove. Both the Revolution and Napoleonic era were sources of pride for the part of France that believed the *patrie* had a progressive mission beyond its borders.

Notes

1 On Bonapartism in particular, see F. Bluche, *Le Bonapartisme* (Paris, 1980). Useful works in English include H.A.L. Fisher, *Bonapartism* (Oxford, 1908), P. Thody, *French Caesarism* (Basingstoke, 1989), and R. Gildea, *The Past in French History* (New Haven, 1994). I have previously explored several of the themes in this chapter in 'Napoleon Bonaparte and the French Revolution', in Pamela Pilbeam, ed., *Themes in Modern European History 1780–1830* (London, 1995), pp. 40–64, and in 'The hero as Houdini: Napoleon and nineteenth-century Bonapartism', *Modern and Contemporary France*, 8: 4 (2000), pp. 457–67.

2 On opposition to Napoleon, see L. de Villefosse and J. Bouissounouse, *The Scourge of the Eagle: Napoleon and the Liberal Opposition* (New York, 1972).

3 The star-crossed paths of de Staël and Constant can be followed in C.J. Herold, *Mistress to an Age: The Life of Madame de Staël* (New York, 1958), D. Wood, *Benjamin Constant* (London, 1993), and Baroness de Staël, *Ten Years of Exile* (New York, 1972).

4 See B. Constant, *Political Writings*, ed. B. Fontana (Cambridge, 1988), pp. 46–7 and 171–3.

5 Baroness de Staël, *Considerations on the Principal Events of the French Revolution* (London, 1821), III, p. 159.

6 For discussion of Restoration writing on the Revolution, see S. Mellon, *The Political Uses of History* (Stanford, 1958), but see also E. Cappadocia, 'The Liberals and Madame de Staël in 1818', in R. Herr and H.T. Parker, eds, *Ideas in History: Essays Presented to Louis Gottschalk* (Durham, N.C., 1965), pp. 183–95.

7 The best description of the Davilliers milieu is to be found in J.-J. Coulmann, *Réminiscences* (Paris, 1862), I, pp. 172–210.

8 B. Constant, *Mémoires sur les Cent-Jours*, ed. O. Pozzo di Borgo (Paris, 1961), especially pp. xliii and 7.

9 The only published study of the Liberal Opposition is P. Thureau-Dangin's *Le Parti Libéral sous la Restauration* (Paris, 1876), but I am currently completing a monograph on the subject entitled *Rewriting the French Revolutionary Tradition*. See also R.S. Alexander, 'Restoration republicanism reconsidered', *French History*, 8: 4 (1994), pp. 442–69, and P. Pilbeam, *Republicanism in Nineteenth-century France, 1814–1871* (London, 1995), pp. 60–94.

10 See S. Neely, *Lafayette and the Liberal Ideal, 1814–24* (Carbondale, Ill., 1991), p. 194, E. Harpaz, ed., *Benjamin Constant et Goyet de la Sarthe: Correspondance 1818–1822* (Geneva, 1973), and G. Lote, 'La Contre-Légende Napoléonienne et la mort de Napoléon', *Revue des études napoléoniennes*, 30 (June 1931), pp. 324–49.

11 See A.B. Spitzer, *Old Hatreds and Young Hopes* (Cambridge, Mass., 1971).

12 See J. Tulard, *Le Mythe de Napoléon* (Paris, 1971), pp. 39–44.

13 See D. Pinkney, *The French Revolution of 1830* (Princeton, N.J., 1972), pp. 289–95, Pilbeam, *Republicanism*, pp. 95–128, and E.

Newman, 'What the crowd wanted in the Revolution of 1830', in J. Merriman, ed., *1830 in France* (New York, 1975), pp. 17–40.

14 See J.P.T. Bury and R.P. Tombs, *Thiers* (London, 1986), pp. 146–53, from which the quotes are taken. See also P. Geyl, *Napoleon: For and Against* (London, 1986), pp. 55–67.

15 The career of Thiers under the July Monarchy can be followed in Bury and Tombs, *Thiers*, pp. 40–100. See also H.A.C. Collingham, *The July Monarchy* (London, 1988), pp. 200–39.

16 See J. McMillan, *Napoleon III* (London, 1991), pp. 7–28.

17 See B.D. Gooch, ed., *Napoleonic Ideas* (New York, 1967); the quotes are on pp. 28 and 31. See also McMillan, *Napoleon III*, pp. 10–17, and Bluche, *Le Bonapartisme*, pp. 193–258. The similarity between Louis-Napoleon's Bonapartism and that of Napoleon at Saint Helena can be seen in P. Gonnard, *The Exile of St Helena* (London, 1909), pp. 117–80.

18 The role of order in imperial progression is stressed in McMillan, *Napoleon III*, pp. 18–34; see also Pilbeam, *Republicanism*, pp. 185–242, Bluche *Le Bonapartisme*, pp. 259–329, and A.-J. Tudesq, *L'élection présidentielle de Louis-Napoléon Bonaparte* (Paris, 1965).

19 On unrealistic expectations, see R. Bullen, 'France and Europe, 1815–48: the problem of defeat and recovery', in R. Bullen and A. Sked, eds, *Europe's Balance of Power, 1815–48* (New York, 1979), pp. 122–44, and L.C. Jennings, *France and Europe in 1848* (New York, 1973).

20 Tocqueville's concerns over the dangers posed by democracy and the growth of central government to pluralism inform virtually his entire corpus of works. The quotes here come from A. de Tocqueville, *Selected Letters on Politics and Society*, ed. R. Boesche (Berkeley, 1985), pp. 143, 158, 255, 285–6.

21 The relation between Louis-Napoleon's domestic and foreign policies can be followed in McMillan, *Napoleon III*, pp. 73–165.

22 The book to read is J. Rothney's *Bonapartism after Sedan* (Ithaca, N.Y., 1969), but also very useful is the discussion in Gildea, *The Past*, pp. 72–89.

23 See M. Larkin, *Church and State after the Dreyfus Affair: The Separation Issue in France* (London, 1974).

24 See Pilbeam, *Republicanism*, pp. 243–63, Tulard, *Le Mythe*, pp. 93–8, 109–10, Geyl, *Napoleon*, pp. 84–101, 150–7, Gildea, *The Past*, pp. 101–6, and S. Hazareesingh, 'The Société Républicaine and the propagation of civic republicanism in provincial and rural France, 1870–1877', *Journal of Modern History*, 71 (June 1999), pp. 271–307.

25 See F. Manuel, *The Prophets of Paris* (New York, 1962), pp. 103–93, and Pilbeam, *Republicanism*, pp. 155–84.

26 Distinctions between Napoleon as agent of the bourgeoisie and agent of state autonomy are less apparent in later works such as 'The class struggles in France: 1848 to 1850' and 'The eighteenth Brumaire of Louis Bonaparte'. See E. Kamenka, ed., *The Portable Karl Marx* (Harmondsworth, 1983) and F. Furet, *Marx and the French Revolution* (Chicago, 1988).

27 For useful background discussion, see Gildea, *The Past*, pp. 264–79; the quote is translated from Tulard, *Le Mythe*, pp. 93–4.

28 See P.-J. Proudhon, *General Idea of the Revolution* (London, 1923), especially pp. 100–69, and *Du Principe Fédératif* (Paris, 1863), especially pp. 49–72, 117–24 and 314.

29 See J. Howorth, 'French workers and German workers: the impossibility of internationalism, 1900–1914', *European History Quarterly*, 15 (1985), pp. 71–97.

30 For a biography of Jaurès, see H. Goldberg, *The Life of Jean Jaurès* (Madison, 1962). On Jaurès and Robespierre, see J. Jaurès, *Histoire Socialiste de la Révolution française* (Paris, 1910) and S. Kernaghan, 'The idealised revolutionary: contemporary French politics and the symbolic importance of Maximilien Robespierre' (M.A. thesis, University of Victoria, 1999), pp. 50–3.

31 P. Brousse and H. Turot, *Consulat et Empire (1799–1815)* (Paris, 1906), especially pp. 14–15, 54, 115.

32 J. Jaurès, *L'Armée nouvelle* (Paris, 1911); for an abbreviated translation, see *Democracy and Military Service*, ed. G.G. Coulton (New York, 1972).

33 The quotes of Jaurès and Jouhaux can be found in Gildea, *The Past*, p. 144.

|3|

Napoleon and the nineteenth-century Right: the Great Commander and the Man on Horseback

The expression 'Man on Horseback' refers to military intervention in the creation or running of a political regime. It also implies a leader whose power derives initially from his position in the military, although it may broaden if he gains popularity. Gaining recognition as a 'Great Commander' thus can serve as a springboard for the 'Man on Horseback' as the 'leadership principle' is carried from the military to the political sphere.

The Man on Horseback has become ubiquitous. According to S.E. Finer, the opportunities for intervention increased dramatically when the French Revolution's assertion of national sovereignty pushed aside older claims to rule, such as those of dynasty. But the question of who best represented the nation left ample room for many claimants, among whom the military was well placed, especially when it could be seen to be defending national independence. A secondary development, professionalization of armies, increased the likelihood of intervention. The key to professionalization lay in separation from civilian society, and development of a particular identity. Thus while the military could make claims to power based on representing national interests, it might be disposed to do so on the basis of its own corporate interests.

Professionalization does not necessarily lead to intervention; a key lies in whether the military recognizes the ultimate sovereignty of civilian authority. The military is less disposed to intervene if political culture has advanced to a point where society is willing to assert civil authority. But in a society wherein civil authority is weak, the military's ability to apply force often gives it great advantages over potential rivals such as political parties, trade unions and religious groups.

Napoleon's reputation has inevitably been affected by the rise of the Man on Horseback. He has often been viewed as the first modern prototype, and the tendency to do so has been enhanced by the inclination of subsequent military dictators or 'strongmen' to associate themselves with him. Yet it is instructive to note that Finer deals with Bonaparte only very indirectly. Perhaps this reflects the author's concentration on later examples, but there was a certain wisdom in leaving Napoleon largely out of the picture.[1]

Napoleon often attributed his rule to his position in the army. Yet this seemingly straightforward proposition raises many questions. In his study of heroism, Thomas Carlyle attributed Napoleonic greatness to the principle of careers open to talent; Bonaparte had progressed through promotion based on merit and then, in so much as he remained great, had applied the principle to state and society. Yet did his rise truly reflect ability? Was he the 'Great Commander' that he claimed to be? If this is granted, did his rise simply reflect military talent, or was there something more to it? Was it solely his position in the army that enabled him to seize political power? Beyond Brumaire, a similar legion of questions arises. If Bonaparte's power sprang from his role as commander, how did this affect the nature of his regime? Was the Empire simply a military dictatorship? Was he so beholden to the army that he was effectively its instrument? Or did other sources of Napoleonic power make the army his instrument rather than the reverse?[2]

In the first part of this chapter we will pursue these questions, but regardless of the outcome, the fact remains that Napoleon has often been seen as the first of modern military dictators. Thus he has been linked to a broad pattern among Men on Horseback. Military regimes do not necessarily reflect right-wing politics; often they spring originally from left-wing aspirations. But dictatorships that cling to power have historically either originated from the political Right, or become increasingly right-wing as the limits of their claims to represent the nation become exposed. It can be argued that under Napoleon the army became an instrument used in favour of the political Right. After all, Bonaparte strangled the First Republic, and, as part of this, rooted out republican elements. The argument that Napoleon converted a republican 'army of virtue' of citizen-soldiers into a professional 'army of honour' has been revivified of late, but can be dated back at least as far as Germaine de Staël. Yet it is crucial to keep in mind that for much of the nineteenth century the army was perceived as more likely to be a tool of the Left than the Right. This was partly a product of the left-wing nature of the cult of Napoleon prior to the Second Empire, and it pertained to much of Europe, not just France. Moreover, the *bête noire* of the Holy Alliance, revolutionary secret societies, often placed their hopes on infiltration of the army, whether in France, Russia, Iberia, or the Italian and Germanic states.[3]

Thus a final question arose: was the 'Man on Horseback' an agent of the Left or Right? Conclusions would inevitably circle back to the origins of power. Napoleon was but one of many strongmen who found their opportunity in breakdown of social and political order. In this scenario, assessment would depend on whether leaders thrust forward by revolution were seen as carrying new aspirations or social forces forward, or as crushing them in the interests of established elites, or of narrow, selfish ambitions. Did the Man on Horseback foster national sovereignty? As we shall see, the traditional Right in fact viewed Napoleon as a left-wing figure, a Jacobin on Horseback. As we discussed concerning the French in the previous chapter, the Left was less certain, but ultimately did accord Napoleon a certain place as an 'heir' of the Revolution. By the end of the century, however, military intervention was no longer associated primarily with the Left. By looking briefly at a sampling of leading nineteenth-century Men on Horseback, we can trace why it was that association with them pushed the Napoleonic reputation steadily to the right.

Talent, it would appear, lies less in the eyes of the beholder than merit. While attempts to identify the precise nature of Napoleon's talent do provoke division, there is little room for serious debate over whether he was talented. This has long been the general perception, despite many attempts at denigration, and Men on Horseback were, therefore, setting themselves a high standard by fostering comparison to him. Yet Bonaparte's career progress was only partly based on martial ability; meteoric promotion also resulted from shrewd political alignment and skill as propagandist. The Napoleonic model thus required both military and political talent.

Similarly, the principle of careers open to talent told only part of the story in the Napoleonic system, once it was established. Wealth, especially landed, was a major advantage when it came to military, social or governmental promotion. According to J.-P. Bertaud, for Napoleon military talent was to be found particularly 'among the high ranks of society'. Elitism was also apparent in selection of the Imperial nobility. Yet what was remarkable to contemporaries was that only 22.5 per cent were drawn from the old nobility; 58 per cent were drawn from wealthy middle-class elements and the remaining 19.5 per cent came from the lower social levels. In comparison to the Revolution, the tendency of the Empire was towards elitism, but if one is to understand the reputation, Napoleonic France must also be viewed in contrast to *ancien régime* France and Europe.[4]

There are good reasons why Napoleon continues to provoke comparison to 'Great Captains' such as Alexander, Hannibal and Genghis Khan. His record was far from uniformly brilliant; it was marred by major defeats. Nor was he a great original; his success lay in synthesizing the ideas of others. All the same, Napoleon's failures were more than balanced by his victories, and the latter gave rise to expectations that dwarfed those of others.[5]

Part of Napoleon's importance lies in his association with the organization of mass warfare in an age which took a major step towards 'total war' in mobilization of human and material resources. Analysts have seen Napoleon as a great exponent of offensive warfare, based on massing of superior force, rapid movement and timely concentration upon the opposition's weak point. He was not much concerned by casualty rates, but his successful campaigns were rapid and decisive. Where he became bogged down, as in Spain or Russia, results were far less impressive, leading to suspicion that limited powers of attention left him vulnerable to wars of attrition. In the first half of the nineteenth century, European commanders tended to draw back from Napoleon's high-risk strategies, yet emphasis on attack remained central to military theory, partly due to the writings of Baron Jomini and Karl von Clausewitz. To some extent, World War One repudiated offensive strategies; yet stalemate on the western front was not replicated in the east. Moreover, German blitzkrieg in World War Two suggested analogies to Napoleonic warfare. Technological developments made for crucial differences, but fascination with Napoleon continued because he retained his position as the leading modern exponent of attack in mass warfare.[6] Much can be made of the debt Bonaparte owed to the Revolution. He inherited tactical advantages in the battalion column, use of skirmishers in large numbers, and superior artillery in weight of fire and manoeuvrability. He thus 'merely adapted ideas which were already there'. The Revolution provided a crop of young generals reared in new techniques, superior junior officers, and a rank and file which was relatively experienced, capable of independent action, and highly motivated. Napoleon further refined such advantages, creating army corps composed of several divisions, often including independent artillery and cavalry divisions. The result was a force with improved communications, greater strategic flexibility and the ability to move more rapidly than opponents. The Revolutionary Army was not, however, without its flaws, some of which continued throughout the Empire. Staff work has been described as 'mediocre', the cavalry was poorly mounted, and Revolutionary generals or Imperial marshals were frequently unreliable. Prior to the coup of Brumaire, the Republic's position was certainly not dire, but French fortunes were consistently in flux and the Directory was far from securing definitive victory.

According to Charles Esdaille, a crucial factor in radical improvement in French military fortunes after 1800 was 'the irreplaceable genius of Napoleon himself'. If at times he scrambled to victory rather than executed a preconceived plan, his campaigns were characterized by 'a single unwavering purpose' – the search for decisive battle. David Gates argues that Napoleon 'excelled at seizing the initiative and imposing his will on his opponents', and that he was 'almost unerringly good at predicting his adversary's responses'. T.C.W. Blanning also insists upon Bonaparte's genius: his confidence and aggression imparted enthusiasm to his men, and his vision and rapid decision-making enabled him to make best use of the assets of the Revolutionary Army. Napoleon derived great advantage from combining his positions as head of the armed forces and of the state. The difficulties encountered among opposing forces, wherein the presence of a prince promoted rivalries and confused command, were

debilitating. Napoleon did not lead from the front; he kept his
headquarters well behind the lines, facilitating centralization of
command and avoiding the diffusion of authority that troubled
his rivals. Moreover, he was better placed to coordinate diplomacy with fighting and his ability to process information rapidly
yielded important advantages.[7]

Perhaps most significant of all was that Napoleon's state
reforms assured the steady supply of men necessary to his aspirations. Conscription had broken down under the Directory; to
redress this involved reforms in local government, accustoming
National Guardsmen to serve outside their immediate locality,
purging and expanding the *gendarmerie*, and using troops of the
line to harass bands of deserters and the local communities that
often supported them. Draft-dodging and desertion remained
persistent, yet bureaucratic routine, improvements in the conscription regime, and coercion of local elites produced startling
results in France until the system collapsed in 1813–14. The
latter was a product of pushing demand too far; even so, what
was most striking was how much Napoleon was able to gain,
especially in comparison to other rulers.

Desertion and draft-dodging have attracted great attention as
acts of resistance to an oppressive state. Yet against such resistance, one must also weigh the often fanatical devotion of the
troops to Napoleon; soldiers gave him a loyalty far from
common in the *ancien régime*. Such loyalty was also largely true
of the Revolutionary Army, but here it is instructive to
distinguish between the Imperial Army and the Revolutionary
Nation at Arms. Precisely how the common soldier responded to
the motivational strategies deployed by the Revolutionary and
Imperial regimes is difficult to assess, but the strategies employed
differed significantly. It can be argued that under Napoleon the
Imperial Army was not a Nation at Arms, which makes sense
given the international nature of the institution. The state did not
seek to motivate soldiers with abstract notions such as virtue,
appealing instead to honour and material interest. Far from
encouraging egalitarian identification as a band of citizen-
soldiers, Napoleon stressed *esprit de corps* and competition for
rank. Those who survived did gain reward, but far more important was the association with 'greatness' that each veteran carried
with him into the village market or café. Propaganda and use of
'the common touch' made Napoleon a cause.[8]

As a prototype, Napoleon set a very high standard. The conditions that gave him opportunity, breakdown of social and political order, were in fact anything but unique; they would become widespread in the nineteenth and twentieth centuries, encouraging a wide variety of emulators. Bonaparte's success was inevitably associated with his role as military commander, yet what made his model so difficult to follow was that his martial skills were matched by his political abilities.

Until the Hundred Days the Empire was effectively a dictatorship. To some extent the regime was based on consultation, but representative bodies could only advise. Authority was vested solely in a sovereign who, while he claimed to represent the nation, justified his rule through plebiscites only when it suited him. While his parliament might occasionally raise difficulties, there was no mechanism by which the Emperor could be held accountable. Similarly, the officials of the state held their power by appointment, not election.[9]

The sovereign was more than titular head of the armed forces; he continuously gave proof of his abilities in battle. Yet according to Bonaparte his political position was separate from his military capacity, and, on the whole, historians have been inclined to agree that the Empire was not a military dictatorship. Certainly the original seizure of power was not simply military; Brumaire was the product of collaboration – the politico-philisophical-military complex. During the Consulate the number of politicians in control was reduced to one, but the relation with the military remained essentially the same. If we view the Empire in terms of personnel, Napoleon had a point. Neither at the ministerial level, nor in the ranks of the administration, was there a preponderance of men drawn from the military. While military officers could prove a useful recruitment source, government and administration did not become a sinecure for the army. If anything the regime was a haven for politicians and technocrats whose positions owed little to the wishes of the army. The qualifications for office were expertise, social standing and loyalty to Napoleon; the Emperor listened to his military as he listened to other groups.[10]

The interests of a particular group can of course be served by the administration of others. Geoffrey Ellis has recently emphasized the extent to which the Empire was organized as a spoils system and certainly the military was at the head of the queue in despoiling conquered territories. In his system of rewards, Bonaparte revealed a very narrow vision of merit; military men were rewarded out of all proportion to their numbers. There was a dangerous circle in this; a value system based on the martial arts encouraged incessant fighting.[11]

That a regime is founded, wholly or in part, by military intervention does not, however, necessarily mean that the regime is military in character. Napoleon at times went well beyond the interests or wishes of the military in his reforms. The Civil Code reflected patriarchal values which rested comfortably enough with military codes, but a leading source of opposition to the Concordat was to be found in the army. State economic direction in the form of the Continental System had military inspiration, but Imperial *dirigisme* was designed for the benefit of society as a whole. Were roads and communication systems improved for military or economic reasons? The answer was both.

No one can miss the way in which the army served as a model for reorganization of government. Reforms were based on centralization of power, chain of command, clear delineation of authority and rapid execution of orders. None of this was perfectly implemented, but it was relatively efficient and at all levels power flowed downwards through delegation. Yet here lies the crux of the issue regarding military dictatorship. Among the types of military regime described by Finer, the Empire seems to fit best in the 'dual' category in that it had two pillars of support – the military and civilian opinion. Napoleon was at the top of both as commander and despot. Yet Finer had organized civilian opinion in mind, in the form of mass parties or pluralist bodies such as trade unions. Here the fit is less comfortable; support for Napoleon was based on personal popularity, attested to by plebiscites, but was not a product of political or social associations. In this sense the Empire had more in common with Caesarism than the modern forms of military despotism. Certainly the regime was not a *junta*. Imperial power was concentrated in the hands of one man, who looked unfavourably upon all rivals – institutional or individual. In this sense, the place of the army differed little from that of the Church.

Moreover, reforms based on military organization were designed to strengthen the state and did so, making it less dependent on the military. The state apparatus inherited by Louis XVIII was far stronger than that which the Directory bequeathed to Napoleon. In the nineteenth century, Bonaparte's encouragement of military professionalism, *esprit de corps* and isolation from civilian society would be enhanced, making the army a less likely source of political intervention. Yet, as Finer has underlined, professionalism means nothing unless the army also recognizes the ultimate primacy of civilian authority. Did it do so under Bonaparte? Finer also observes that military intervention is most likely during periods of 'low political culture', when commitment to civil institutions is weak. Certainly the Directory qualified, but the Restoration did not. Through its provision of order, the Napoleonic state had restored faith in civil institutions and Napoleon thereafter buttressed this by his propaganda at Saint Helena – order was a means to liberty. In this sense, the Empire was a 'caretaker government', something which military dictatorships have ever since claimed to be, but only rarely actually been.[12]

To nineteenth-century conservatives, Napoleon was a 'Jacobin on Horseback' who had continued the Revolution's onslaught on the old political and social order. True, he had sought to recreate social hierarchy, but this was not the nobility of the *ancien régime* with its independence based on corporate privilege. He had improved the fortunes of the Catholic Church with the Concordat, but there was no freedom in a relation which subordinated Church to state. He had sought to gain legitimacy through dynastic alliance, but none of this was sanctified by divine will or the weight of historical tradition.

Alongside the cult of Napoleon developed the Black Legend. Outside France the Empire could readily be linked to plunder and the gamut of demands exacted by incessant warring. Inside France such motifs also had a certain currency due to the economic crises of 1811 and 1813. Of greater potential, however, was the image of Ogre – an insatiable creature who fed on the lives of hundreds of thousands through callous warmongering. Like the Jacobins before him, Napoleon was a Godless destroyer whose alleged principles were but a mask for personal ambition. In fact he was utterly immoral: at the age of nine he had sexually abused a cousin and thereafter he had violated the innocent when he was not availing himself of prostitutes. He came by this naturally; after all Madame Letizia was the 'Mother of Joy' who had secured her son's future through the pleasures she provided Marbeuf. Moreover Napoleon was scheming, ungrateful, cruel and a physical coward who repeatedly betrayed those who served

him. Like the Revolution, Napoleon was a scourge sent forth to
remind all of the folly of tampering with God's old order.[13]

The basic elements of the Black Legend are to be found in the
memoirs of Chateaubriand, although this source is less consistently hostile than pamphlets such as his *De Bonaparte et des
Bourbons*, written in 1814 when it was necessary to speak in the
name of 'legitimacy' against 'a tyranny which was still alive'. In
his memoirs, Chateaubriand fought the renascent Bonapartism
of the 1820s and 1830s, deploying 'facts' against myth.
Corrupted by the 'original stain' of the execution of Enghien,
Napoleon's ambition was the work of the 'Prince of Darkness'.
His claims to liberalism and nationalism were a hoax; 'tyranny
personified', he knew only how to destroy. The Napoleonic cult
was based on ignoring the misery the Ogre had strewn in his
path, sacrificing and humiliating France while pitting his ego
against the world.[14]

Much of the Black Legend originated abroad, in the writings of
Germans such as Arndt and Kleist, Italians such as Barzoni and
Leopardi, or Russians such as Glinka and Derzhavin. Wars of
liberation were fought against a demon who spread misery with
his 'venomous serpents'. In the 'German Catechism' of Kleist,
Napoleon is 'the source of all Evil and the end of all Good', a
'patricidal demon, spawned by Hell'. Braccini, a Tuscan,
attacked Bonaparte as a bloodthirsty tiger feeding on his Italian
slaves, and at Venice popular songs poured scorn on Napoleon as
a schismatic agent of the Devil. While much of this was essentially Francophobic in character, the Empire came under criticism
specifically as 'a despotic military state'. The latter quote from
Arndt, however, reveals a certain liberal influence which would
decline in the more stridently nationalist attacks of later German
writers such as Sybel and Treitschke.[15]

Early mixing of liberal and conservative elements was especially apparent in Britain. The thread that tied together all the
Napoleonic wars was the clash of two empires, and British unity
was never more apparent than during the invasion threat of
1803–5. It was no coincidence that several of the blackest marks
of the legend, mass poisoning of his own troops at Jaffa and
treacherous slaughtering of Turkish prisoners at El Arish, can be
traced back to works such as R.T. Wilson's *History of the British
Expedition to Egypt*. Accounts of such horrors were disseminated
widely by prominent journals such as *The Times*, and occasional
diatribes such as the *Anti-Gallican*.

The conservative view sprang naturally from Edmund Burke's prediction that the Revolution would lead to military tyranny through its destruction of the old order: 'In the weakness of one kind of authority, and in the fluctuation of all, the officers of an army will remain for some time mutinous and full of faction until some popular general . . . shall draw the eyes of all men upon himself'. Napoleon, from the Tory perspective, was a rogue upstart, an adventurer capable of any atrocity. He was a natural leader of Jacobin France, revealing the base designs that lay behind hollow principles and the abstract formulae of the Godless Enlightenment. Behind Gillray's famous satirical caricatures of 'Boney' lay the message that all things uncouth were to be expected of a man of such origins.[16]

For Whigs, the Martello towers of Channel coast defence meant something different. To them, the Frenchman on Horseback (whether Robespierre or Napoleon) was a liberticide; for Coleridge, Southey and Wordsworth, it was the new, not the old, order that was being destroyed. Wordsworth, as poet laureate, wrote the following in his 'Ode written during the negotiations with Buonaparte in 1814':

> O France! beneath this fierce Barbarian's sway
> Disgraced thou art to all succeeding times;
> Rapine, and blood, and fire have mark'd thy way
> All loathsome, all unutterable crimes.

The poet had travelled far indeed from his 'The Prelude' of 1789, when 'twas a time when Europe rejoiced, France standing on the top of golden hours, and human nature seeming born again'.

From 1815 onwards unity in anti-Napoleonism would slowly disintegrate, as writers such as Byron and Macaulay moderated assessment in a line which led to Carlyle's flawed hero. Macaulay found it difficult 'to understand how a man of very great talents, who had been born in an obscure rank . . . should have been selfish, arbitrary, capricious and intolerant of restraint to a degree very unusual even in despots surrounded by flatterers'. Because it promoted talent, the Revolution was the source of Napoleonic power, but he had used the Revolution to promote personal despotism. His original sin lay in the destruction of liberty, but this was compounded by his attempt to re-establish hierarchy. Cruikshank's depiction of Bonaparte bestriding Saint Helena with cloven hoofs remained characteristic of British cartoons, but growing antagonism towards the Holy Alliance improved Napoleon's stock; by the late 1820s the epithet 'Waterloo Man' was by no means flattering of Wellington.

Only a small minority joined John Cam Hobhouse, friend of Byron and Constant, in the view that during the Hundred Days a former military despot had returned as a true representative of the people. That John Bull should not kick a man when he was down (by despatching him to Saint Helena), however, found a wider audience. The *Memorial*, in which Las Cases spent a good deal of time refuting the more scurrilous allegations of authors such as Wilson, helped to soften opinion. In 1827 the radical William Hazlitt would write a sympathetic biography, but Alfred Tennyson mined a richer vein when he raised the traditional alarm in 1852:

> O where is he, the simple fool,
> Who says that wars are over?
> What bloody portent flashes there
> Across the straits of Dover?
>
> Four hundred thousand slaves in arms
> May seek to bring us under:
> Are we ready, Britons all,
> To answer them with thunder?

French Empire meant slavery.[17]

For the British, as for most continental Europeans, the most powerful image of Napoleon was that of the conqueror. Both the Left and Right saw that the Napoleonic regime sprang from the opportunities presented by revolution, but thereafter their appraisals differed. For the traditional Right, the threat of this Man on Horseback lay in their belief that he had continued the Revolution's work of destroying the rule of the old order's social elite. Such associations would make conservatives very reluctant to place their fortunes in the hands of Men on Horseback, until the latter were no longer identified with social or political revolution.

There is irony in beginning discussion of association of Napoleon with other Men on Horseback with a set of examples drawn from Haiti; after all, Napoleon had sought to crush the independence of the former colony of Saint Domingue with an expedition despatched in late 1801. For a state which came to symbolize black equality, Napoleon was the consummate villain, a man who wanted to 'annihilate the government of the blacks'. His abolition of slavery in 1815 counted for little against his renewal of it in 1802, and his luring of Toussaint Louverture to France to imprison and leave him to perish was an act of base treachery.[18]

Yet from its onset until the Duvalier regime brought the military to heel through use of the paramilitary *tontons macoutes* in the 1950s and 1960s, the army has played an often decisive role in Haiti. According to David Nicholls: 'Authoritarianism has been a constant feature of Haitian politics since independence. Governments have been dictatorial and the pattern has been that of military command.' Nicholls argues that Haitian society and politics have long been riven by perceived racial divisions between a commercial elite of mulattoes and generally poor rural and urban blacks. Regimes have varied in the extent to which they have claimed to, and did, represent such interests, but according to Murdo MacLeod, 'the praetorian, Napoleonic figure seems to be somewhat of a constant'. Whereas regimes more closely identified with mulatto interests have tended to maintain at least a façade of parliamentary government, regimes identified with black interests have inclined more towards authoritarianism based on paternalism and the cult of the leader.[19]

Our four Men on Horseback, Toussaint, Jean-Jacques Dessalines, Henry Christophe and Faustin Soulouque, were all military commanders before they became head of their regimes. Each owed his position to political instability enabling seizure of power; each cultivated the leadership principle; and all were highly authoritarian. Of the four, however, only Christophe and Soulouque held power long enough to consolidate their rule, and thereby invite comparison to Napoleon. The regime created by Toussaint has been described as a 'military despotism': Toussaint was named governor-general for life and the constitution of 1801 concentrated authority in his hands while turning local government over to army officers. After French duplicity removed Toussaint in 1802, Dessalines gradually fought his way to the top, having himself crowned Emperor in October 1804. His constitution again concentrated power in the leader, and administration fell partly to a council of state composed of generals. Within two years Dessalines had himself been betrayed, ambushed by rebel troops, prior to the division of

Haiti into a republic led by General Pétion in the south, and, ultimately, a monarchy ruled by Christophe in the north.[20]

Toussaint did at times style himself the 'Black Napoleon' and recently Martin Ros has developed parallels between the two in *Night of Fire: The Black Napoleon and the Battle for Haiti*. Yet the author emphasizes that similarities were superficial, whereas differences were fundamental. The two shared charismatic leadership and the role of the army was pronounced in their political systems. However, whereas Napoleon was a false liberator, Toussaint was genuine. While Napoleon failed in plans for world conquest, Toussaint's objective, black emancipation, was achieved. Better still, Napoleon was a pale imitation of Toussaint: the former could have learned a great deal from Toussaint's use of guerrilla tactics, Toussaint's troops moved faster than those of Bonaparte, and the Imperial Guard was simply copying Toussaint's Blue Cossacks in cultivating moustaches and beards. In an arresting reversal of imagery, Napoleon is thus depicted as an inferior version of his rival.[21]

As Nicholls notes, Toussaint has by no means been viewed uniformly by Haitians as simply a liberator, yet ultimately both he and Dessalines did free Haiti by overthrowing French rule. Whatever else the Directory might have been, it was French; Brumaire was essentially a palace coup rather than an act of liberation. The adoption of the title Emperor by Dessalines could lead to certain analogies, but the most striking feature of Dessalines was his blood lust for French whites. British-inspired rumours about Napoleon's actions in Egypt could provoke comparison, but allegations of Napoleonic cruelty paled before the hatred born of slavery.[22]

Similarities are stronger if we turn to Christophe, King Henry I from June 1811 to October 1820, and Soulouque, Emperor Faustin I from August 1849 to January 1859. Christophe, in fact, held British monarchy in higher esteem than the French variant, yet his creation of a hereditary court nobility, for which he designed the attire, passion for monument building, and coronation were all decidedly Napoleonic in tone. So too was the authoritarian nature of his rule, wherein military discipline was imposed on society, alongside fundamental reforms such as his rural code (part of the Code Henry) and attempts to found an educational system. Unlike the Pétion Republic in the south, where plantations were divided among smallholders, the plantation system was maintained in the monarchy. The army oversaw production, and one-quarter of the proceeds went to the state, so that the Crown treasury dwarfed that of the Republic.[23] Points of comparison among Soulouque, Napoleon I and Louis-Napoleon abounded. All three were underestimated by the politicians, who thought they could be made puppets. The repression deployed by Soulouque, after he had been named President of the Republic of Haiti in March 1847, was reminiscent of the Bonapartes. By the end of 1849 Soulouque had transformed Haiti into an Empire, recreating an extensive nobility, adding a Legion of Honour, and modelling his coronation on that of 1804. Soulouque was as much a warrior as our first three examples, and until his fall in late December 1858 his reign was marked principally by fruitless attempts to conquer Santo Domingo. There were in fact legitimate geo-political reasons for trying to secure what might have become a launching pad for renewed imperial intervention by France, Britain or the United States, but 'Soulouque's international reputation was . . . one of a self-indulgent petty tyrant, driven by lust for Napoleonic grandeur'. According to Robert Walsh, effectively the American consul-general: 'The Haitian Government is a despotism of the most ignorant, corrupt and vicious description, with a military establishment so enormous that while it absorbs the largest portion of its revenue for its support, it dries up the very sources of national prosperity'. We are very close here to the image of the Ogre.[24]

Although it was with Louis-Napoleon specifically in mind that French caricaturists Honoré Daumier, Cham and Nadar made Soulouque the butt of their satire, they interpreted both contemporary emperors as the heirs of Napoleon I. Indeed, the form given Soulouque in cartoons, when it was not entirely racist in depictions of bestiality, signified Napoleon I rather than his nephew. Thus in a cartoon of 1850, Nadar placed Soulouque atop the statue of Napoleon on the Vendôme Column, lampooning the Haitian's efforts to 'make himself over into a new Napoleon'. For the press, the most capital of crimes lay in repression of freedom of expression, but the key was that Soulouque served to reveal the true meaning of the Napoleonic heritage, in a manner similar to Hugo depicting 'Napoleon the Little' as a form of expiation for his uncle.[25]

In all of this reflection, the element of despotism based on, and serving only, the military came increasingly into focus. Gone was the liberal Bonaparte of 1815, and fast disappearing was the image of a national unifier ruling in the interests of all. Our four Haitian 'Men on Horseback' all fell due to internal division rather than foreign intervention. More importantly, none of them gave much credibility to the Napoleonic claim that concentration of power in the hands of a general would eventually lead to liberty.

Spain and her former colonies have contributed much of the vocabulary used to describe military intervention; *pronunciamento* (declarations designed to influence government policy, usually with more than a hint of potential rebellion) and *caudillo* (a military chieftain whose power base often lies in one wing of the army and often is restricted to certain regions) are but two of the more familiar terms. From a vast array of Men on Horseback, we can select Antonio Lopez de Santa Anna and Baldomero Espartero. Both were initially associated with left-wing aspirations, but the rule of neither promoted social or political revolution.[26]

General Santa Anna was the leading political figure in Mexico from Independence in 1821 to 1855. He had played an important role in freeing the former colony of New Spain, and his revolt against Iturbide (Agustin I) in 1823 was vital to thwarting the latter's attempt to establish an empire. He would hold the office of president frequently, establishing quasi-dictatorships between 1841 and 1845 and again between 1853 and 1855. In the latter period his rule became increasingly monarchical, although Mexico remained formally a republic. Thus although he did not quite strangle a republic in the cradle, his relation to parliamentary democracy was akin to that of Napoleon, and several of his acts were designed to evoke memories – creation of a Legion of Honour, and use of plebiscite to prop up his rule.

Santa Anna, his partisans and his opponents fostered comparison. Napoleonic pictures, statues and books filled Santa Anna's haciendas. After defeat at the battle of San Jacinto in April 1836, he informed the Texan General Sam Houston, 'Sir, yours is no common destiny; you have captured the Napoleon of the west'; back in Mexico City liberal journalists sneered at the 'little Napoleon'. While his first dictatorship was being overthrown in 1845, he pleaded to Congress for exile rather than execution in the following terms: 'Napoleon, after having outraged Europe, was exiled to Saint Helena'. Whether in victory or defeat, analogy to Napoleon served to puff his status.[27]

Illustration 3.1 Honoré Daumier, lithograph in *Le Charivari*, 15 June 1850. The picture depicts Soulouque plunging a critical European journalist into a cauldron of burning oil.

Certainly there were similarities. By invading Spain in 1808 and seizing the throne, Napoleon had triggered a succession of revolts which eventually gained Mexican independence, but also entailed heavy loss of life, 'the rise of uncontrolled militarism', an 'explosion of regionalism' and the spread of 'banditry and political violence'. Thereafter the Republic had to be defended: against armed intervention by Spain in 1829 and France in 1838, and during the frequent wars with Texas and then the USA, including the invasions of 1846–47. Times were propitious for a *caudillo* who could associate himself with patriotism. Santa Anna was not an armchair general; he was a mediocre commander, but he was courageous and did more than his fair share of fighting. As with Napoleon, support from his troops could extend into broad popularity following victory, but defeat could damage his fortunes.

The two also shared much in method. Both recognized the importance of propaganda, and sought to prevent expression of alternative accounts when they had the power to do so. Santa Anna's proclamation to his troops in June 1821 was typical: 'Comrades! You are going to put an end to the great work of reconquering our liberty! You are going to plant the eagle of the Mexican empire, humiliated three centuries ago on the plains of the Valley of Otumba, on the banks of the humble Otumba, where the Castilian flag was first unfurled.' Less public was his statement as president that: 'A hundred years to come my people will not be fit for liberty. They do not know what it is; unenlightened as they are, and under the influence of a Catholic clergy, a despotism is the proper government for them.'[28]

In the many hostile accounts of Santa Anna the equivalent of an Ogre image is strong, based on exorbitant fiscal exactions and the slaughter of young soldiers. Especially reminiscent are charges that had Santa Anna pursued a more moderate course in dealings with Texas, war with the USA and subsequent territorial losses might have been avoided. For Anglo-Saxons there was the horror of *deguello* (execution of all prisoners taken under arms) after the battle of the Alamo; for Mexicans there was dissipation of the revenues of the Gadsden Purchase on lavish display.[29]

It would not be difficult to compile an equally lengthy list of differences. No one can miss the significance of the army in Napoleonic France, but France was never the playground for the military that was Mexico. No Mexican regime could be founded without military backing, officers dominated most regimes, and the military enjoyed privileges (*fueros*) which removed it from civilian authority. According to E. Gruening, in 1821 there was roughly one officer for every two soldiers in Mexico City; in sixteen of the years between 1823 and 1845 annual military appropriations exceeded the total national revenue. In certain regards Mexico was the perfect example of Finer's model of 'low political culture' wherein its organization makes the army unrivalled by any civilian group. Yet what is most notable is that into the vacuum created by the collapse of colonial rule surged not just the army, but many regionally based armies led by their military chieftains.[30] Santa Anna was but one of many *caudillos* whose fortunes were linked to the intense regionalism that blocked unification. Even while in power, he never enjoyed the unity of command and rule held by Bonaparte, and hence he could not provide the elements of consolidation and stability given France by Napoleon. Whereas the rule of law recovered in France, no such progress came to Mexico under Santa Anna. Instead, his 'Age' is associated with 'chronic political upheaval', at least partly attributable to the demands of the army. Among contemporaries his name became 'synonymous of efforts to foment anarchy for private ends'. Moreover, while Santa Anna posed as a statesman-general, he in fact had little idea of how to govern; being above party masked bankruptcy in terms of social or economic policy.[31]

When authors refer to Napoleon in relation to Santa Anna, they do so as a means to heighten the elements of military despotism, callous ambition and corruption. Both are seen as agents who blocked progress toward liberal democracy while despoiling their nations. Thus Santa Anna's flight before invading American forces conjures visions of the retreat from Moscow. No such associations are made in terms of figures such as General de Herrera, a contemporary of the 'Napoleon of the West', but one who is associated with moderate liberalism, dedication to the republic, and sincere interest in the people of Mexico. It is Santa Anna who brings Napoleon to mind, reflecting him in a very disreputable light. Allusions of course are frequent in Hanighen's *The Napoleon of the West*, but while reference to the 'prototype' may serve to belittle Santa Anna, Napoleon emerges simply as a more accomplished villain.[32]

Spain in the era of the *pronunciamento* (roughly from 1814 to 1874) presents us with a cavalry of Men on Horseback, all seemingly riding in different directions. For every faction – absolutist, Liberal, Carlist, Moderate, Progressive or Democrat – there was at least one *caudillo*. Of those who ran regimes, none of Generals Espartero, Narváez, O'Donnell or Prim established military dictatorships. They sought to establish constitutional monarchies which, to varying degrees, recognized the principle of representative government through a variety of parliaments and franchises. In essence, from the 1830s onwards power was shared among the Bourbon dynasty, the army and the dynastic parties.[33]

Amidst an extraordinary succession of regimes, certain features emerged. The impact of Napoleon's invasion of 1808 was to weaken the authority of the Spanish Bourbons, providing a vacuum into which a variety of contenders surged. Whether a new regime was founded on the basis of foreign intervention, revolution, palace intrigue or *coup d'état*, the military always played a leading role. Henry Maine calculated that between 1812 and 1875 there were 'forty military risings of a serious nature'. The army was not, however, a homogeneous entity; each political group had its general and vice versa, although neither could be said to be in control of the other. When in power generals tended to go their own way. On the other hand, politicization of the military meant that appointments were often based on patronage and political alignment, rather than ability. After the War of Liberation had been consummated by the Restoration of Ferdinand VII in 1814, the Spanish regular army may have been 'lean and mean', but it was not much of a 'fighting machine'.[34]

Nevertheless, the army was always able to contest civilian authority. During the War of Liberation, officers frequently challenged the rule of regional and national civilian *juntas*, and during the Liberal interlude of 1819–23, army interests were successfully defended against attempts to reduce military expenditure. After French intervention in 1823 had again restored Ferdinand, he conducted the inevitable purge, but thereafter the state took care that its military was provided with better pay and better material conditions. The outbreak of ultraroyalist Carlist revolt in the 1830s then assured that subsequent constitutional regimes would be highly reliant on the army. Generals, in turn, needed to assure supplies and salaries, and this increasingly led them to assert political control.[35]

The regular army grew dramatically and its toll on budgets was enormous; during the First Carlist War (1833–40) it increased from 40,000 to 200,0000 and gobbled up 80 per cent of state revenues. By 1866 there were 302,000 men in uniform, with 100,000 in reserve. Moreover, relentless promotion meant that the army was ludicrously top-heavy; in 1872 one commentator 'complained that the Spanish army was commanded by enough officers to take charge of an army of two million men'. The role of Catholic clergymen in the Carlist rebel armies, and the fact that state revenues increasingly derived from the sale of nationalized Church properties, combined to assure that most generals were opposed to *ancien régime* reaction; hence army intervention usually upheld liberal regimes until the 1870s. But its role of enforcing order gradually pushed the army in a conservative direction.[36]

All *caudillos* lived in Napoleon's shadow, but the context in which they seized power was more complicated. Napoleon had enjoyed a great advantage in that his victories were gained outside France. For this reason he possessed a preponderant claim on patriotism uniting Frenchmen against foreigners. In Spain spoils must be gained to the disadvantage of other Spaniards, including other *caudillos*.

The most Napoleonic was General Espartero. He was not a military genius and his victories in the Carlist Wars have often been attributed to luck, although it is perhaps more fair to say that he had the sense not to engage until he possessed overwhelming force. He was brave: 'Espartero . . . was in advance of all, cheering and encouraging his men, and exposing himself to the hottest fire'. While his bulletins may have struck some as ridiculous, they served their purpose: 'Whoever has seen him on horseback . . . in the midst of his soldiers, will tell of the enthusiasm which his proud posture and warlike improvisations inspire'. Ultimately he wore down Carlist opponents and his greatest triumph, the Convention of Vergara of 1839, came when a Carlist army transferred allegiance for the promise of being placed on the state payroll.[37]

Espartero's origins were humble; the son of a village carter, he had fought his way up through the ranks. Promoted to command of the Army of the North during the Carlist revolt, he cultivated hero worship among soldiers and the general populace with posters and cigarette papers that bore his image. Success, self-promotion and a judicious marriage brought him great wealth, but by constantly posing as a 'son of the people', he became the symbol of popular aspirations. Equally important was the clique of loyal officers he built by showering promotions and public honours whenever possible. Other *caudillos* did the same, but rivals such as Narváez lacked popular appeal. When in September 1840 Espartero entered Barcelona, 'more than 80,000 persons filled the streets to acclaim him'.[38]

Espartero first grasped power in 1840 after allowing revolution to oust the Queen-Regent Maria-Christina. Espartero modelled his inaugural speech as Regent on Bonaparte's as First Consul. He claimed to be 'above party' and refused definite alignment with Moderate or Progressive Liberals, although it was with the latter that he was associated. As Prime Minister and Regent for Isabella II, Espartero, however, soon clashed with Progressives who called for reduction in army expenditure. The general could not allow his chief source of patronage to be debilitated; gradually he resorted to filling most of the cabinet with his personal cronies. Allusions to military despotism led to measures against the press. By 1841 O'Donnell and Narváez were already plotting revolt in alliance with Moderates and the exiled court faction surrounding Maria-Christina in Paris. These attempts from the Right failed but conspiracy continued; thereafter a revolt led by radicals and Prim in Barcelona necessitated Espartero's laying siege to the Catalan capital. By 1843 an unholy but sadly typical alliance of Moderates and Progressives had brought Espartero down, paving the way for an extended period of Moderate rule dominated by the more conservative Narváez.[39]

A second episode of vainglory came in 1854 when a faction of Moderates, headed by General O'Donnell, combined with Progressives in a revolution against the increasingly absolutist pretensions of the court. After his first fall, Espartero had lived in exile for several years in London, where it was fashionable to view him as a great champion of Spanish liberalism. Allowed to 'vegetate' in his garden at Logrono from 1848 on, Espartero's status as hero for the Left rose, if only by way of contrast with the likes of Narváez. According to a British diplomat, 'Like Napoleon in France, his portrait is universal in the huts of the poor'.[40]

There were vital differences between 1854–55 and 1840–43. Once bitten, Espartero was more than twice shy over Progressive demands for reform. Mostly he involved himself in ceremonials, while assuring the Left that as a 'son of the people' he would never allow the forces of reaction to recover. Meanwhile O'Donnell shrewdly entrenched himself in the War Office and acted as chief spokesman of the army when politicians began to talk about fiscal retrenchment. In fact, Espartero's main following in 1854 lay in the civilian militia; regular officers viewed the latter as a rival and seedbed of republican, socialist anarchy. Marx described Espartero as playing Don Quixote to Isabella's Dulcinea and there was some truth to this; had Espartero supported it, Spain would probably have become a republic in 1854. But no one, least of all Espartero, knew what he wanted, beyond grandstanding at parades. Opportunity was thus frittered away while Moderates, O'Donnell and the court planned the inevitable counter-revolution of 1855; in the meantime Espartero gave his backing to repression of democratic clubs and popular elements within the militias. After Espartero and Progressives had been shunted aside, Spain's fortunes would subsequently be determined by struggles between palace reactionaries and conservative Moderates led alternately by O'Donnell and Narváez, until Prim arose to engineer expulsion of the Bourbons in 1868.[41]

Ultimately the reflection cast on Napoleon by Espartero was less negative than that of Santa Anna. Espartero could in fact act harshly when challenged, but he was less brutal and tyrannical than his Mexican counterpart. Neither had much by way of political competence beyond posturing, but Espartero did at least tolerate representative government, provided that parliaments left him alone to run government in the areas that mattered most to him. More importantly for Espartero's hero status, the regimes that followed were indeed less progressive, based on the rule of an even more narrow section of the elite, the Crown and, of course, the army. Marx perhaps had the liberal Bonaparte of 1815 in mind when he wrote of Espartero: 'Extensive and violent epochs of reaction are wonderfully fitted for re-establishing the fallen men of revolutionary miscarriages'.[42]

Yet in the long run, Espartero was part of a package of problems which beset modern Spain. It could hardly be said that parliamentary government prospered under him; he did not enable civil authority to assert supremacy over the military and his accomplishments as a state builder were negligible. All of the *caudillos* allowed parliament to survive, but by preventing it from being effective, they did much to discredit it. In terms of stability, Espartero was less a solution to a problem than a cause to which all *caudillos* contributed.[43]

José Ortega Y Gasset, in a series of essays published in 1937 as *Invertebrate Spain*, cited the military as an example of a group which thought only in terms of its selfish interests, hindering development of a national identity which went beyond merely living side by side with, and exploiting, others. He dated the army's 'particularism' as beginning with the disillusionment that set in with the military after humiliating defeat in the Spanish-American War of 1898. From then on, the army detached itself from other groups, in a process similar to what Finer identifies as professionalization. Yet it seems more accurate to push the point of departure back to the Wars of Liberation. Generals covered all points of the political compass prior to the 1870s, yet none of the liberal *caudillos* did much to prevent military demands from debilitating development of Spanish state, society and economy throughout the nineteenth century. As latter-day Napoleons, they contributed to the instability and decline for which Spain became notorious.

Santa Anna played a similar role in Mexico. While his wars with foreign opponents gave him opportunity to claim patriotism, ultimately he did little to favour, and much to disfavour, national interests. Haitian 'Men on Horseback' could at least claim to be fighting for independence and freedom from slavery. Yet figures such as Soulouque also became identified with political regression or 'immaturity' in the development of representative government. Napoleon's image suffered through association with the increasing number of generals who intervened, sometimes in the name of order and sometimes in the name of liberty, but consistently in the interests of one small group within society.[44]

When scholars underline the extent to which the First Empire was organized to the advantage of the military, they revitalize what has long been a traditional view of Napoleon. Comparison with subsequent figures, however, suggests that Napoleon was far more than just a 'Man on Horseback'. His political support base extended well beyond the military, and while the army played a great part in his rule, he was never completely beholden to its interests. Perhaps more importantly, Napoleon was a great state builder and, for better or worse, his reforms were to prove remarkably enduring. One of his great legacies was that France would not succumb to military dictatorship in the nineteenth century. Nevertheless, the image of Napoleon as prototype for military strongmen has been very strong; it will continue to be so because it is grounded in a partial but plausible interpretation of him.[45]

Notes

1 See S.E. Finer, *The Man on Horseback* (Harmondsworth, 1975), particularly pp. 187–204.
2 See T. Carlyle, *On Heroes and Hero-worship* (Oxford, 1968), pp. 312–19.

3 See J. Lynn, 'Towards an army of honour: the moral evolution of the French army, 1789–1815', *French Historical Studies*, 16 (Spring 1989), pp. 152–82, Baroness de Staël, *Considerations on the Principal Events of the French Revolution* (London, 1821), II, pp. 173–6, D. Porch, *Army and Revolution: France 1815–48* (London, 1974), and P. Pilbeam, 'Revolutionary movements in Western Europe', in P. Pilbeam, ed., *Themes in Modern European History 1780–1830* (London, 1995), pp. 125–50.

4 See G. Ellis, *Napoleon* (London, 1997), pp. 193, 132–6, J. Tulard, *Napoleon* (London, 1985), pp. 192–5, and J.-P. Bertaud, 'Napoleon's officers', *Past and Present*, 112 (August 1986), pp. 91–111.

5 There is a vast literature on Napoleon as commander, but for a sampling see D.G. Chandler, *The Campaigns of Napoleon* (New York, 1966), P.J. Haythornthwaite *et al.*, *Napoleon: The Final Verdict* (London, 1996), O. Connelly, *Blundering to Glory* (Wilmington, Del., 1987), J.R. Elting, *Swords around a Throne: Napoleon's Grande Armée* (New York, 1988), and G. Rothenberg, *The Art of Warfare in the Age of Napoleon* (Bloomington, Ind., 1978).

6 See K. von Clausewitz, *On War* (New York, 1943), Baron de Jomini, *The Art of War* (Philadelphia, 1862), and J.F.C. Fuller, *A Military History of the Western World* (New York, 1955), II, pp. 405–542.

7 See C.J. Esdaille, *The Wars of Napoleon* (London, 1995), pp. 40–70, D. Gates, *The Napoleonic Wars 1803–1815* (London, 1997), especially pp. 3–9, and T.C.W. Blanning, *The French Revolutionary Wars 1787–1802* (London, 1996), especially pp. 145–53.

8 A. Forrest, *Conscripts and Deserters: The Army and French Society during the Revolution and Empire* (Oxford, 1989), and I. Woloch, 'Napoleonic conscription: state power and civil society', *Past and Present*, 111 (May 1986), pp. 101–29.

9 See I. Collins, *Napoleon and his Parliaments, 1800–1815* (London, 1979).

10 On the *Brumariens*, see M. Lyons, *Napoleon Bonaparte and the Legacy of the French Revolution* (London, 1994), pp. 29–42; on military dictatorship, see D.M.G. Sutherland, *France 1789–1815* (London, 1985), pp. 336–65.

11 See Ellis, *Napoleon*, pp. 136–41, and Sutherland, *France*, pp. 366–97.

12 See Finer, *The Man on Horseback*, pp. 5–27, 71–80, 149–51.

13 The Black Legend was spread in memoirs, newspapers and especially pamphlets; see J. Tulard, *L'Anti-Napoléon* (Paris, 1965), and G. Lote, 'La Contre-Légende Napoléonienne et la mort de Napoléon', *Revue des études napoléoniennes*, 30 (June 1931), pp. 324–49.

14 See R. de Chateaubriand, *The Memoirs of Chateaubriand*, ed. R. Baldick (Harmondsworth, 1965), especially pp. 243–8, 262–352. See also J. Tulard, *Le Mythe de Napoléon* (Paris, 1971), pp. 45–8, 93–101, and P. Geyl, *Napoleon: For and Against* (London, 1986), pp. 127–39.

15 See Tulard, *Le Mythe*, pp. 48–51, Ellis, *Napoleon*, pp. 199–209, T.

Ziolkowski, 'Napoleon's impact on Germany: a rapid survey', *Yale French Studies*, 26 (Fall–Winter 1960–61), pp. 94–105, and E. Millar, *Napoleon in Italian Literature, 1796–1821* (Rome, 1977), pp. 119–21 and 129–35.

16 Tulard, *Le Mythe*, pp. 51–2, and Ellis, *Napoleon*, pp. 208–14. The passage from Edmund Burke can be found in his *Reflections on the Revolution in France*, ed. T. Mahony (New York, 1955), p. 258. For examples of English caricature, see M. Duffy, *The Englishman and the Foreigner* (Cambridge, 1986), pp. 314–79, and M.D. George, *English Political Caricatures* (Oxford, 1959), pp. 53–165.

17 For the passages of poetry, see R. Gibson, *Best of Enemies* (London, 1995), pp. 111–12, 167, 202–3. See also George, *English Political Caricatures*, pp. 165–9, 173–4, 222 and 235–40, T.B. Macaulay, *Napoleon and the Restoration of the Bourbons* (London, 1977), pp. 49–50, and F.J. MacCunn, *The Contemporary English View of Napoleon* (London, 1914), especially pp. 183–292.

18 See R. and N. Heinl, *Written in Blood* (Boston, 1978), pp. 99–122, and C.L.R. James, *The Black Jacobins* (London, 1980).

19 D. Nicholls, *From Dessalines to Duvalier* (Cambridge, 1979), p. 245, and M.J. MacLeod, 'The Soulouque regime in Haiti, 1847–1859: a reevaluation', *Caribbean Studies*, 10 (1970), p. 35.

20 See G.F. Tyson, ed., *Toussaint L'Ouverture* (Englewood Cliffs, N.J., 1973) and C.E. Frick, 'Dilemmas of emancipation: from the Saint Domingue insurrections of 1791 to the emerging Haitian State', *History Workshop Journal*, 46 (1998), pp. 1–15.

21 M. Ros, *Night of Fire: The Black Napoleon and the Battle for Haiti* (New York, 1994), especially pp. 57–81, 115–31, 146–152, 169–81.

22 See Nicholls, *From Dessalines to Duvalier*, pp. 32, 91–100, 120, 172 and 206.

23 See Heinl and Heinl, *Written in Blood*, pp. 145–64, and H. Cole, *Christophe: King of Haiti* (London, 1967), pp. 191–278.

24 Heinl and Heinl, *Written in Blood*, pp. 194–212, and MacLeod, 'The Soulouque regime', pp. 35–48.

25 E. Childs, 'Secret agents of satire: Daumier, censorship, and the image of the exotic in political caricature, 1850–1860', *Proceedings of the Annual Meeting of the Western Society for French History*, 17 (1990), pp. 334–46.

26 For further discussion of vocabulary, see Finer, *The Man on Horseback*, p. 164, S. Payne, *Politics and the Military in Modern Spain* (Stanford, Calif., 1967), pp. 14–15, R. Carr, *Spain 1808–1975* (Oxford, 1982), pp. 124–5, and E. Christiansen, *The Origins of Military Power in Spain* (Oxford, 1967), p. 1.

27 For background, see L. Bethell, ed., *The Cambridge History of Latin America* (Cambridge, 1985), pp. 51–94, 423–70. Among biographies, W.H. Callcott, *Santa Anna* (Hamden, Conn., 1964) is readable and relatively balanced; see pp. 126–7, 311. F.C. Hanighen, *Santa Anna: The Napoleon of the West* (New York, 1934) is resolutely hostile and condescending towards Mexico generally. The quotes of Santa Anna are taken from F. Robinson, *Mexico and her Military Chieftains* (Glorietta, N.M., 1970), pp. 172, 198.

28 See Callcott, *Santa Anna*, pp. 25, 108–9.
29 See for example the contributions of L.B. Simpson and J. Sierra in W.D. Raat, ed., *Mexico* (Lincoln, Nebr., 1982), pp. 60–83, 105–21, and that of N. Benson in J.E. Rodriguez O, ed., *The Independence of Mexico* (Irvine, Calif., 1989), pp. 275–307. See also Callcott, *Santa Anna*, pp. 122–38, 296–8.
30 See E. Gruening, *Mexico and its Heritage* (New York, 1928), pp. 289–331.
31 See Callcott, *Santa Anna*, p. 276, and M. Costeloe, *The Central Republic in Mexico, 1835–1846* (Cambridge, 1993), pp. 2–15.
32 On Herrera, see T.E. Cotner, *The Military and Political Career of José Joaquin De Herrera, 1792–1854* (New York, 1949). On 'Moscow', see L.B. Simpson's contribution to Raat, ed., *Mexico*, p. 79. See also Hanighen, *Santa Anna*, pp. 8, 33, 48, 53, 72–3, 155, 173, 185, 193, 216, 266.
33 Useful background reading can be found in Payne, *Politics and the Military*, pp. 14–30, Carr, *Spain*, pp. 79–319, Christiansen, *The Origins*, and K. Marx and F. Engels, *Revolution in Spain* (New York, 1939).
34 See J. Brandt, *Toward the New Spain* (Philadelphia, 1933), p. 35.
35 See Carr, *Spain*, pp. 105–154, 214–18, and Christiansen, *The Origins*, pp. 1–66.
36 See Carr, *Spain*, pp. 155–80, Brandt, *Toward the New Spain*, p. 30, and V.G. Kiernan, *The Revolution of 1854 in Spanish History* (Oxford, 1966), pp. 18–33.
37 See E. Holt, *The Carlist Wars in Spain* (London, 1967), pp. 96, 189–203, Marx and Engels, *Revolution*, pp. 102–4, and G. Fernández, 'The making of Spain's first *Caudillo*' (Ph.D. dissertation, Florida State University, 1974), pp. 431, 552.
38 See Carr, *Spain*, pp. 183–209, Christiansen, *The Origins*, pp. 67–100, and C. Marichal, *Spain (1834–1844)* (London, 1977), p. 145.
39 See Carr, *Spain*, pp. 210–27, Christiansen, *The Origins*, pp. 99–155, and Marichal, *Spain*, pp. 144–204.
40 See Kiernan, *The Revolution*, p. 47, and Carr, *Spain*, p. 250.
41 See Carr, *Spain*, pp. 227–310, Kiernan, *The Revolution*, pp. 33–252, Marx and Engels, *Revolution*, pp. 108–9.
42 See Marx and Engels, *Revolution*, p. 107.
43 See Christiansen, *The Origins*, pp. 102, 106.
44 See J. Ortega Y Gasset, *Invertebrate Spain* (New York, 1974), pp. 46–57. Finer's *The Man on Horseback* is, of course, littered with examples drawn especially from Spain and her former colonies from roughly the turn of the twentieth century onwards. See also A. Cobban, *Dictatorship* (London, 1939), pp. 144–58.
45 See Ellis, *Napoleon*, especially pp. 125–141.

4

Prototype for Hitler and Mussolini? Napoleon and fascism

Was Napoleon a forerunner of twentieth-century fascist leaders? The answer depends on how one defines 'fascist', and there is vast and detailed academic debate concerning fascism, both as an ideology and as a historical phenomenon. However, exact definition is less important to us than general understanding. For our purposes, we need only identify basic features of fascism in order to consider to what extent they were to be found in Napoleonic rule. This will be undertaken at the start of the chapter and analysis will be kept very general.

Given the extent of anachronism involved, few historians would seriously contend that Napoleonic rule was fascist. Yet it has often been maintained that fascism resulted from the combination of several long-term developments, some of which originated in the Revolutionary era. Could it be that Napoleonic rule marked a significant transition in the process? Towards the other end of the nineteenth century, analysts of the proto-fascist French New Right routinely note that Bonapartism was a tributary of this new phenomenon. In the second part of this chapter, we will discuss where Bonapartism fits in the long-term development of fascism.

Association of Napoleon with fascism has not, however, come about simply as a result of academics searching for the historical roots of a political system or ideology. Far more influential has been the force of circumstance. The threat of European hegemony posed by Nazi Germany and, to a lesser extent, Soviet Russia triggered memories of the wars fought against Napoleon. In this context, Napoleon was frequently linked to twentieth-century dictators, though detailed, comparative biographies were relatively few. In the latter, emphasis fell on parallels of circumstance and similarities of character, rather than on analysis of political systems. In a sense, such works followed the lines of the 'Great Man in History' approach, although their message was similar to that of the Black Legend. Working against this, at least in academic circles, has been preoccupation with systems rather than individuals, and this has tended to underline the vast gulf between the Napoleonic and fascist regimes. Yet, perhaps the bottom line is that no other modern European leader has posed the question of world conquest as did Napoleon and Hitler. The reputation of Napoleon has inevitably been darkened by such association.

As a historical phenomenon, fascism took form according to context, and often its advocates spoke more about what they planned to destroy than what they proposed to create. On the other hand, some of fascism's basic features were shared by other ideologies; it was the sum total of its constituent parts that gave fascism its distinct character. That precise definition is difficult can be seen in the swirling debates over whether various French groups were fascist. Happily, our concern militates against too much specificity; all we need do is identify basic characteristics associated with fascism. They can be grouped together as follows.

1 Fascist regimes arose amidst a backlash against liberal, parliamentary government. Although they rose to power partly by democratic means, upon gaining control they eliminated political rivals, effectively establishing one-party rule.
2 Fascism made a cult of its leader, who, as head of the party, gave strong, decisive action to redress the nation's problems and provided clear direction for the future. The 'leader' or 'Führer' principle was then extended throughout the government, military and economy.
3 Fascism tended towards totalitarianism, accepting no limits as to what the state could do. In theory, at least, fascism rejected

attempts to limit the powers of the state through individual rights or collective liberties. Pluralism was severely diminished, although, in a one-party state, the party did play a coordinating role in organizing mass support. This did not mean, of course, that all social or economic organization disappeared. But such organizations as did remain depended upon state approval or toleration.

4 Fascist states fed upon extreme nationalism. In international relations, this could make them extremely aggressive. In domestic politics, fascism was guided by an extremely narrow concept of what constituted the true or 'integral' character of the nation. Integral nationalism fostered scapegoating of allegedly foreign groups, practices or cultures, and this served to eliminate critics, while channelling discontent away from the regime.

Was the Empire a step towards fascism? Historians are rightly concerned to avoid anachronism, but tracing phenomena back to their origins is the very woof and stuff of history. Moreover, the Napoleonic period followed the Revolution, generally recognized as a watershed from which flowed a diverse range of developments. Thus, just as one can see elements of liberal democracy and fascism both emerging in the Revolution, one can also see them evolving under Napoleon.[1]

Bonaparte certainly exploited disillusionment with parliamentary government to establish the authoritarian regime that emerged as the Empire. His charges of corruption against the Directory were aimed at the nature of the regime itself. We can perhaps see this in social terms as a turning against democracy, yet there was not much by way of democracy left when he seized power. What appears more evident is that Bonaparte put forward the arguments of strong government untrammelled by division of power.

Bonaparte commenced his imperial progress by taking part in an old-fashioned *coup d'état*. Thereafter, however, the means by which he subverted the Republic had a modern ring. They involved measures of dubious legality and, at times, application of force. But the key to his concentration of power lay in the growing popularity his victories yielded. Popularity, registered in plebiscites, enabled him to push aside potential opponents with relative ease. He may well have subsequently based his rule on elite administration, but it was the plebiscites that allowed him to reduce representative government to a largely consultative function. This process can be labelled as Caesarism and it is certainly true that Bonapartist rule had nothing to do with party organization. His power was individual, but it was also based on a direct appeal to the nation and derived its legitimacy from the concept of national sovereignty. Circumstance rendered Napoleon rather more than the traditional Caesar.

Certainly the Empire made a cult of its leader, surpassing, say, the worship surrounding the Sun King. While Louis XIV might claim that he was the state, his authority ultimately derived from dynastic succession. Bonaparte intended to establish similar forms of legitimation, but the basis of his rule always lay in his personal claim to be the choice of the French. Much of his charisma derived from frequent exercise of command; battle illustrated his capacity for rapid decision-making, unhindered by the 'claptrap' of political debate. The public, accustomed to rapid change by the Revolution, was also treated to a whirlwind of domestic reform, so that stability did not appear as stasis. The regime was dynamic, but unlike during the 1790s, France appeared to have a leader with a firm grip on the tiller.

Hero worship of the Emperor became increasingly personalized, based less on what he stood for than on the leader himself. Bonaparte's penchant for likening himself to famous forerunners meant that he cultivated association with a seemingly incongruous variety of 'heroes', but such comparison consistently elevated him above all contemporaries. The messianic strands of nineteenth-century Bonapartism originated in Napoleonic rule, apparent in the catechism imposed upon the Catholic Church, and creation of Saint Napoleon. Yet, while the painter Gros's *Bonaparte Visiting the Victims of the Plague at Jaffa* suggested divine powers of healing, Napoleon was quick to inform the clergy that his power derived from Mars; hence his reminder to Pope Pius VII that it was unwise to irritate the modern Charlemagne. Important as the other aspects of his persona of leader were, it was especially the role of warrior that set a dangerous precedent for others to follow. It can be argued that Napoleon, Hitler and Mussolini all 'over-reached' themselves. However, Napoleon's direct command of his military had real credibility; the attempts of Hitler and Mussolini to play 'warrior' were based on delusion.

Napoleonic rule was 'one person' rather than 'one party' in nature. He did not rise to power as the leader of a party, and indeed his likening of party to faction played upon reaction against civilian organization. His government repressed all political and most social organization, not just opposing associations. On the other hand, Bonaparte, through his plebiscites, retained a formal tie to the notion of social contract. He was inclined to recognize this only when convenient, and only where France was concerned, but it did distinguish his rule from that of previous Caesars. In this regard he can be viewed as a transitional figure amidst the emergence of nationalism. That he claimed the Imperial throne, unlike Charlemagne, as Emperor of the French also gives the impression of transition: he was neither entirely pre-modern fish nor wholly modern fowl.

The Empire lacked an element occasionally identified as linking the Revolution and fascism: the cult of the martyr. While the Revolution celebrated figures such as Marat as symbols of sacrifice, there was very little of this during the Empire. Several explanations suggest themselves. Napoleon was not much given to worship of others, even as embodiments of an abstraction. Moreover, the subject of sacrifice, given problems of conscription and mass slaughter, was a sword which could cut both ways. On the whole, the ethos of Napoleonic rule was to celebrate material improvement, rather than to gird the people for further sacrifice.

All roads led to Napoleon; the symbols of his regime were linked to his personal rule, and while the tricolour was retained from the Revolution, it was the Eagle that truly represented the regime. The *Marseillaise* disappeared as national anthem. How could it be suited to Napoleon's personal agenda – empire? Moreover, while the Revolution and fascism celebrated abstractions such as liberty, unity or those who sacrificed themselves for the fatherland, this was a form of 'the people worshipping the people'. In this sense, Robespierre, Mussolini and Hitler were conductors for the mass orchestra. Napoleon was not just conducting; he was the object of veneration.[2]

Bonaparte expanded not just the authority, but also the 'reach' of the state. Much has rightly been made of the widening horizon of governmental endeavour brought by the liberal and Jacobin phases of the Revolution. Many such projects were however aborted; Bonaparte proved much better at delivering the goods, thereby fostering expectations of what the state should undertake. Balzac had a point in portraying Napoleon as the idol of bureaucrats; the Imperial regime possessed boundless enthusiasm for economic management. Nationalization of private property played little part in this, but the regime's penchant for public works and mania for statistical analyses were good indicators of where it was headed.[3]

There was an ominous side to state expansion, although it was often darker in potential than execution. The originality of the Napoleonic police state should not be overestimated; the Habsburg Joseph II had major claims in this regard, and much of the repressive apparatus of the Napoleonic regime derived from *ancien régime* and Revolutionary precedents. The state did become more capable of sticking its nose into private affairs, but generally did so with caution. Policing responsibilities were divided among several ministries and lack of coordination limited the repressive capacities of the state. Even Fouché, despite his sinister reputation, was hardly a zealot in Napoleon's service, occasionally interpreting orders with a latitude tantamount to ignoring them.[4]

The main objective was to cripple criticism. Control of expression was most evident in destruction of the free press, but it was extended in varying degrees to all forms of publication, generally by preliminary censorship and printing regulations. Those who went beyond the pale were banished from Paris or exiled from France. Bonaparte was aware of the importance of public opinion as no Bourbon had been, and hence a central role of the administration was to monitor the public, so as to be able to intervene when necessary. In this sense the regime did listen, and in fact criticism could, to a limited extent, be expressed through private channels – through patronage networks or via reports generally processed by the Council of State. But the ethos of the regime was less to represent than to direct opinion, and hence much effort went into propaganda. Commissioning works by artists such as David, Gros and Ingres was part of the process, but doubtless more consequential was direction given to the parish clergy as to what they should report each Sunday.[5]

Perhaps because challenges were not very great, the regime was not terribly savage. Much has been made of the execution of Enghien, and liberals such as Constant were highly critical of the substitution of military for civilian justice in the repression of banditry in the countryside. Even the most notorious symbols of Bourbon despotism, *lettres de cachet*, were revived. Yet when all is said and done, state disregard for the rule of law was exceptional; the number of Imperial political prisoners paled by comparison with both the Montagnard Red Terror and the

Restoration White Terror. As a police state the Empire was benign when compared to fascist regimes.[6]

Perhaps the strongest reason for distinguishing between fascism and the Empire lies in Napoleon's renewal of social hierarchy. In this regard, the Empire had more in common with traditional conservatism than fascism. Typically, Bonapartist elitism was a synthesis: Napoleon created a full court nobility, but hereditary nobility was rarely granted, and the legal and fiscal privileges of *ancien régime* nobility were eschewed. More substantive was Napoleon's policy of building his regime on the 'masses of granite' – local notables whose prominence was largely based on land ownership. The latter were targeted for inclusion in departmental or local councils, and participation in parliament. While none of these bodies held independent power, notables did wield considerable influence in their advisory capacity. In short, the notables were to serve as intermediaries between the average citizen and the state. It is perhaps possible that Hitler had similar plans in mind for the SS, but even were this the case, Napoleon had progressed much further in institutionalizing return to social hierarchy.[7]

For those who would build empires, nationalism can pose problems. Napoleon frequently appealed to patriotism, especially when he wished to extract sacrifices from his citizens/subjects. This could apply to satellites such as the Kingdom of Italy as well as to France, and to some extent attempts to combat parochialism fostered national consciousness, especially in military academies. Yet Napoleon was aware that patriotism could rapidly slide into chauvinism, dividing those whom he wished to unite under his rule. There was the rub; patriotism could be useful for conquering, but it could be lethal for collaboration within the Empire.[8]

Passing familiarity with the history of Haiti reminds one that racism was not exactly foreign to Europeans prior to the pseudo-scientific trappings it acquired in the second half of the nineteenth century. Similarly, Napoleon's administrators mixed a great deal of chauvinism with their Enlightenment views of progress. Yet when all is said and done, cosmopolitanism was not shorn from patriotism under Napoleon, as it would be later in the nineteenth century. If the 'oppressed peoples' of Europe were irritatingly slow to renounce the tyrants of the *ancien régime*, nevertheless they were scheduled for enlightenment rather than elimination or enslavement.[9]

Matters become more complicated when the Napoleonic kaleidoscope fixes upon the Hundred Days. In the face of renewed Allied attack, patriotism bounded forward, manifest most clearly in the federative movement. The federations have generally been interpreted in terms of renewed Revolutionary *élan* and there is much truth to this; old Jacobins played an outstanding role in organizing the associations. But many old Jacobins had evolved from democrats to nineteenth-century liberals, having shed their optimistic views of the power of the 'people' and become more preoccupied by preservation of civil order. Moreover, they were but one component of a broad anti-Bourbon coalition which included Bonapartists. Revolutionary Bonapartism's essence was captured by Joseph Cambon, former member of the Committee of Public Safety, when he founded the federation of the Hérault: 'Patriots of 1789! Let us banish all of the nuances that divided us during the course of the Revolution. . . . Let us form no more than a single and unique arm [*faisceau*] . . .'.

As expressed in 1815, patriotism still retained a cosmopolitan element of war against despots: *fédérés* would combat the Allied potentates who intended to trample 'the sacred rights of peoples', as they had done in Poland, Saxony, Italy and Belgium. But amidst anger at the Allies for 'the extravagant pretention' to fix 'the forms of our government', xenophobia was also gaining force, born of invasion and occupation in 1814. In their appeal for support, the *fédérés* of Picardy called on anyone who hesitated to 'travel our countryside: the bloody traces they left during their passage will make you tremble with horror'. At Strasbourg Jean de Bry, prefect and regicide, proclaimed that the *fédérés* were awaiting the Prussians, notorious for having 'surpassed the barbarians themselves in cruelty against women, old men and defenceless children'.

When he was exploiting Revolutionary *élan*, Bonaparte targeted internal enemies and this was strongly echoed in the federative movement. A consequence was that the dynastic, hierarchical structures cultivated during the Empire were weakened. Whereas the Bourbons were rejected because they did not recognize that thrones were made for, and with the consent of, the people, Napoleon was championed because his reign was the expression of the will of the nation. More strident, however, than aversion to the Bourbons was opposition to social privilege. According to the *fédérés* of Nantes, *ancien régime* nobles were 'the shame of civilization'; for those of Riom, noble pretensions were 'odious'. Perhaps the most vilified group of all were the *émigrés* who had fled France during the Revolution. Here too, Bonaparte had given the lead, but more important was general questioning of whether these figures could be considered 'truly French'. From their departure, they had connived with foreign enemies and fomented domestic counter-revolution rather than surrender their privileges. All the ills besetting France could be ascribed to them. While targeting of *émigrés* had a certain basis in genuine conspiracy and was as old as the Revolution itself, the growth of scapegoating 'unnatural' Frenchmen marked a serious reversal of the unifying policies Bonaparte had pursued from Brumaire onwards.

After Waterloo, opposition to Bonaparte was organized in parliament by Joseph Fouché as a means to force the Emperor to abdicate again. In response, lower-class *fédérés-tirailleurs* from the *faubourgs* of Saint-Antoine and Saint-Marçeau gathered at the Elysée, indicating their willingness to attack the Chamber of Representatives. Here we find evidence of the sort of Caesarism that would haunt politicians during the Third Republic. Yet, the *fédérés-tirailleurs* were exceptional; in the provinces liberalism was just as evident as authoritarianism. The two elements thus developed in parallel.[10]

The emergence of the New Right in the 1880s brought together previously antagonistic elements, and initially struck contemporaries as little more than a temporary expedient to destroy the conservative republican establishment that appeared to be entrenching itself. But the New Right did not prove ephemeral, and in some regards it can be viewed as a transition towards fascism. Defeat by Prussia in 1870–71 had unleashed a virulent strain of nationalism, characterized by longing for revenge and desire for 'moral regeneration' based on purging France of 'impure' elements. Scapegoating became a hallmark of the New Right; Jews were the leading target, but various groups were despised for their international associations. Corruption and 'decadence' haunted the imagination of the New Right, and much of their invective was hurled at the parliamentary system. Regeneration required strong government, and thus authoritarianism was another trait of integral nationalism.

The volatile mixing of these compounds first became evident in the Boulanger Affair of 1886–89. Named as Minister of War in 1885, General Boulanger attracted attention by his willingness to

Illustration 4.1 Engraving from the *Moniteur* of 16 May 1815. It depicts a review of the *fédérés* of the Parisian *faubourgs* of Saint-Antoine and Saint-Marceau.

match the German Chancellor Bismarck in sabre-rattling. He also cultivated popular support among soldiers and civilians. Some of his reforms were practical: revision of mobilization plans and introduction of the Lebel rifle. Others were pure dash: permitting soldiers to grow 'republican' beards and painting sentry boxes red, white and blue. When troops were deployed to break up strikes, Boulanger reported that they were sharing their rations with starving workers.

If this was not quite the 'whiff of grapeshot', republican politicians had good reason to suspect demagogy; between 1886 and 1889 over 370 songs in honour of 'General Revenge' thrilled hearts in music halls. Alongside this was the usual propaganda – posters, brochures, toys and a variety of food products adorned by the General's name. All of this came straight out of Popular Bonapartism, and there were other worrisome reminders. When Boulanger was dismissed as Minister, he began to champion a vague platform of constitutional revision based on strengthening the executive. More strikingly, he repeatedly ran for parliament in a series of by-elections, resigning after each victory. In effect, this was to imitate a plebiscite, but supposedly weak politicians then took decisive action: electoral laws were adjusted and Boulanger was tricked into fleeing the country when false rumours of pending arrest were leaked.

More important than the man was the movement that supported him. Much of Boulanger's early backing came from the extreme Left – disaffected radical republicans and socialists. From Boulangist victory they expected extensive social reform, if not revolution. Hence the movement had an anti-bourgeois ethos based on denouncing exploitation of the 'little man' by international (read Jewish) capitalism. Much of the muscle involved in massive street demonstrations came from Paul Déroulède's League of Patriots, providing a paramilitary element. They wanted an authoritarian republic with a charismatic leader who would restore France to her former primacy in Europe.

Complicating matters was the participation of royalists; certain Bonapartist, Bourbon and Orleanist leaders provided extensive funding and timely refusal to run candidates against Boulangists. In fact, the left wing of Boulangism was kept in the dark as to such contacts, adding to the confused character of the movement. Whether this duplicity heralded a fascist tendency to compromise with conservatives after social revolution had enabled seizure of power remains a matter of debate. One way or another, the combination of authoritarianism backed by paramilitary leagues, mass political organization, rhetoric of social revolution, and xenophobic nationalism marked a disturbing transformation in modern politics.[11]

However, after the Boulanger Affair petered out, the extreme Right was characterized by endless splintering. While integral nationalism attracted leading intellectuals, their contribution was to add further complexity by offering endless variations on what constituted being 'truly' French. Moreover, twentieth-century ultranationalist leaders such as Pierre Taittinger (president of the Jeunesse Patriotes) and Colonel de La Rocque (leader of the Croix de Feu) were even paler imitations of Bonaparte than Boulanger. Tiger Clemençeau (in World War One) and General De Gaulle (in World War Two) established much better claims to the Bonapartist mantle of unifier, but in this they embodied the element of Napoleon's reputation that made his legacy problematic for integral nationalist intellectuals.[12]

Few writers expressed the sense of decline after 1870 more sharply than Maurice Barrès; his reaction was to elevate patriotism as the highest of all values. As a Boulangist and, later, as leader of the League of Patriots, Barrès preached a brand of nationalism which fostered xenophobia, and to this he added a vague socialism based largely on protectionism, anti-Semitism, and discrimination against immigrant workers. Particularly pronounced in his works was the theme of sacrifice, especially apparent in the cult he made of young, dead soldiers during World War One. In his pantheon of heroes, pride of place went to Napoleon in the novel *Les Déracinés*, originally published in 1897. The author's vision had not much changed in 1922; in his preface to *Memoirs of a Napoleonic Officer*, Barrès refers to Napoleon as a genius because of the devotion to defence of France he inspired among youth.[13]

Other ultranationalist intellectuals, especially those associated with Action Française, found this less than satisfactory. Action Française took a variety of forms after its founding during the Dreyfus Affair, ranging from a newspaper to an intellectual movement, to a political party, to a student paramilitary league called the Camelots du Roi. Determining the relation of Action Française to fascism has always been complicated, partly because its guiding spirit from 1899 onwards was Charles Maurras. The latter combined integral nationalism and anti-parliamentarianism, two obvious components of fascism, with royalism and social elitism, more clearly associated with traditional conservatism. Similarly, while they might admire forceful leadership capable of directing mass energy, intellectuals such as Jacques Bainville retained a dry rationalism which rested uncomfortably with the appeal to emotion apparent in Barrès and integral to nationalism generally.[14]

In *Napoléon* (1931) and again in *L'Empereur* (1939), Bainville provided an interpretation which gave substance to his assertion in *Dictators* (1937) that it would have been better had Napoleon 'never been born'. For Bainville, dictatorship was not necessarily an evil. In *Dictators* his admiration for Mussolini was apparent, and while he recognized that Hitler was 'France's most formidable antagonist', the author also evinced respect for a man who knew what he wanted and used mass aspirations to get it: 'he has succeeded in winning for himself a position above all others, a position which sometimes makes us think of Bonaparte'. Yet, if Napoleon was 'one of the most perfect examples of dictator', this did not mean that he was good for France. Bainville was much less impressed by the inspirational qualities of Napoleon than Barrès, and more inclined to ask hard questions. What was the upshot of the Empire? Like de Staël, Bainville noted that France was smaller in 1815 than it had been in 1799. Unlike the great liberal, however, Bainville was less impressed by the sacrifices rendered than that they had been squandered. Bainville did find much to admire in the authoritarian elements of the Napoleonic regime, yet Imperial expansion had been driven by a chimera. After Trafalgar Napoleon had tried to combat British domination of the seas with mastery of the continent, but this was impossible, leading directly to Waterloo and all the resultant humiliation. Along the way, the Emperor had triggered nationalism abroad, preparing the way for German unification by ignoring traditional French policies of fostering the particularism of petty German states.[15]

Similar arguments could be found in Maurras's *Napoléon avec la France ou contre la France?*, published in 1932. Barrès and Maurras had frequently worked in close collaboration, and perhaps this explains why the latter did not draw the line clearly between Napoleon and patriotism until Barrès had died. There were, however, political motives behind Maurras's diatribe. The various extreme-right groups were in competition for a following, and attacking Napoleon's reputation served the purpose of criticizing overtly Bonapartist groups such as Taittinger's Jeunesse Patriotes. After granting that Bonaparte was a military genius, Maurras swiftly moved on to contrasting 'facts' with illusions. Napoleon was a false patriot because he was a son of the Revolution, apparent in the centralizing administrative reforms of Year VIII and the Civil Code; while the former sapped civic life, the latter fostered depopulation (presumably through egalitarian inheritance laws). Moreover, as a Corsican, Bonaparte was not truly French; indeed his role was similar to Jews in the Bolshevik Revolution. Having spread anarchy through promotion of revolution, Napoleon and the Jews had then profited by their own clan ties to surge to power while all others were divided. Such were the 'facts'.

In case anyone missed the point, in 1937 Maurras republished *Napoléon* alongside panegyrics of Louis XIV and Joan of Arc. In the Maurrasian scheme of things, the Sun King was a better model of patriotism than Napoleon because he gave France lasting grandeur. Joan was, however, the figure who best served ultranationalist arguments; Louis XIV could hardly be presented as the sort of disinterested sacrificial lamb of patriotism that Barrès celebrated. Barrès too had made much of Joan, but Maurras was more insistent that she was a heroine of nationalism, but not democracy. She was a symbol of unity based on royalist legitimacy, not liberalism.[16]

Léon Daudet also granted that Bonaparte was a military genius in *Deux Idoles Sanguinaires: La Révolution et son fils Bonaparte*, published in 1939, but he was otherwise scathing. Execution of Enghien demonstrated that Bonaparte was a true heir of the bloody tyrants of the Committee of Public Safety. Adoption of the trappings of monarchy by a Corsican clansman was little more than farce; in fact Napoleon had little idea of what he was doing, and 'the great drama of his destiny was to have had so many killed *For Nothing*'. From the standpoint of 'Teaching, national defense, morality, finance and national economy, democracy and demagogy hailed from the same sources and ended in the same effects. One must either fight them and their common revolutionary source, or perish.'[17]

In academic debates over whether the New Right was an extension of Bonapartism or whether 'this new revolutionary right had little in common with Bonapartism', much pivots on which elements of Bonapartism one identifies as integral. In the shifting context of modern politics, Bonapartism, like Revolutionary tradition, tended to fragment, with dissident elements realigning with other groups. Traditional right-wing Bonapartism flowed into a conservatism which could be authoritarian when confronted by social revolution, but which also accommodated itself to liberal democracy during stable periods. This element had very little to do with fascism, a point upon which leading scholars, otherwise divided, seem to agree. Yet there also was a Bonapartism of the Left which, in its emphasis on national sovereignty and egalitarianism, would appear to have had more in common with the revolutionary element of the New Right. It was for this reason that groups such as the Jeunesse Patriotes wished to plug themselves into a Bonapartist tradition.[18]

What became of left-wing Bonapartism? Doubtless some of the elements of Bonapartism flowed into the extreme Right, but Bonapartism was too closely attached to its originator for it to be convincingly placed within integral nationalism. The latter was based on exclusion of 'foreign' elements, of which Napoleon could be considered one. Ultimately the ethos of the Empire was outward-looking, based on a belief, shared with republicanism, that France's 'mission' was to enhance 'progress' throughout the world. Thus Imperial integration was far distant from integral nationalism. The latter was a product of insecurity, whereas during the First Empire France still possessed the confidence to claim greatness. It was, of course, such claims that made Revolutionary and Imperial France dangerous to her neighbours, but they also gave her a certain grandeur utterly lacking in the Far Right. Bonapartism of the Left went back to its republican origins.

The subject of dictatorship inspired a great deal of writing in the 1930s as the democracies of the Paris Settlement crumbled. Historians began to analyse dictatorship from its classical origins, while distinguishing its modern character through examination of its relation to the concept of popular sovereignty. Bainville's *Dictators* did warn against placing too much power in the hands of one man, but the author also argued that dictatorships were necessary because good representative governments were 'rare', and most of the governed were 'imbeciles'. Lurking behind his position was the characteristic Action Française argument that dynastic monarchs were less subject to the whims of public opinion, and therefore better placed to serve the true interests of the nation. Thus while the author praised Mussolini, he also concluded that those who wanted to bring fascism to France should think again: 'The Gallic cock is not designed by nature to suck the dugs of the Roman wolf'.[19]

Very different was the perspective of the British historian Alfred Cobban in *Dictatorships*, published initially in 1939 and then again in early 1943. With the tide flowing against parliamentary democracy, Cobban viewed dictatorship as an unnecessary evil. Like Bainville, he saw in Napoleon the first modern dictator, linking his uncontrolled power to rejection of failing parliamentary government. Napoleon was not simply a Caesar, because his power was at least partly based on mass approval; nor was he simply a tyrant, since state Terror was seldom used. Where Napoleonic dictatorship did, however, retain a certain pre-modern heritage lay in the Rousseauean concept of the General Will, with its tenet that power must be unitary. Sovereignty remains undivided, although it is transferred from the monarch to the 'people'. The latter is seen as a single entity and once its Will has been determined, there can be no limit to it. Thus parties and dissent are viewed as seditious once the General Will has been expressed. This combination of national sovereignty with unitary rule is lethal for liberalism and pluralism, wherein there is a 'majority will', but dissent and opposition are respected as integral parts of representative government.

Cobban saw a direct link between modern dictatorship and totalitarianism. Given their mass base, modern dictators needed to assure that economic problems did not alienate support. In a largely agrarian economy, Napoleonic economic policy was rudimentary, consisting largely of providing order and confidence. It was only with the advent of industrial revolution and its associated social problems that dictators began to intervene more directly. By the twentieth century, however, dictators were regulating their economies heavily, though to varying degrees. Nevertheless, the objectives of expanding control were always political, and closely tied to expansionist programmes. Writing when he did, Cobban naturally emphasized the territorial aggression of modern dictatorships. Napoleon made no statements about France being 'hungry for land' or 'living space', but the whole ethos of the Empire lay in conquest. We have previously noted a certain British tradition of emphasizing Napoleonic territorial aggrandizement and its link to boundless ambition, and Cobban's chapter on the First Empire flows from this stream of writing, although he avoids the simplistic images of bloodthirsty tyranny. The timing of the second edition of the work, when American participation in the war in Europe was so crucial, was perhaps not coincidental.[20]

There certainly could be no doubt as to the timely nature of Carola Oman's *Napoleon at the Channel*, published at Garden City, New York, in 1942. Historical parallel was the message: 'We may think that the ruthless ambition of Hitler . . . is a visitation of horror such as the world has never previously endured; but history shows us we are wrong in believing so. Napoleon was an equally disturbing force.' Oman's work falls into the genre of 'portrait of a people at war'; the heroes of the tale are the British going about their daily lives, as during the Blitz, aware of the menace across the Channel, but unwilling to submit. Specific analogies abound. With 'childlike innocence', Britain disarms after Amiens. Desire for peace has led to a disastrous treaty and it takes time for British ministers to recognize 'they had misconceived the First Consul's intentions'. Fortunately, semaphore telegraphs are the equivalent of radar and there is always the British Navy. Yet Tilsit foreshadows the Molotov–Ribbentrop pact of August 1939, and Britain's role is essentially to endure disappointment until Spain begins the process of continental resistance and Napoleon makes the mistake of invading Russia. Napoleon's plans were 'vast'; after a three-year campaign, he would be 'Master of the Universe'.[21]

The impact of contemporary events is also pervasive in Pieter Geyl's *Napoleon: For and Against*. The latter has justly become a 'classic' of historiography, but R. Holtman has a point in advising that it be read after acquiring a good grounding in 'Napoleonic facts'. The work was originally conceived as an article in 1940, but while a journal editor was reviewing it, Holland fell to Germany. When Geyl used the article for lectures at the Rotterdam School of Economics in September, students were alive to analogies between Napoleon and Hitler, as were Geyl's fellow inmates, one month later, in the Buchenwald concentration camp. After Buchenwald and forty months of further internment in which he was able to continue his studies, Geyl published the first Dutch edition of the book in late 1944.[22]

Thus we have a richly scholarly work imbued with the reflections of personal experience. In the preface, the author addresses the latter element directly: '"I always hate to compare Hitler with Napoleon." So, listening to the B.B.C. the other day, I heard that Winston Churchill had been telling the House of Commons, only to continue with a "but" and to enter upon the comparison all the same. So it is with all of us, and so it is with me.' In terms reminiscent of George Orwell, Geyl then briefly summarizes some of the more striking parallels. Hitler and Bonaparte are both children of a revolution convinced 'that it is bringing a new world, a new order', and that 'all the standards, all the laws of the past have become antiquated'. Napoleon used this conviction to break not just all organized expression of independent opinion, but 'free thought itself'. Enslavement was scheduled for all: Napoleon 'was a conqueror with whom it was impossible to live; who could not help turning an ally into a vassal' and who 'decorated his lust of conquest with fine-sounding phrases of progress and civilization'.

There were differences. The principles of 1789 were 'radically different and in some respects diametrically opposed' to those of the Nazi New Order. Napoleon did not 'embody in their purity' the principles of 1789, but his system 'remained true, from first to last, to conceptions of civil equality and human rights'. Yet 'methods of compulsion and atrocities are inseparable from the character of the dictator and conqueror'. Napoleonic rule was perhaps softened by 'the mild manners of a humane age', and Napoleon's personal character was not to be compared to that of Hitler. While Napoleonic France had its dark side, it did not have 'the annihilation of all opposition parties in jails or concentration camps', and 'the worst that our generation has had to witness, the persecution of the Jews', had no parallel in Napoleon's system. Yet when all was said and done, the difference between the Napoleonic and Hitlerian systems was one of 'degree', not 'principle'. One could not have put the case for the prosecution much better, and it was strengthened by an approach which was scrupulously even-handed in citing witnesses both for and against. Although the image of Ogre does appear, its unsubstantiated elements are shown for what they are – the false assertions of enemies.[23]

Whether one concluded 'for or against', comparison of the two dictators was inevitable in reading Geyl's work, and such association would remain a major part of Napoleon's reputation in the decades following World War Two. Given the prominence of Charles de Gaulle on the world stage, there were, of course, other points of comparison, especially among French historians or political analysts. But among many writers, the inclination to view the Revolutionary–Napoleonic era as a first world war, apparent in Oman, continued. While robust British imperialism diminished, at least some vindication could be found in the defeat of a warlord. Clash of empires, with freedom on one side and tyranny on the other, also suggested analogies between the Napoleonic era and the Cold War. The many studies of totalitarianism of this period added Stalin and the Soviet Union to the list that began with Napoleon. It would take time for scholars of fascism to break from this combination by insisting that anti-communism vitiated such association; even so there is by no means any consensus that the two extremes were intrinsically different. Perhaps more pertinently, Cold War assured that the issue of appeasement remained red hot. Was *détente* with Soviet Russia not a familiar mistake?[24]

In *Amiens and Munich: Comparisons in Appeasement*, published in 1978, Ernst Presseisen focused on British policy almost exclusively and took little account of the wide body of debate over Amiens discussed in Geyl's *Napoleon*. Particularly noteworthy was the way in which Bonaparte and Hitler emerged as one-dimensional characters: 'Can Hitler and Napoleon be so readily equated? In many respects they are of course not the same, but where the European continent was concerned their visions were remarkably alike.' They were products of revolution, and they practised a form of diplomacy for which British elites were ill-prepared. British statesmen misread the character of the two and the nature of their regimes; given 'the visions of these tempestuous figures, . . . appeasement had small chance of success'. The 'career of Bonaparte and the record of Hitler were replete with treachery', and 'coexistence with Bonaparte or Hitler was impossible'. Appeasement only whetted the appetites of two tyrannical warlords, who, at least from the standpoint of foreign relations, were essentially the same.[25]

Geyl had expressed reservations about lumping the characters of Napoleon and Hitler together, but in *Napoleon and Hitler: A Comparative Biography*, published in 1988, Desmond Seward entered where Geyl had chosen not to tread. The work basically consists of identifying similarities. In terms of career, both find their opportunity in revolution. They initially promote themselves as agents of an ideological 'middle way', but immediately establish police states. Neither wants 'total' war, but British opposition forces it. Early victories foster blind ambition, and dreams of empire begin. Neither is sufficiently secure to tolerate perception of defeat; hence they refuse to compromise, bringing ultimate destruction. Along the way they sacrifice all to preservation of their own power. The author also puts forward a catalogue of common character traits. Hitler and Bonaparte are 'outsiders' – *parvenus* and foreigners; both are opportunists and egotism is the key to all they do. In the case of Napoleon, the Civil Code is simply something he manipulates for his own purposes. Treatment of the Jews does present a difference, but this is not due to character. Napoleon has imbibed some of the ideas of enlightened despotism, and for him to have thought in racist terms would have been an anachronism. Ultimately Seward returns to Geyl's point – differences are of degree and not kind; Hitler simply had better opportunities for control provided by modern science and mass communications.[26]

Comparison to Hitler thus revivifies the image of the tyrant, and, taken on their own, Seward's portraits are compelling. Yet no work on either figure is likely to be taken on its own, and comparison to Geyl alone begins to reveal problems. There is nothing wrong with calling in Pitt, de Staël or Madame de Rémusat as witnesses for the prosecution, but Geyl's 'against' Napoleon reminds us of how poorly the defence has been represented. Should Taine be the leading expert witness? This is not to say that the work or its premises are to be rejected outright, but the author runs too close to what Geyl had said of Bainville: 'It is true that by . . . keeping obstinately to a single leading idea, one can write an exceedingly readable book. . . . But as for objective truth – no.' Familiarity with Napoleonic literature rapidly alerts one to which elements of the 'debate' have been ignored. Passing reference to Bonaparte's relatively 'benign' policies towards the Jews, or rapid dismissal of the Civil Code as something that Louis XIV 'instigated', hardly constitutes serious consideration of where these elements fit into the thesis. Napoleon is quoted as stating: 'We want a European legal code, a European appeal court, a single currency, a single system of weights and measures. I shall make the European nations into one nation and Paris the world capital.' How does this relate to the spoils system subsequently described? Perhaps all of this can be accommodated to the portrait of unprincipled tyrant, but to proceed largely by ignoring contrary evidence is not the way.[27]

A problem with association with Hitler is that Napoleon is apt to emerge as merely the lesser of two Ogres. Perhaps for this reason, Alan Schom in *Napoleon Bonaparte*, published in 1997, avoids direct reference. Yet the text begs comparison. Napoleon is a compulsive liar and utterly irresponsible to anyone because 'he had neither shame nor a sense of guilt'. He is a megalomaniac bordering on lunacy: his invasion of Egypt is mad, 'so totally unrealistic in its preparations'. Assassination attempts early in the Consulate cause him to 'retrench psychologically'; Spain and epileptic fits demonstrate that 'Napoleon was going downhill rapidly'. As his Empire collapses, 'Bonaparte did not seem to grasp the reality'; at the time of the first abdication 'all was chaos in Napoleon's mind'; during the Hundred Days he was 'living in his fantasy world'. He develops a 'bunker mentality': 'By February 1809 Napoleon was hermetically sealed off from the rest of society by his self-imposed isolation at the Elysée and by the fact that he had no real friends with whom he could discuss matters'. An attempt at suicide is, however, bungled, and by the end, the British have 'the most hated war criminal in Europe' in their possession. Other comparisons do arise: Napoleon was the 'most destructive man in Europe since Attila the Hun', but Schom's final paragraphs, with their references to the Dreyfus Affair and German nationalism, point to a more recent psychopath.[28]

In the absence of overt comparison, the Napoleonic Ogre flourishes, dominating from a powerful opening image to the epilogue, seldom long absent, and even thrusting the tyrant into the background. Therein, however, lies the problem. By now we are well familiar with the Ogre. He should never be forgotten and descriptions of carnage do serve a point. When the author sticks to narrative and drops his Taine-like invective, the impact is impressive. Yet, in his preface the author states that his objective is to achieve balanced insight. There is, however, little balance apparent; so strong is the image of Ogre that the other elements of Napoleon's reputation are either shunted aside or simply ignored.

Perhaps the best way to illustrate the point lies in comparison with Frank McLynn's equally weighty *Napoleon*, published in 1998. Here too the Ogre stalks, but he is accompanied by examination of Napoleon in the context of the Revolution and, perhaps more importantly, Napoleon's enemies. Whereas McLynn gives serious consideration to the reliability of witnesses such as Laure Junot (the Duchess d'Abrantes), one finds little such discrimination in Schom. Given that the principal theme of Schom's work is war, it is remarkable how little discussion is actually given to diplomatic history, beyond praise for Nelson, Wellington and a British character which, of course, Napoleon never understood. Why was there incessant war? Because Napoleon was an Ogre. Because he was an Ogre, civilian France desperately wanted to be free of him; hence the Flight of the Eagle was purely a matter of military betrayal of the Bourbon King who brought peace. Those civilians who rallied to the 'retread Emperor' must have been very stupid; after all, the Ogre 'had done everything he could as emperor to eradicate every trace' of the Revolution. As for the rest of Europe, she could 'sigh with relief' upon news of his death in May 1821. Perhaps, but by that stage revolt against those who had triumphed over Napoleon left little time for sighing.[29]

In 1944 Geyl expressed fear that the parallel between Hitler and Napoleon would extend to the former gaining a legend similar to that of the latter. Despite Holocaust denial, Geyl's nightmare has not been realized. On the other hand, the favourable elements of Napoleon's reputation have continued to hold their own against the darker side.[30]

Passage of time has tended to strengthen the significance of the caveats placed on comparison by Geyl. The more one learns of the totalitarian regimes, the more one is struck by the differences of degree and the element of anachronism. Although analogies between Napoleon and Hitler were frequent in A.J.P. Taylor's *From Napoleon to Stalin*, published in 1950, in *Totalitarian Dictatorship and Autocracy*, written by Carl Friedrich and Zbigniew Brzezinski and published in 1956, Stalin and the element of party have become central to discussion, whereas reference to Napoleon is largely incidental. Discussion of Hitler, Mussolini or Stalin inevitably entails consideration of their political systems, and the latter were rooted in their own time period.[31]

Where analogy proves more enduring lies in the element of character. Much can be made of certain apparently common elements, particularly that of the outsider becoming increasingly isolated from reality until a degree of madness sets in. But this variant of 'absolute power corrupting absolutely' is very common, and, in Napoleon's case, the argument concerning madness has to be stretched to a breaking point. Certainly stress and manic work habits brought moments when he broke down, but this was far short of madness and the periods of exile soon revealed his continued penchant for clever calculation.

The element of leadership amidst revolution will probably always produce a degree of association, and the image of insecure 'outsider' who became 'more French than the French' or more

'German than the Germans' will hold a certain intrinsic fascination until authors draw more attention to 'insiders' who gained
power under revolutionary circumstances. Has anyone asked
whether Atatürk was more Turkish than the Turks? For obvious
reasons, the Georgian Stalin did not associate himself with any
Napoleonic tradition; the term 'Bonapartist' was one of oppro-
brium in Soviet Russia. The case concerning the two fascist leaders was, however, more complex. Both emphasized identification
with their own national revolutions in a way which separated
them from the attempts at Bonapartist association made by figures such as General Pilsudski of Poland. But when they thought
of themselves in historical terms, both Hitler and Mussolini did
recognize a certain lineage.

For Hitler, such reflections were more private than public. He
was, of course, aware of circumstantial parallels, noting that he
too could inspire fierce loyalty while informing an officer (in
reference to his own relationship with Ludendorf): 'Napoleon
also surrounded himself with insignificant men when he was
setting himself up as consul'. Hitler's visit to the Invalides in June
1940 does remind one of the qualified respects Bonaparte paid to
Frederick the Great. Yet references to Napoleon basically demonstrated that Hitler was unique. Before disaster struck in Russia,
Hitler underlined that 'We have mastered a destiny which broke
another man a hundred and thirty years ago'; then again,
Napoleon was 'only a human being, not a worldshaking event'.[32]

The sense of rivalry was more acute in Mussolini. In the early
1920s the future *Duce* already expected to be 'greater than
Napoleon'; by 1944 he habitually compared the vicissitudes of
his career to those of Napoleon and Christ. Why aim low? He
was not above copying Napoleonic body language while posing,
although Bonaparte was seldom to be seen stripped to the waist
racing along a beach. Of the three plays Mussolini falsely
claimed to have written, one was entitled *Napoleon*. He and his
apologists liked to make comparisons publicly, always pointing
to the *Duce*'s superiority: 'Where Mussolini appears really great
as a modern statesman . . . is in the judicial, political and social
organization which he created. . . . He has a double superiority
over Cromwell and Napoleon . . . [in that he] has ruled the
country without giving anybody the possibility of thinking that
he does it for personal gain or egoistic ambition.' Perhaps this
sense of rivalry was part of Mussolini's undoing; it was one
thing to proclaim that the subjugation of Ethiopia was 'far

greater than the conquests of Napoleon', but quite another to think that he was an equally able warlord.[33]

The images of Hitler and Mussolini are sufficiently powerful that they do not need any association with Napoleon to heighten effect, and gradually comparisons have diminished since the immediate post-war era. In Alan Bullock's *Hitler: A Study in Tyranny*, originally published in 1950, Napoleon's shadow still hovers: 'In This Age of Unenlightened Despotism Hitler has had more than a few rivals, yet he remains, so far, the most remarkable of those who have used modern techniques to apply the classic formulas of tyranny'. Similarities of circumstance remained striking for the author: Hitler gained a hegemony over Europe 'comparable to that of Napoleon at the height of his fame'. Yet, the author also stresses that Hitler's rise was rooted in specifically German history. Moreover, as time passes it has been the element of 'modern techniques' that has drawn most attention. In 1992 Bullock published *Hitler and Stalin: Parallel Lives*; while reference to Mussolini is relatively frequent, Napoleon is absent. Partly this results from the point that three of the four lives were intertwined, but the same can be said of the circumstances in which they lived. A similar trend is apparent in other biographies. There is but a single, brief reference to Napoleon in William Carr's *Hitler*, published in 1978, and none at all in the first volume of Ian Kershaw's *Hitler*, published in 1991.[34]

Because Mussolini himself invited comparison, association with Napoleon is more likely to appear in historical accounts. What is notable, however, in Dennis Mack Smith's *Mussolini's Roman Empire* and *Mussolini*, published in 1976 and 1981 respectively, is that the author himself eschews comparison. Works on Italian fascism, as opposed to its leader, are even more reticent over analogy. In Gaetano Salvemini's *The Origins of Fascism in Italy*, written in 1942, the Napoleonic spectre is present, but only in a fleeting fashion. The author distinguishes between the march on Rome and Bonapartist coups, and while he describes Bonapartist rule as a 'totalitarian system', his emphasis on the modern nature of corporatism underlines a major difference. A. James Gregor's *Italian Fascism and Developmental Dictatorship*, published in 1979, makes no comparison of systems, and no mention of Bonaparte is to be found in Philip Morgan's *Italian Fascism 1919–1945*, published in 1995.[35]

While most historians can agree as to which was the 'good' side in World War Two, consensus comes less readily concerning the Revolutionary–Napoleonic wars. The *ancien régime* is not, of course, without its advocates, but a full embrace of Napoleon's enemies is difficult unless one simply ignores what they represented for the vast majority of European people. In this context, Napoleon will always be viewed in terms of the regimes that preceded and followed him. There is a place for the Ogre in Napoleon's reputation, and at times circumstance will give it preponderance. Yet there also remains a place for Napoleon as 'son of the Revolution', albeit a prodigal one.

Moreover, Napoleon's reputation as state builder has begun to push to the fore, spreading from studies of France to Europe in an age of integration. For Taylor in 1950, the attempts to unite Europe linked the two dictators in that Napoleon's Empire was essentially a sham, composed of institutions in which Napoleon himself did not believe. Certainly Napoleon was a nepotist, although in a fashion which would have embarrassed Hitler, Mussolini or Stalin. There seems little doubt that the Nazi New Order never advanced beyond Albert Speer's hopes for integration; it consisted wholly of plunder and extermination. At the end of the day, the Holocaust speaks more profoundly than invasion of Russia. The Napoleonic Ogre had his spoils system too, and we should never forget it. Yet, as will be discussed in Chapter 8, there was more to the Napoleonic Empire than that. Here too, altered historical circumstance facilitates perspectives which emphasize differences rather than similarities between Napoleon and fascism.[36]

Notes

1 Among many works, see J.L. Talmon, *The Origins of Totalitarian Democracy* (London, 1952), G.L. Mosse, 'Fascism and the French Revolution', *Journal of Contemporary History*, 24: 1 (1989), pp. 5–25, and J. Leith, 'The French Revolution: the origins of modern liberal culture?', *Journal of the Canadian Historical Association*, 2 (1991), pp. 177–93.
2 See Mosse, 'Fascism', pp. 8–9, 16–20.
3 See I. Woloch, *The New Regime* (New York, 1994), J.-F. Perrot and S. Woolf, *State and Statistics in France, 1789–1815* (London, 1984), and R.S. Alexander, '"No minister": French restoration rejection of authoritarianism', in D. Laven and L. Riall, eds, *Napoleon's Legacy* (London, 2000), pp. 29–47.
4 See E. Arnold, *Fouché, Napoleon and the General Police* (Washington, 1979).
5 See R. Holtman, *Napoleonic Propaganda* (Baton Rouge, La., 1950)

and also his *The Napoleonic Revolution* (Baton Rouge, La., 1978), pp. 163–78.

6 See M. Sibalis, 'Prisoners by *Mesure de Haute Police* under Napoleon I: reviving the *lettres de cachet*', *Proceedings of the Annual Meeting of the Western Society for French History*, 18 (1991), pp. 261–9, and F. Bluche, *La Bonapartisme* (Paris, 1980), pp. 88–9.

7 See J. Tulard, *Napoleon: The Myth of the Saviour* (London, 1985), pp. 181–95, G. Ellis, *Napoleon* (London, 1997), pp. 125–54, and M. Lyons, *Napoleon Bonaparte and the Legacy of the French Revolution* (London, 1994), pp. 160–77.

8 See Holtman, *The Napoleonic Revolution*, pp. 179–93.

9 See S. Woolf, 'French civilization and ethnicity in the Napoleonic Empire', *Past and Present*, 124 (1989), pp. 96–120. For further discussion of the nature of French Empire generally, see Chapter 8.

10 See R.S. Alexander, *Bonapartism and Revolutionary Tradition in France* (Cambridge, 1991), pp. 14, 66–94, 206–9.

11 For concise discussion, see R. Tombs, *France 1814–1914* (London, 1996), pp. 447–53. For more detail see F. Seager, *The Boulanger Affair* (Ithaca, N.Y., 1969), W. Irvine, *The Boulanger Affair Reconsidered* (Oxford, 1989), P. Hutton, 'Popular Boulangism and the advent of mass politics in France, 1886–90', *Journal of Contemporary History*, 11 (1976), pp. 85–106, and B. Fulton, 'The Boulanger Affair revisited: the preservation of the Third Republic, 1889', *French Historical Studies*, 17: 2 (Fall 1991), pp. 310–29.

12 For recent discussion, see R. Gildea, *The Past in French History* (New Haven, 1994), pp. 298–329, R. Soucy, 'French fascism and the Croix de Feu: a dissenting interpretation', *Journal of Contemporary History*, 26 (1991), pp. 159–88, W. Irvine, 'Fascism in France and the strange case of the Croix de Feu', *Journal of Modern History*, 63 (June 1991), pp. 271–95, and K. Passmore, 'The Croix de Feu: Bonapartism, national populism or fascism?', *French History*, 9: 1 (March 1995), pp. 67–92.

13 See M. Barrès, *Les Déracinés* (Paris, 1897), pp. 215–35, and *Memoirs of a Napoleonic Officer, Jean-Baptiste Barrès* (London, 1925). See also C.S. Doty, *From Cultural Rebellion to Counterrevolution: The Politics of Maurice Barrès* (Athens, Ohio, 1976) and Z. Sternhell, 'National Socialism and antisemitism: the case of Maurice Barrès', *Journal of Contemporary History*, 8: 4 (1972), pp. 47–66.

14 Among many works, see J. Blatt, 'Relatives and rivals: the responses of the Action Française to Italian fascism, 1919–26', *European Studies Review*, 11: 3 (July 1981), pp. 263–92, and S. Wilson, 'The "Action Française" in French intellectual life', in J. Cairns, ed., *Contemporary France: Illusion, Conflict and Regeneration* (New York, 1978), pp. 139–67.

15 J. Bainville, *Napoléon* (Paris, 1931), *Dictators* (London, 1937) and *L'Empereur* (Paris, 1939). The quotes come from *Dictators*, pp. 101, 112, 258.

16 C. Maurras, *Jeanne d'Arc, Louis XIV et Napoléon* (Paris, 1938). See also M. Hanna, 'Iconology and ideology: images of Joan of Arc in

the idiom of the Action Française, 1908–24', *French Historical Studies*, 14: 2 (Fall 1985), pp. 215–39.

17 L. Daudet, *Deux Idoles Sanglantes, la Révolution et son fils Bonaparte* (Paris, 1939).

18 For the main lines of debate, see R. Rémond, *Les Droites en France* (Paris, 1982), especially p. 44, and Z. Sternhell, *Neither Right nor Left* (Berkeley, 1986). A useful introduction can be found in Passmore, 'The Croix de Feu', pp. 67–72.

19 Bainville, *Dictators*, pp. 225, 261–2.

20 See A. Cobban, *Dictatorship* (London, 1939), especially pp. 79–95.

21 C. Oman, *Napoleon at the Channel* (Garden City, N.Y., 1942), pp. v–vi, 57–8, 99, 119–21, 132–6, 215–20, 227, 254.

22 Holtman's comments are in his *Napoleonic Revolution*, p. 217.

23 P. Geyl, *Napoleon: For and Against* (London, 1986); the quotes come from the preface.

24 See Irvine, *Boulanger Affair*, p. 14.

25 E. Presseisen, *Amiens and Munich: Comparisons in Appeasement* (The Hague, 1978), pp. 6–7, 17–20, 29, 58, 67, 111, 128–31. The author was using lines of investigation apparent in M. Gilbert, *The Roots of Appeasement* (New York, 1966) and A.J.P. Taylor, *The Trouble Makers* (Bloomington, Ind., 1958), pp. 11–39.

26 D. Seward, *Napoleon and Hitler: A Comparative Biography* (London, 1988), pp. 125–6, 216–19, 219–32, 295–303.

27 Seward, *Napoleon and Hitler*, p. 179, and Geyl, *Napoleon*, p. 343.

28 A. Schom, *Napoleon Bonaparte* (New York, 1997), pp. 30, 82, 281, 462, 489, 493, 552, 557, 656–7, 699–701, 719–22, 768, 775 and the epilogue. See also the review of Adam Gopnik in the *New Yorker*, 24 November 1997, pp. 106–14.

29 Schom, *Napoleon*, pp. 714, 786.

30 See Geyl, *Napoleon*, pp. 9–10.

31 See A.J.P. Taylor, *From Napoleon to Stalin* (London, 1950), and C.J. Friedrich and Z.K. Brzezinski, *Totalitarian Dictatorship and Democracy* (New York, 1956). One looks in vain for reference to the first 'modern' dictator in S.J. Lee, *The European Dictatorships 1918–1945* (London, 1987).

32 See A. Bullock, *Hitler: A Study in Tyranny* (London, 1952), p. 617, and J. Fest, *Hitler* (New York, 1974), pp. 157, 177, 212, 636, 642–6.

33 See D. Mack Smith, *Mussolini* (London, 1981), pp. 21, 106, 131, 188–9, 203, 311, the same author's *Mussolini's Roman Empire* (London, 1976), pp. 46, 85, 250, and A.J. Gregor, *Italian Fascism and Developmental Dictatorship* (Princeton, N.J., 1979), p. 239.

34 See Bullock, *Hitler*, pp. 735–8, and his *Hitler and Stalin: Parallel Lives* (New York, 1992), W. Carr, *Hitler: A Study in Personality and Politics* (London, 1978) and I. Kershaw, *Hitler* (London, 1991).

35 See Mack Smith, *Mussolini and Mussolini's Roman Empire*, G. Salvemini, *The Origins of Fascism in Italy* (New York, 1973), especially pp. 384, 414–15, Gregor, *Italian Fascism*, and P. Morgan, *Italian Fascism, 1919–1945* (London, 1995).

36 See Taylor, *From Napoleon to Stalin*, pp. 24–32.

|5|

The Great Man: Napoleon in nineteenth-century literature and art

Napoleon's greatest empire lay in the nineteenth-century imagination. The sheer volume of works in which the meaning of his life is discussed or illustrated is simply stunning. For this reason, consideration here must be highly selective. Emphasis will fall on literature, although reference will also be made to the visual arts. Moreover, discussion in this chapter will be confined to 'high' culture – classic works read or seen principally by social elites. Academics have at times assumed that 'classic' works fostered Popular Bonapartism; yet it is improbable that illiterate peasants were much affected by such sources. Elite and Popular Bonapartism did, however, spring from the same source, and hence we will commence with discussion of the arts during the Napoleonic epoch.

The theme of the 'Great Man in History', with its emphasis on human will and accomplishment, flourished throughout the nineteenth century; it was only towards the turn of the century that it began to lose its ascendancy. Napoleon was, of course, the prime contemporary example of the significance of a single being. Yet, from very early on, there was a pronounced tendency to make him something other than human. He would be rendered as a demi-god or demon, as an embodiment of broad historical forces who carried the future within him, or an as archetype, especially of the human will. In very little of this did he emerge as an ordinary mortal struggling against mundane, human frailties. There were a number of reasons for such depiction. Attempts to reveal the 'true' Napoleon were by their very nature political, and almost inevitably highly partisan. Impassioned dispute over the 'meaning' of his life favoured portraits that pushed his character to extreme dimensions, and this was exacerbated by his association with forces that continued to cause great disruption over the course of the century. Napoleon had himself promoted such identification and set the tone for dispute, and his followers and adversaries responded in kind.

Napoleon sought to immortalize himself through direction of how he was represented. According to one expert: 'Every painting and every object seems intended to celebrate his glory'. There is much truth in this, but there is also hyperbole. While he could influence the arts, Napoleon could never entirely control them. Napoleon is often associated with the artistic movement known as neo-classicism, and certainly contemporary inclination to imitate ancient Greek and Roman models served him well. But the origins of neo-classicism can be traced back to the first half of the eighteenth century, and by the time of the Revolution the movement had largely pushed aside earlier fascination with Chinese or Indian culture. Neo-classicism provided the context for Napoleon to go about his work, rather than the reverse.

Similarly, Romanticism had little to do with Napoleon's wishes. Because Romanticism emerged partly as a break from neo-classicism, and because it flowered amidst German nationalism, it is tempting to see some sort of opposition between Napoleon and Romanticism. Yet Bonaparte's notorious taste for the fictional Celtic bard Ossian, reflected in paintings by Gérard, Guérin, Girodet and Ingres, points in the direction of Gothic revival. In so much as Bonaparte had aesthetic values, he preferred a simplicity which would foster whatever message he wanted conveyed. Pragmatic as he was, he was not wedded to the tenets of any artistic movement.[1]

The collapse of noble patronage in France brought about by the Revolution did create a vacuum into which the state could enter in pursuit of cultural domination. Due to his growing state revenues, Bonaparte possessed vast opportunities to channel the arts and he was eager to revitalize the luxury industries for which France was famous. Napoleon was 'good news' for Jacob *frères* (leaders in furniture design and production), Sèvres porcelain and Lyonnais silks, and, in turn, he was celebrated by these great disseminators of Imperial style. As French political control expanded, such opportunities could be exploited in much of Europe; some five hundred Napoleonic busts per year were produced at Carrara. Yet there were limits to Napoleon's influence. He considered 'Great tragedy . . . the school of great men' and wanted to foster neo-classical theatre. Many playwrights were willing to oblige, but the Parisian public remained unmoved. Nor did all artists respond to the Napoleonic siren. Cherubini refused to indulge Bonaparte's taste for melodic Italian *opera seria*. He was therefore snubbed when it came to state honours, but this did not prevent recognition where it counted – Beethoven.[2]

In literature, history enjoyed a certain pride of place. Bonaparte promoted Clio, and the volume of works steadily increased. To facilitate scholarship, France's national archives and library were reorganized and their holdings expanded. Reorganization of the Institut saw creation of the Class of History and Ancient Literature; soon thereafter followed commissions designed to keep the Institut from becoming a forum for criticism of the regime. Patronage was not, however, limited to Institut members; commissions, prizes or sinecures were also directed at less renowned scholars. In combination with censorship, such means served to shape the character of historical writing. Certain themes were predictable, typified by an essay written in 1800 by Joseph-Marie Portalis (*fils*). According to Portalis, the relation between the Great Man and his people is symbiotic. While he shapes the character of his people, the Great Man also derives his genius from that people. The Great Man is both a thinker and man of action; desire to fulfil his destiny makes him impervious to common misfortune and provides him with the will necessary for accomplishments of transcendent importance. History progresses through a pattern in which dynasties are founded by Great Men who embody progressive forces; when dynastic lines become decadent, revolution occurs, moving progress forward, but also bringing anarchy. In the midst of disorder, the people turn to their new hero.

While it is largely true that, until 1815, Napoleon sought to draw a veil over discussion of the Revolution in the newspaper press, this was less the case concerning literature. Bonaparte was convinced that contemporary history was of more immediate relevance, and hence there was no policy of stopping discussion at 1789. Officially inspired studies of Caesar and Charlemagne were, of course, larded with reference to the founder of France's fifth dynasty. Presentation of the Bourbons was not entirely negative, especially where Henry IV was concerned, but the dynasty was portrayed as weak and incapable of providing unity by the time of Louis XVI. Nor was the Revolution all bad; it was a necessary eruption of emerging forces ultimately misled by a bloodthirsty Robespierre and corrupt Directory. Given her monarchical tradition, France turned to a 'Saviour' and in the Emperor she found her modernizing Charlemagne.

Perhaps more consequential was Napoleon's insistence that history take an important place in school curricula. Most of the regime's educational efforts were aimed at the elite, with creation of the Université between 1806 and 1808 serving as a vehicle to centralize and unify teaching. Of particular note was a commission established to stipulate which school textbooks would be used. Despite resistance from Fontanes, Grand Master of the Université and a determined classicist, Napoleon's emphasis on contemporary times became increasingly apparent in textbooks which presented the same themes as those of official or semi-official history. Thus when writers such as Hugo converted to the cult of Napoleon in the 1830s, their myth-making had a familiar ring to many members of the elite.[3]

Contemporary visual arts perhaps played a greater part in establishing the cult than literature, and Napoleon is inevitably associated with what is known as the French Empire style. While Empire style was no more a product entirely of Napoleon's will than neo-classicism, it did broadly reflect his intentions. He wanted grandeur – monumental structures of massive proportion, but with classical simplicity of line. On the other hand, Imperial furnishings should be sumptuous. Partly this reflected a trend towards conspicuous display already apparent in Thermidor, but it was also attuned to lavish Napoleonic pomp and ceremony.[4]

There was, however, something more subtle at play. Bonaparte's mania for designing costume was apparent among the Imperial nobility, state administration, clergy and members of academic or educational institutions, and his military officers became the peacocks of the age. Yet, against this backdrop, Bonaparte himself cultivated a modest image, symbolized by the famous *bicorne* (cocked hat), greatcoat and black boots. Simplicity of attire amidst foppery underlined that it was the talent of the Great Man that made him outstanding. Much of the European elite would dismiss Bonaparte as a charlatan who sought to mimic nobility of mind and manners, but remained a coarse imposter. At the core of Empire style, however, lay Napoleonic achievement – a direct threat to those who enjoyed privilege based on birth alone.[5]

If the Empire was to be a 'golden age' of the arts, it followed that Paris must be a showpiece, and a notorious result of such ambition was the looting of art treasures. There was nothing new in this, but Bonaparte systematized plunder and it was not simply a matter of economic asset stripping. Dominique Vivant Denon, Director-General of Museums, was but one of many 'culture vultures' who circled above the army, assuring that removal of treasures was based on aesthetic as well as economic criteria. He was not the average mercenary. The modern Louvre (named the Musée Napoleon from 1803 to 1814) probably owes more to him than anyone else; he played a major part in spreading 'Egyptomania' with his *Voyages dans la Basse et la Haute Egypte* (dedicated to Bonaparte in 1802), and his role was not so very different from that of Lord Hamilton, to whom the British Museum owes rather more than does Italy.[6]

Bonaparte wished to be remembered as a great builder, and when one takes into account the regime's many public works, it is difficult to deny his claim. Many of the more famous projects lay in additions: massive extensions to the Louvre, the covered arcades of the rue de Rivoli, the chapel and *salle des spectacles* of the Tuileries, and alterations to the Luxembourg Palace and former Palais Bourbon. Partly due to the costs of warfare, several projects, including a palace for the King of Rome, reconstruction of Versailles, and the great Arc de Triomphe, had to be shelved. In the latter case this mattered little; the completed Arc commemorates Napoleon rather than the July Monarchy, and is complemented by the Arc du Carrousel, even if the bronze horses of Saint Mark were removed by the Austrians in 1815. The Bourse, the Madelaine (originally named the Temple of Glory) and the Vendôme Column provide further reminders of Imperial neo-classicism.[7]

Empire style was spread especially through the decorative arts and here we find certain features which look decidedly Napoleonic. The great purveyors were Charles Percier and Pierre Fontaine. Their works of interior decoration at Malmaison, Saint Cloud and the Tuileries set a standard which was disseminated throughout Europe by their *Recueil des décorations intérieurs.* Spread initially by establishment of the Bonaparte clan as rulers throughout Europe, Empire style was then taken up to varying degrees by admirers such as Bernadotte, Czar Alexander, Fredrick William III of Prussia, Wellington and the Prince Regent.

Fontaine and Percier gave Empire style an elegance based on simplicity of line and in the *Recueil* they warned against indiscriminate combination of unrelated motifs. Yet, according to one expert, Empire style was 'heavy-handed, self-conscious' and meant to 'dazzle by its luxurious materials and exact craftsmanship'. One of the more notorious examples of decorative self-celebration was the Emperor's Table of Marshals, which featured 'a grandiose Sun-Napoleon glittering with the Byzantine pomp of his regal vestments and standing at the centre of thirteen radiating tongues of flame that ended in portraits of the Marshals of the Empire'. Moreover, below the simplicity of structural lines lurked a jumble of motifs – Egyptian, Greek and Roman often combined in porcelain, silver, furniture and statuettes, so that Greek gryphons were to be found peering at Egyptian sphinxes. While the origins may have been classical, the effect was not. At one level, this can be taken as a sign of a *parvenu* bourgeoisie newly engaged in pursuit of fashion; works such as Joseph Beunat's *Recueil des desseins d'ornements d'architecture* enabled the less-fabulously wealthy to indulge tastes for grandeur. On the other hand, it also reflects a Napoleonic inclination to associate himself and his Empire with anything that attracted attention.[8]

Desire to immortalize Napoleon is especially apparent in painting; Napoleon was truly blessed by the presence of David, Gros, Gérard, Girodet, Prud'hon and Ingres. Among sculptors, Corbet and Houdon also contributed, but to less effect, and Canova was reluctant. As a whole, it was painting that added most to myth-making.

Certain characteristics can be seen in the paintings of Jacques-Louis David. Consistent throughout his work is preoccupation with the heroic, generally captured in some transcendent moment or act. Yet in the paintings of the pre-Revolutionary and Revolutionary periods, in works such as *The Oath of the Horatii* or *The Tennis Court Oath*, the figures portrayed are essentially vehicles for the principle (patriotism) celebrated. The same can be said of the *Assassination of Marat*; while visual focus is on the martyr, he remains a symbol of the suffering people. In David's

Napoleonic paintings, Bonaparte also is symbolic: of France, glory, or selfless dedication. Yet, a transition has occurred; Napoleon remains at least as memorable as the principle he embodies. This effect results from the singular, and unearthly calm of the Hero amidst the forces surrounding him. In *Napoleon Crossing the Saint Bernard Pass*, one is, of course, reminded of other 'Greats' – Hannibal and Charlemagne. Yet, equally impressive is David's accomplishment of what the Hero wanted: the image of the Conqueror 'serene upon a fiery horse'. It is this serenity, as though extraordinary feats are in the natural order of things, that lifts Napoleon beyond the reach of mere mortals. David's *Napoleon in his Study* presents the Emperor in a more mundane light: he is subject to ageing and perhaps weariness; yet the same calm is present amidst Herculean labours.

Similar features are apparent in the paintings of Antoine-Jean Gros. Among the many versions of a heroic moment, his *Bonaparte Visiting the Victims of the Plague at Jaffa* gained the most renown. In it, Bonaparte is shown to be impervious to such worldly dangers as the plague. While he is to be found among his people, through thick and thin, he is not quite of them; otherwise he and his followers might be subject to defeat. Defeat does lurk at the edges in Gros's *Napoleon at Eylau*, wherein emphasis shifts to an Emperor moved by suffering. Perhaps this marks a transition in the later Imperial years, leading towards Géricault's *Wounded Cuirassier* of 1814–15. Yet these two works are exceptional in a general chorus of victory. Moreover, in neither is it Napoleon who is shown to be vulnerable, although his followers are; in *Eylau* the Emperor retains his ethereal calm amidst chaos.[9]

Allegory abounds in the art of the period and is richly varied. Napoleonic imagery was uniform only in linking Bonaparte to greatness, whether by stars, bees or the 'N'. Indiscriminate allegory, in turn, reflected Bonaparte's own expansive imagination. This is not to say that he necessarily appreciated all of the recondite symbolism in, say, Jean-Antoine-Dominique Ingres's *Napoleon Enthroned*. The Emperor preferred a simple, clear message in individual works, but collectively whatever pointed towards glory was welcome – allusions to Alexander the Great, Julius Caesar, Augustus, Justinian, Christ, Mohammed, Charlemagne, whomever. Notably lacking, however, was association with recent figures. Reference to some other contemporary hero would have reduced the significance of a man who wished to be seen as the harbinger of a new age. Napoleon was the

Illustration 5.1 Jean-Antoine Gros, *Bonaparte Visiting the Victims of the Plague at Jaffa*, 1804, painting, Paris, Musée du Louvre.

choice of the people and this distinguished him from all contemporary rivals. Yet he was also the latest in a chain of Great Men which reached back into the mists of time. It was this combination that made him unique.[10]

Given the nature of such representation, it is not surprising that Napoleon's opponents responded by creating the equally extreme Black Legend. Chateaubriand, as discussed in Chapter 3, based much of his initial onslaught on allegations in the often scurrilous pamphlets of British and *émigré* writers such as Goldsmith. Yet there were two lines of attack in British opposition, and while one of these was retained in subsequent British literature, it was largely lost on the continent. One could depict Napoleon as a demon, or belittle him through association with common vice. The belittlement theme could already be seen in, and perhaps sprang from, the cartoons of contemporary caricaturists such as Gillray and Cruikshank, wherein Napoleon appears like a mischievous schoolboy run wild. The contrast with, say, Goya's tragic depictions of the impact of the Giant of War bestriding Spain could not be more pronounced. While Goya's Giant represents war generally, association with war's leading agent is obvious and takes us into a realm beyond human.

De Staël and Chateaubriand led the continental onslaught, initially deploying both belittlement and demonizing. Napoleon was an upstart, lacking in good manners: what good could come of a man notorious for bolting his meals? At points both authors contested whether Bonaparte was even talented; he owed his success to propaganda and dupery. There was, however, little glory in subduing an insignificant opponent, and hence belittlement gave way to demonizing. As the embodiment of liberty struggling with tyranny, de Staël invested Napoleon with inhuman qualities. It was not just the barbarity of an Attila; Napoleon was similar to Milton's 'Sin'. He was immoral, propagating the triumph of materialism and self-interest over principle and virtue. Chateaubriand's depiction evolved in reaction to the growing cult of Napoleon. Certain elements of belittlement – Napoleon as charlatan – remained consistent, but gone was contestation of Napoleon's ability, and once the point was admitted, Bonaparte rose from mediocrity to history's greatest warrior. Still, he remained a scourge, God's agent of chastisement and, ultimately, an evil giant among men.[11]

A contrast to such approaches can be found in Walter Scott's

Illustration 5.2 James Gillray, cartoon engraving entitled 'Destruction of the French Gun-Boats – or – Little Boney and his Friend Talley in High Glee', 22 November 1803. In the speech bubble 'Boney' expresses his joy that so many French 'Cut Throats' have been killed by John Bull's firepower. This 'beats the Egyptian Poisoning hollow!'

The Life of Napoleon Buonaparte (1827). Where the British are concerned, the work is predictably partisan, yet the author's claim to treat his subject with 'impartial justice' is not entirely unfounded. Scott views the Napoleonic system as based on 'force and fraud', and emphasizes that Napoleon tarnished his image through criminal acts such as the execution of Enghien and the massacre of prisoners at Jaffa. Yet he also rejects many of the accusations of contemporary *libelles*. Napoleon is not depicted as innately cruel and he is described as having many positive virtues in private life. His talents as commander and administrator are acknowledged, and Scott grants that France and Italy enjoyed significant benefits from his rule.[12]

Consistent throughout the work is Scott's insistence that Napoleon was neither demon nor deity. Allusions to classical tyrants and Satan are not lacking, but many of Scott's metaphors are drawn from common life. In discussing justifications given for looting art, Scott comments: 'The fingering connoisseur who secretes a gem cannot plead in mitigation that he stole it, not on account of the value of the stone, but the excellence of the engraving'. In challenging whether voter abstention constituted approval of the plebiscites, Scott remarks: 'This argument, is not more valid than the defense of the soldier, who, having stolen a necklace from an image of the Virgin, replied to the charge, that he had first asked the Madonna's permission, and, receiving no answer, had taken silence for consent'.[13]

Particularly striking is Scott's treatment of the theme of Destiny, which he consistently discusses in terms of appearance. After Marengo it 'seemed that his mere presence in Italy was of itself sufficient at once to obliterate the misfortunes of a disastrous campaign. . . . It appeared as if he was the sun of France . . .'. At the height of his power, Napoleon increasingly justifies his despotism on the basis of providence, 'often holding out to others, and no doubt occasionally considering himself, in his own mind, as an individual destined by Heaven to the high station which he held'. Given circumstance, this was understandable: 'It seemed as if Napoleon had been wafted on to this stupendous pitch of grandeur by a power more effectual than that of any human assistance'. That Napoleon developed inordinate belief in his own mission was a 'natural error': he 'felt, and justly, that he was the sole projector of his gigantic plans, and also, in a great measure, the agent who carried them through'. Yet this was delusion; in the Russian campaign 'ill-founded trust

in the prominence of his own personal influence' led him into
'gross neglect of the usual and prescribed rules of war'. His fall
had little to do with Destiny; it was a product of that most
familiar of human vices – pride.[14]

Napoleon's image was also brought to earth in William
Makepeace Thackeray's *Vanity Fair* (1848). The work's subtitle,
A Novel without a Hero, says much about it; at the outset
Thackeray advises the reader who is 'a lofty man of genius, and
admires the great and heroic in life and novels' to 'go elsewhere'.
Yet, if the novel lacks a hero, it does possess a main protagonist
who embodies many of the conventional British reflections upon
Napoleon. Rebecca Sharp is not overtly cast from a Napoleonic
mould in the sense of, say, Stendhal's Julien Sorel. Yet, there is
clear association, illustrated by Thackeray's woodcut initial
commencing Chapter 64. Thackeray first reveals her character by
having Becky momentarily remove the mask of propriety, utter-
ing 'Vive la France! Vive l'Empereur! Vive Bonaparte!', much to
the shock of her companion Amelia Sedley. According to the
author, this was tantamount to crying 'Long live Lucifer!', but
Thackeray's tone is typically ironic. Shortly thereafter Becky
reveals 'I'm no angel' and Thackeray adds 'And, to say the truth,
she certainly was not'. We are a long way here from the inflated
prose of Chateaubriand.

Becky's career is described as a campaign of (romantic) conquest, and her besotted husband Rawdon believes 'in his wife as
much as the French soldiers in Napoleon'. Her 'talents and
accomplishments are of a high order'; she is an intelligent,
resourceful and ruthless schemer who seeks to exploit whatever
opportunity provides. Unprincipled, she pursues worldly ends to
the detriment of spiritual growth, and hence her central place in
a novel of vain pursuits. She is a consummate social climber, and
while at times she may be an eagle among pigeons, her charla-
tanism involves constant struggle in a world of equally accomplished swindlers. Thackeray, however, is little inclined to what
F.E.L. Priestley terms the 'sentimentalization of vice'; Becky is as
much a producer as a product of the society the author satirizes.
Still, her 'vices' are of an obviously human kind, whether she is
plying Jos Sedley with wine in pursuit of marriage, plundering his
cowardice at Brussels (in a novel famous for depicting everything
but the battle at Waterloo), or subsequently poisoning him to
secure his life insurance and thereby provide for her 'pious
retirement'.[15]

Illustration 5.3 William Makepeace Thackeray, initial wood-block print commencing Chapter LXIV of his *Vanity Fair*, 1848.

On the continent, Napoleon retained his superhuman mystique. Initially Romanticism was hostile as authors such as Alphonse de Lamartine, Victor Hugo and Alfred de Vigny aligned with Bourbon Restoration, and this element never did disappear entirely. The Lamartine who in 'Ode aux Français' (1817) attacked the Vendôme Column as a celebration of unjust war, again inveighed against the First Empire as a perversion of the liberal Revolution in his *History of the Restoration* (1851–53).

For Vigny, Napoleon personified 'to what depths of wicked cal-culation genius could sink when moved by personal ambition'. In *Servitude and Grandeur of Arms* (1835), Vigny celebrated the 'unassuming heroism and disinterestedness' of the common soldier through contrast with the cruel tyrant who betrayed them.[16]

A general transition in Romanticism from antagonistic to wor-shipful is often associated with Victor Hugo. Hugo's 'progress' began in 1823 with the ode 'A mon Père' (his father was an Imperial general), and advanced with a tribute to Imperial veterans in 'A la Calonne' (1827). It continued with recognition of Bonaparte's all-pervasive influence in 'Lui' (late 1827), and culminated in the early 1830s as propagation of the cult. Hugo's conversion was, however, more symptomatic than causal of growing Bonapartism. Time and the Emperor's absence had proved propitious for hero worship. Napoleon himself appraised how exile worked to his benefit: 'The universe is looking at us; we remain the martyrs of an immortal cause. Millions of men weep for us, and glory is in mourning. Adversity was wanting to my career. If I had died on the throne amidst the clouds of omnipotence, I should have remained a problem to many men.'[17]

He would in fact remain a problem long afterwards, but his death did produce a certain relenting even among those who remained doubtful. An international cast of poets (including the Briton Shelley, the Austrian Grillparzer, the German August Lamey, the Swede K.A. Nicander, the Italians Manzoni and von Chamisso, the Russians Pushkin and Lermontov, and the Frenchmen Béranger, Hugo and Lamartine) found in Napoleon's passing inspiration for their meditations. Of the many works, those of Manzoni and Lamartine have perhaps gained the most fame, but all bore testimony to the centrality of Napoleon to contemporary political and ideological convictions.

Neither Alessandro Manzoni's 'Il Cinque maggio' nor Lamartine's 'Bonaparte' was written simply in praise of the pass-ing Caesar. Yet both poets saw in Napoleon an instrument of divine will, a man chosen to push the world forward. If for Lamartine Bonaparte was mostly a scourge, Manzoni's testimony to Napoleonic greatness was more favourable: 'My poetic inspiration saw him while triumphing on the throne and kept silent. . . . Free from servile adulation and from cowardly offense at the sudden disappearance of such a light, now I raise my voice with emotion and dedicate to his ashes a song which may not perish.' Other poems were more adulatory, but a common theme was reverence, not so much for Napoleon himself, but for his significance. Such a reflective mode proved fertile ground for O'Meara's *Napoleon in Exile* and the *Memorial*, with their message that Napoleon had represented the 'modern' forces of liberalism and national sovereignty, to take root in the early 1820s.[18]

If his path to the cult was circuitous, no one did more for the cult during its heyday of the 1830s and 1840s than Hugo. In Napoleon as state builder the author found an embodiment of France's entire history; as a general he personified French glory. He saved the Revolution and his Empire carried enlightenment to the rest of Europe; it was only God's inscrutable will that brought defeat at Waterloo – no mere mortal could triumph over an individual whose genius and accomplishments lay outside the realm of nature.[19]

What most distinguished the Romantic contribution to the cult was a pervasive longing for past glories. Certainly there was little that was novel in identifying Napoleon as the great individual struggling against society, or as the source of energy capable of infusing others with resolution. What was new was the sense of loss and futility; if there were budding Napoleons, they were isolated and alienated. The influence of Germanic *Sturm und Drang* (storm and stress) is obvious, yet alongside the sorrows of nineteenth-century versions of Goethe's young Werther was the haunting example of Napoleon, producing a certain tension between hope and despair. Elevating Bonaparte to deity could inspire, but it could also produce alienation among individuals incapable of triumphing over the multitude of contemporary pygmies ensconced in power.[20]

In his *Confession of a Child of the Century* (1836), Alfred de Musset presents us with the antithesis of the idealized Napoleon. The main character is a tortured soul, incapable of overcoming the disillusionment of his first affair. Finding little that is true in the universe, he slides into dissipation until he is temporarily spared self-loathing through confrontation with genuine love. Yet his life is destined to futility; his most positive step lies in inaction – inability to murder his mistress and withdrawal so that she may be saved by a better man. Overlapping this tale of the failure of individual will is a kind of generational insecurity complex. Musset and his character had contracted the *mal de siècle* ('sickness of the age'), caught between great forebears and a brave new world yet to unfold. The gods had intervened, cutting short the glories of the Empire and leaving France 'the widow of Caesar'. An 'anxious youth' awaits the return of the 'spirit of Caesar', but it never comes in the silence that follows Napoleon's shaking 'of the world'. For this generation all illusions fall, leaving them prey to idleness and *ennui*. Reflected by such offspring, the Napoleonic Giant takes even greater proportions.[21]

Honoré de Balzac and Stendhal (Henri Beyle) also carried the cult to middle-class readers. Stendhal's Julien Sorel, in *The Red and the Black* (1831), and Fabrice, in *The Charterhouse of Parma* (1839), are both cut from a Napoleonic cloth. Julien, in particular, portrays the alienation of young men denied opportunity in a world wherein true talent counts for little. He is first presented reading the *Memorial*, and thereafter he frequently measures the progress of his career against that of Napoleon: 'Bonaparte, starting as a poor and obscure lieutenant, had made himself master of the world, with his sword alone'. Yet the world has changed: 'When Bonaparte made his name . . . the soldier's trade was necessary and fashionable. Nowadays there are forty-year-old priests who draw salaries of a hundred thousand francs, three times as much as the famous division commanders of Napoleon.' Thus the young eagle learns that aspiration must be masked in hypocritical humility and caballing intrigue. Although Julien struggles to retain the 'sacred fire with which one makes oneself a name', upon meeting the Bishop of Agde, he 'has no more dreams of Napoleon'. Ambition remains, but it has been shorn of heroic character.[22]

While Stendhal's caustic portrayal of Restoration society may seem an endorsement of Bonapartism, the author's attitude to the cult was rather more complex. His *Life of Napoleon* is an *apologia*, written to counter de Staël's *Considerations*. As such it falls into the heroic mode with its denial of alleged crimes, emphasis on the Emperor's sincerity and generosity, and argument that social disorder required strong measures. Other writings, however, reveal a more measured assessment. For Stendhal, Napoleon's greatness lay in the rational governmental model that he created and infused with energy. Yet, Stendhal did share Lamartine's mistrust of militarism, partly because as an Imperial administrator he had encountered too many overbearing officers. As with many great writers, Stendhal said different things at different times, but the ultimate impression given in his works is that Napoleon was larger than life.[23]

The most comprehensive biographer of Napoleonic mythology

was Balzac. At various points in his *comédie humaine*, one sees how the Emperor is glorified in different ways by army veterans, bureaucrats, peasants and even nobles.

Particularly striking is that the Emperor is the yardstick by which all greatness (for better or worse) is measured: Nucingen is the Napoleon of finance (in *César Birotteau*); Gaudissart becomes the Napoleon of boulevard theatres (in *Cousin Bette*) and Vautrin is the Napoleon of rogues (in *Père Goriot*). More than anywhere else, the theme of Bonaparte as archetype is apparent in the works of Balzac, and most powerful of all is his identification of Napoleon as the embodiment of the human will.

From a historical perspective, one can see the attraction of investing a single being with the ability to channel, if not entirely control, circumstance. For contemporaries, the Revolution of 1789 had unleashed profound, rapid and bewildering change. On the other hand, Bonaparte could be viewed as a 'self-made' man who by force of will not only rose to the top, but also imposed order upon anarchy. In the *comédie humaine*, plot frequently pivots upon the struggle of an individual to conquer his or her world. While Balzac may not have approved of contemporary mores, he did present a society which had its rules for the pursuit of success. The role of the fictional protagonist is first to discover (or fail to discover) these rules and then to exploit (or fall victim to) them.[24]

Of the many characters who fall into this pattern, two of the more memorable are to be found in *Père Goriot* (1834) – Vautrin and Eugène de Rastignac. The worldly Vautrin wishes to serve as young Rastignac's mentor and confronts him with two stark options: 'You must cut a path through this mass of men like a cannon-ball, or creep among them like a pestilence. . . . Men give way before the power of genius, they hate it . . . but they give way if it persists.' If he wishes to succeed, Rastignac must shed illusions: 'There are no such things as principles, there are only events; there are no laws, there are only circumstances: the man who is wiser than his fellows accepts events and circumstances in order to turn them to his own ends'. There is, however, a familiar model who can be emulated: 'In a million of this herd of human cattle there are ten sharp fellows to be found who climb above everything, even above laws. . . . But you will have to fight against envy, slander, mediocrity, against the whole world. Napoleon came up against a Minister of War called Aubry who just failed to send him to the colonies.'

Whether Rastignac ultimately takes the tempter's path is left ambiguous; in the conclusion he declares war against Parisian society, but he has already rejected Vautrin's plans for fortune. The 'little eaglet', whom Vautrin predicts will become 'a ruler among men', takes his own route, but whether this constitutes rebellion through return to virtue or through assertion of individual choice is left unclear. One way or another, Vautrin's version of the social contract amounts to dealing with society only upon one's own terms – no altruism is included in this form of extremely rugged individualism. The contrast here with, say, Thackeray, for whom moral issues never quite went out the window, is striking. On display is a line of thought wherein an individual's will to power can place him or her beyond the bounds of common morality. Napoleon has become the model for a doctrine which appears a good deal like moral relativism, but which has more to do with substituting the principle of *raison d'état* (overriding state interest) with belief that a Great Man cannot be adjudged by the rules governing all others. The Hero is the harbinger of progress, and hence he has the right to act in accordance with the fulfilment of his individual mission.[25]

Such themes were by no means confined to French authors. Reflections on Napoleon became a frequent source of inspiration for the Russian Alexander Pushkin, in whom one can see a progression similar to that of French Romantics. In 1814 Napoleon was the 'scourge of the universe' to be taunted with the question 'Where are you, the favourite son of fortune and war'? Perspective had changed, however, when news of Bonaparte's death arrived in 1821: 'A marvellous destiny has been accomplished. A great man has been extinguished.'

The image of Napoleon in the works of Pushkin and his 'successor' Mihail Lermontov is complex. Like Musset, the two Russians are famous for their presentation of the 'superfluous man' caught in the *mal de siècle*. In this context, Napoleon is linked to ambition in a manner similar to Balzac, but such ambition often leads to tragedy. In Pushkin's verse novel *Eugene Onegin* (1831), Eugene comments: 'We all aim at being Napoleons/ The millions of two-legged creatures are for us merely a tool'. In the short story *Queen of Spades* (1834) the physical resemblance of the main protagonist Hermann to Napoleon is underlined; moreover the young officer is 'reserved and ambitious', keeping 'strong passions and an ardent imagination' in check with 'firmness of disposition'. In Lermontov's *A*

Hero of Our Time (1840), references to Bonaparte are few and the anti-hero Pechorin is more obviously in the Byronic mould of lady killer (literally). Yet Pechorin, having driven his horse to death in fruitless pursuit of 'perished happiness', then collapses into 'the sleep of Napoleon after Waterloo'.[26]

Part of the apparent ambiguity in the authors' use of Napoleonic allegory lies in ironic treatment of the 'Great Man' theme. In her search for the true character of Onegin, his (of course, lost) lover ruminates: 'Perhaps he is all imitation, / An idle phantom or, poor joke'. Similarly, Lermontov introduces a victim of Pechorin in the following unRomantic terms: 'His object is to become the hero of a novel. So often has he tried to convince others that he is a being not made for this world and doomed to suffer in secret, that he has almost succeeded in convincing himself of it.' At points Pechorin, the man of the 'penetrating and oppressive', but 'serene' glance, will be treated to the same withering irony.[27]

An author can, however, jest and yet remain in earnest. If the tone of Pushkin and Lermontov at times resembles that of Thackeray, the two Russians are closer to Stendhal. In his poem 'The Hero' (1830), Pushkin responded to questioning of the authenticity of accounts of Napoleon's visit to the plague victims of Jaffa as follows: 'The deceit that uplifts us is dearer to me than a whole host of base truths'. Lermontov, upon learning of the transportation of Napoleon's ashes from Saint Helena, responded with the poem 'The Last Resting Place', wherein he argues that the Emperor should remain 'guarded by the ocean, which is like him unconquerable and great'. Ultimately what the two authors saw in Napoleon was an embodiment of aspiration, an ideal which was as universal as it was God-given.[28]

Matters are different when we encounter the 'glittering eyes' of Feodor Dostoevsky's Raskolnikov. There were many targets for the diatribes of *Crime and Punishment* (1865–66), ranging from Benthamite utilitarianism, to utopian socialism, to the diverse expressions of Russian nihilism. Similarly, passages in the work attack Louis-Napoleon's *Histoire de Jules César*, and the character and circumstances of Raskolnikov are designed to echo those of Balzac's Rastignac. Yet, within this firestorm of intellectual attack, Dostoevsky's variation on the Napoleonic theme remains consistent and penetrating. Raskolnikov has thought himself into believing that ends justify means and that a crime may be committed for the 'greater good'. His symbol for this is

Napoleon and his reason for murder is that he wants to test whether he is a Napoleon. In this sense, Napoleon (or the ideas associated with him) is the axe that kills an old moneylender and her sister: 'there are persons who . . . have every right, to commit any wrong or crime, and . . . laws, so to say, are not made for them'. All Great Men are 'law-breakers and transgressors', but 'if it is necessary for one of them . . . to march over corpses, or wade through blood, then in my opinion he can in all conscience authorize himself to wade through blood'.[29]

From the outset, however, Raskolnikov is not Napoleon as thus conceived; in executing his plan, reason entirely deserts him as he blunders from mistake to mistake; it is only chance that prevents his immediate failure. In his torturous path to redemption thereafter, Raskolnikov comes to recognize that he has not in fact acted for the greater good, but rather out of selfish desire: 'I wanted to make myself a Napoleon, and that is why I killed her. . . . I wanted to have the courage, and I killed . . . I only wanted to dare . . . that was the only reason.' Yet, all along Raskolnikov could not subdue his conscience: 'If I worried for so long about whether Napoleon would have done it or not, it must be because I felt clearly that I was not Napoleon'. Until he returns to faith, Raskolnikov's will, intelligence and ability count for nothing. For Dostoevsky, Napoleon as construed within the Great Man theme is but a product of human pride and, hence, one of many false idols produced by eighteenth- and nineteenth-century rationalism. Neither as man nor symbol does Napoleon exist beyond good or evil.[30]

Passage of time could enhance the appeal of using Napoleon as a universal symbol, but this varied in relation to the position of Bonapartism in France. With the election of Louis-Napoleon as President of the Second Republic in 1848, association of Napoleon I with a specifically French, and threatening, tradition was restored. French official promotion of Napoleon worship was in fact nothing new in 1848, but the July Monarchy had been relatively discreet in using it to rally domestic support, while pursuing pacific policies abroad.[31]

Initially, the July Monarchy simply sought to tap the cult. Paintings of Bonaparte were exhibited at the Luxembourg Palace in October 1830, and in 1831 the state commissioned some 165 medals commemorating the reign of Napoleon. Thereafter, however, especially in the reconstitution of Versailles as a national museum, a more calculated approach was developed by Louis-Philippe. In essence, the martial element of the reputation was emphasized, whereas the image of Napoleon as great ruler was ignored. Perhaps the best example was to be found in Emile Seurre's statue, placed atop the Vendôme Column in 1833: the Napoleon of official choice was the Little Corporal of greatcoat and cocked hat rather than the former neo-classical emperor. Similar emphasis could be seen in the works of Horace Vernet, who became the most famous of officially inspired painters of Napoleon in the 1830s. Vernet made Bonaparte the focus of the many battles he depicted, but his choice of scenes illustrated moments of little historical significance. Art critics attacked Vernet's vignettes, but they served the purposes of the regime better than depictions of 'transcendent moments' associated with the modern forces that Napoleonic victory allegedly represented.

Non-official art, however, worked against such strategies. In the lithographs of Dennis-Auguste-Marie Raffet and Nicholas-Toussaint Charlet, and paintings of Paul Delaroche, Napoleon became the inspired genius, struggling to promote progress. In the more aggressive works, Bonaparte became Godlike and the theme of resurrection was pronounced, as exemplified by François Rude's sculpture *The Awakening of Napoleon*. Such imagery was directly threatening to the July Monarchy because there was an obvious Bonapartist pretender from 1836 onwards.

Change of policy could be observed during the return of Napoleon's ashes, although the ceremonies have often been interpreted as the culmination of Orleanist dabbling in the Napoleonic cult. The initiative for the return lay in the misguided policies of Thiers, who sought a diversion from demand for political reform in May 1840. The King was reluctant, and became increasingly perturbed as Thiers risked war with the other European Powers in the Egyptian Crisis, beginning in July. In this context the danger of conjuring the cult became obvious as lingering resentment over the Vienna Settlement and Bonapartism combined. Alarm was then heightened in August by Louis-Napoleon's second attempt to seize power. By this stage there could be no going back, but shoddy preparations and per-functory execution revealed that, for the regime, commemoration had become an exercise in laying a ghost. State commissions of art celebrating Napoleon thereafter virtually ended, but opposition politicians increasingly sought to exploit the cult through the newspaper press or in parliamentary speeches. The ghost refused to be interred in the Invalides, as the regime plunged into deepening unpopularity in the 1840s.

Lermontov had complained that the return of Napoleon's remains would diminish the universal element of his reputation. He was correct in the short term, but this was due mostly to the return of a Bonaparte to power in 1848. Louis-Napoleon and his followers developed the Bonapartist propaganda machine gradually, but they aimed for the widest possible audience, using various elements of the Napoleonic cult. For the peasantry, emphasis could be placed on the Napoleon who had defended them from the depredations of local nobles, the clergy, and the 'red menace' of the cities. For urban workers, propaganda could stress that Napoleon had attended to all material interests and provided full employment. For the elite, Bonapartism could stress that Napoleonic rule had restored forceful government and respect for religion, the family and property after the chaos of the 1790s. And for one and all, there was the Napoleon who had fought for France to the bitter end.

If such propaganda contained contradictory messages, it was consistent in its celebration of an individual. Despite its twists and turns in policy, the fortunes of the Second Empire thereafter rested heavily upon the popularity of Napoleon III, much of which had been inherited from the cult of his uncle. To nurture the latter, a commission was established in 1854 to publish Napoleon's correspondence. By the time a second committee had finished in 1869, thirty-two volumes had been published. Massive as it was, the edition was also selective, designed to reinforce the image of a Hero guiding the progressive forces unleashed by the Revolution. While this 'spin' was obviously inspired by the *Memorial*, it also derived from the propaganda of the First Empire, combining the theme of the Great Man with that of representing the nation. Berlioz's eulogistic cantata *L'Impériale*, first performed at the Paris Universal Exhibition of 1855, captured the spirit: the 'Liberator' rules with the blessings of God and nation, but is the 'Heir of our Caesar's'.[32]

The Second Empire did bring a sustained attempt to broaden the Napoleonic reputation while extending glory to the supporting cast. Louis Visconti's tomb of the Emperor in the crypt of the Invalides celebrated the martial Napoleon, but the political achievements of the Civil Code and Concordat were commemorated in the surrounding bas-reliefs of the gallery. The Little Corporal was transferred from the Vendôme Column to

Courbevoie, and replaced by a statue of Napoleon as Roman Emperor by Augustin Dumont. Baron Haussmann's urban renewal provided numerous opportunities for naming avenues and streets after First Empire luminaries, ranging from members of the Imperial family to nineteen of Napoleon's marshals. Yet when all was said and done, the effect was like Napoleon's Table of Marshals; while others might reflect it, it was the Emperor who radiated glory.[33]

In his *Histoire de Jules César* (1865), Louis-Napoleon projected his uncle's radiance upon classical Rome. There was no need for an emperor to veil his references; analogy was made explicit in the preface. Men such as Caesar, Charlemagne and Napoleon are sent by Providence to clear the path for civilization to follow. They come when only they can provide a just appreciation of the needs of the moment and the problems of the future. They represent a principle – love of the public good – and it is this that enables them to rise above the selfish intrigues of faction, gaining public acclamation. Personal rivalries are overcome by moral authority and those who seek to block the rise of the Man of Destiny simply push him towards supreme power. Neither the murder of Caesar nor the exile of Napoleon can thwart destiny; in his good works, the Great Man has revealed the future.[34]

A danger of association with a demi-god is that one is apt to be compared and found wanting. The fall of the First Empire was seldom attributed to personal failure; the Gods had intervened or the followers had betrayed the martyr. For Louis-Napoleon, however, mixed foreign policy results in Italy, a fiasco in Mexico, and humiliation at Sedan turned comparison to his uncle into a liability. For those who remained smitten with the cult, each defeat revealed the unworthiness of the successor; for others, disaster was a reminder of the fruit born of warmongering in 1814–15. The Second Empire fell with remarkable ease in September 1870.

The Franco-Prussian War revealed that *la grande nation* was no longer the leading continental power, and for roughly two decades anti-Napoleonism predominated in French elite culture. Thus the ground was again prepared for viewing Napoleon as a universal rather than specifically French figure. He remained closely tied to the 'Great Man in History' theme, but, more significantly, it was at this point that his status as the leading embodiment of human will became permanently entrenched.

Among many authors who fostered this, we can settle for two of the more famous.

Few thinkers have been as iconoclastic as the German philosopher Friedrich Nietzsche, yet in his writings Napoleon is consistently treated with profound respect. This is not to say that Napoleon was Nietzsche's model for his Superman; Goethe was a more likely prototype. But Nietzsche frequently cites Bonaparte as the leading historical example of genius: the 'most powerful man, the creator', whose 'strong will and ample spirit' confirms 'belief in the autocracy of the individual'. Nietzsche insisted that such a figure was not merely a product of circumstance. Although the Revolution helped to clear a path for Napoleon, he was the heir of neither 1789 nor the *ancien régime*; he was part of a much older tradition and represented the triumph of personal ability and will.[35]

Napoleon was the best answer to what Nietzsche saw as the triumph of the common herd and its predilections for egalitarian mediocrity. The 'intensity, coherence and inner logic' of Napoleon's dream had led him to carry 'his ideal against the ideals of other men' and remake 'them in his own image'. He was not, however, without flaw. Nietzsche felt few qualms over Napoleon's ruthless actions; these were necessary and evil only if one accepted common values. Unfortunately, to lead the herd Bonaparte had resorted to superstition, and this had corrupted him. Great Men were naturally masters of dissimulation, but Napoleon had come to believe in his own Destiny, thus attributing his success to something other than ability and will. For this reason, his capacity for self-criticism had declined, bringing ultimate ruin.

Several Napoleonic themes reach their culmination in Nietzsche. Especially noteworthy is the author's stripping away of the religious character previously ascribed to Great Men by Carlyle. For Nietzsche, any attribution of greatness to the will of God reduced the autonomy of the individual, denying the emergence of the Superman after recognition that God is dead. For progress to ensue, the will to power must replace religion as source of motivation. Nietzsche's recognition that Napoleon had fallen into the trap of believing his own 'moral imposture' reminds one strongly of Walter Scott, except, of course, that Scott shared none of the German author's extreme secularism.

At various points Nietzsche paid his respects to Dostoevsky, yet his placing Napoleon beyond good and evil ran very much contrary to *Crime and Punishment*. To Nietzsche, Raskolnikov would have been simply an example of what happens when a Great Man cannot rise above the common herd. If one fails to assert one's alternative values, one is branded a criminal, and although a certain respect is due to the act of rebellion against mass mediocrity, the key factor lies in insufficient will to power. Given his assertion that values are culturally relative, Nietzsche's position does have a certain logical consistency, but Dostoyevsky was no great apostle of the primacy of reason or exponent of removing God from human motivation.

Ultimately most striking about Nietzsche's Napoleon is the frank elitism underlining celebration of the individual will. His identification of Bonaparte as the antithesis of the irrational power of the masses is the direct opposite of Popular Bonapartism's premise of Napoleon as the people's choice. In this light, Napoleon represents the greatest threat to mass democracy. As Nietzsche well knew, intellectual currents were running against elevation of individual will above worldly circumstance, and celebration of the Hero as a force for taming the common herd. Nevertheless, there were exceptions, most notably in a genre which straddled the line between elite and emerging mass culture – detective fiction.

Professor Moriarty was not, of course, the first 'Napoleon of crime'. Indeed there is a good deal of Balzac's Vautrin about him: he is a man of the shadows, organizing 'half that is evil' and 'nearly all that is undetected' in the London of the 1890s. Moriarty 'sits motionless, like a spider in the centre of its web, but that web has a thousand radiations'. More pertinent, however, is that the Professor is a *doppelgänger* for Sherlock Holmes, and it is appropriate that 'the most dangerous criminal and the foremost champion of the law of their generation' should have toppled to their apparent doom in the 'cauldron of swirling water' below Reichenbach Falls. It was, after all, the Treaty of Reichenbach that had assured the fall of Napoleon.

Both Moriarty and Sherlock are variants of the 'Nietzschean superior man', even though Arthur Conan Doyle described Nietzsche's philosophy as 'openly founded in lunacy'. The difference between Conan Doyle and Thackeray, when dealing with characters directly associated with Napoleon, could hardly be greater, and we are in fact much closer to Coleridge's identification of Bonaparte as the quintessential 'evil genius'. Although Conan Doyle's sketch of Moriarty in *The Final Problem* (1894) is thin, his linkage to Holmes gives us the essentials of the Professor's character: he is a genius, being the intellectual equal of his antagonist, and he is unswerving in relentless application of his will. Neither is much troubled by convention; Sherlock's bohemianism frequently cuts him out from the common herd, and both can be a law unto themselves when it suits them. The good Doctor Watson, an archetype of Victorian convention, serves as a foil for such creatures because they are both beyond merely good. In the opposite paths they take, Sherlock and the Professor illustrate the possibilities of the Great Man.[36]

When all is said and done, Napoleon has come to stand for what can be done by an individual through application of will. Because his life was so monumental, and because through his propaganda he had successfully identified himself with forces reshaping modern Europe, the nineteenth-century 'debate without end' was expressed in extreme terms. He was either an agent of Lucifer, or God's gift to progress. There was a certain line in British writing which insisted that he was no more than human, but this was exceptional and seldom heard on the continent, where Romanticism took up where neo-classicism had left off, in combat with the equally hyperbolic Black Legend.

Adoption of Napoleon as a universal symbol by non-French Europeans varied in relation to whether Bonapartism was in power in France. Prior to 1848, it was especially Russian writers who joined the French in exploring the 'Great Man' theme, taking up or attacking an argument which held that certain individuals could not be judged by the laws or mores governing all others. From 1848 to 1870, Louis-Napoleon was able to direct the imagery surrounding his uncle, emphasizing the familiar argument that Napoleon I was a force of world progress, but this held less appeal abroad when France was actually ruled by the heir of the Napoleonic cult. After the fall of the Second Empire, the Black Legend recovered in France, and it was in the writings of a German that the Napoleon as Great Man theme culminated.

Nietzsche's Napoleon reflected a desire to assert the supremacy of an individual over mass democracy as a mechanism for control of modernization. There was always a reactionary element to the Napoleonic theme, based on Bonapartism's image as a source of stability. Nietzsche's Napoleon was, however, but a variation on a theme, and the Great Man school was not necessarily reactionary. For many of his admirers, Napoleon symbolized the ability to understand and direct change, rather than simply block it. Given the bewildering degree of upheaval, this in itself was an extraordinary attribute, and many saw something divine in it. Over the course of the nineteenth and twentieth centuries, forces such as national sovereignty gradually became established and increasingly commonplace. They therefore diminished as striking aspects of 'the life', and less central to the reputation. What remained essential was the individual who had imposed his will upon circumstance to achieve such extraordinary accomplishments. While this may have been particularly attractive to elite culture in the nineteenth century, the appeal of Napoleonic greatness was by no means confined to the elite. Destruction of the *ancien régime* and creation of mass society broadened the horizons, and to some extent prospects, of individual aspiration. Every individual, even the most ideologically committed determinist, struggles with day-to-day circumstance and seeks to influence it. The great exemplar of individual mastery thus holds universal interest. Sherlock Holmes and his innumerable progeny point to the fascination of an individual who can make sense of a mystery, and put life in order. Intellectual trends in elite culture were increasingly leaving the Great Man theme behind by the turn of the nineteenth century, but the Superman carried on the heroic work of the Great Man in popular culture.

Notes

1 See A. Gonzalez-Palacios, *The French Empire Style* (London, 1970), especially pp. 7–9, A. Boime, *A Social History of Modern Art II: Art in an Age of Bonapartism 1800–1815* (Chicago, 1990), introduction and pp. 315–628, W. Friedlaender, *David to Delacroix* (Cambridge, Mass., 1952), pp. 1–11, and T. Wilson-Smith, *Napoleon and his Artists* (London, 1996), pp. 1–84, 150–93. For a conventional discussion of the relation between Napoleon and Romanticism, see M. Cranston, *The Romantic Movement* (Oxford, 1994), pp. 77–84, but by way of contrast see W. Vaughan, 'The visual arts', in D.G. Charleton, ed., *The French Romantics*, I (Cambridge, 1984), pp. 324–5.
2 See M. Polowetzky, *A Bond Never Broken: The Relations between Napoleon and the Authors of France* (London, 1993), pp. 46–61, J. Charpentier, *Napoléon et les hommes de lettres de son temps* (Paris, 1935), pp. 60–98, and W. Miller, 'Napoleon and Cherubini: a discordant relationship', *Consortium on Revolutionary Europe Proceedings* (1989), pp. 260–9.
3 The above passages are largely based on J. Burton, *Napoleon and*

Clio: Historical Writing, Teaching and Thinking during the First Empire (Durham, N.C., 1979), but see also Charpentier, *Napoléon*, pp. 99–129, 176–201. A similar, but more famous, line of thought to that of Portalis can be seen in G.W.F. Hegel, *Philosophy of History*, trans. John Sibree (New York, 1956); see especially the introduction and p. 31.

4 See Boime, *Social History of Modern Art II*, pp. 12–14.

5 See Wilson-Smith, *Napoleon*, pp. 134–49, and K. Le Bourhis, ed., *Costume in the Age of Napoleon* (New York, 1990).

6 See D.M. Quynn, 'The art confiscations of the Napoleonic wars', *American Historical Review*, 50: 1 (October, 1944), pp. 437–60, R. Maras, 'Napoleon and levies on the arts and sciences', *Consortium on Revolutionary Europe Proceedings* (1987), pp. 433–46, and M. Byrd, 'Denon and the Institute of Egypt', *Consortium on Revolutionary Europe Proceedings* (1989), pp. 438–43.

7 Wilson-Smith, *Napoleon*, pp. 100–33, Gonzalez-Palacios, *French Empire Style*, pp. 69–76, Boime, *Social History of Modern Art II*, pp. 14–25.

8 The quotes are from, respectively, Boime, *Social History of Modern Art II*, p. 20, and Gonzalez-Palacios, *French Empire Style*, p. 83.

9 See Friedlaender, *David to Delacroix*, pp. 12–106, Boime, *Social History of Modern Art II*, particularly pp. 35–95, 200–10, 315–18, 628, Wilson-Smith, *Napoleon*, pp. 85–100, 150–93, Gonzalez-Palacios, *French Empire Style*, pp. 17–69.

10 See J. Connolly, 'The origin of the star and the bee as Napoleonic emblems, and a reflection on the *Oedipus* of J.A.D. Ingres', *Consortium on Revolutionary Europe Proceedings* (1984), pp. 131–46.

11 See M. Descotes, *La Légende de Napoléon et les écrivains français du XIXe siècle* (Paris, 1967), pp. 11–112, and J. Boorsch, 'Chateaubriand and Napoleon', *Yale French Studies*, 26 (Fall–Winter 1960–61), pp. 55–62.

12 W. Scott, *The Life of Napoleon Buonaparte, Emperor of the French* (Paris, 1827), I, pp. i–iv; III, p. 9; IV, pp. 43–4, 95–100; V, pp. 115–24; VI, pp. 42–65; IX, pp. 317–54.

13 Scott, *Life*, III, pp. 152–7; IV, pp. 86–93; V, pp. 163–4; VI, pp. 29–30.

14 Scott, *Life*, IV, p. 293; VI, pp. 25–30; VII, pp. 51–4, 431–5.

15 W.M. Thackeray, *Vanity Fair: A Novel without a Hero*, ed. F.E.L. Priestley (Toronto, 1969). See in particular the introduction and Chapters 2, 34 and 64. On Thackeray's treatment of Waterloo and the indirect Napoleonic presence generally, see the introduction to the edition edited by G. and K. Tillotson (Boston, 1963).

16 See Descotes, *La Légende*, pp. 113–50, 187–223, and Albert Guérard, *Reflections on the Napoleonic Legend* (London, 1924), pp. 188–203. For translation of *Servitude et grandeur militaires*, see A. de Vigny, *The Military Condition* (London, 1964); the quote is on p. 153. See also W. Fortescue, *Alphonse de Lamartine* (London, 1983), pp. 92, 122, 198, 248, 261–2.

17 Quoted in H.A.L. Fisher, *Bonapartism* (Oxford, 1908), p. 70.

18 See S. Cro, 'Alessandro Manzoni and the French Revolution' and E.

Gerato, 'Manzoni's "Il Cinque maggio" and Lamartine's "Bonaparte"', both in *Consortium on Revolutionary Europe Proceedings* (1989), pp. 383–91 and 863–8, and K. Cornell, 'May 5, 1821 and the poets', *Yale French Studies*, 26 (Fall–Winter 1960–61), pp. 50–4.

19 Descotes, *La Légende*, pp. 187–223, and Guérard, *Reflections*, pp. 219–29, 230–7.

20 Of the many works on Romanticism, I have drawn mainly from J. Barzun, *Classic, Romantic and Modern* (London, 1961), G.R. Ridge, *The Hero in French Romantic Literature* (Athens, Ga., 1959), and P.T. Comeau, *Diehards and Innovators: The French Romantic Struggle: 1800–1830* (New York, 1988).

21 A. de Musset, *Confession of a Child of the Century* (Paris, 1905), especially pp. 2–21. See also Ridge, *The Hero*, pp. 5–6, 115–28.

22 Stendhal, *Red and Black*, ed. R.M. Adams (New York, 1969), pp. 13, 19, 59, 73, 85, 111.

23 See Descotes, *La Légende*, pp. 153–85, Guérard, *Reflections*, pp. 211–13, and Fortescue, *Lamartine*, pp. 78–9.

24 See Descotes, *La Légende*, pp. 225–67, Guérard, *Reflections*, pp. 213–19, 253–68, and S. Gemie, 'Balzac and the moral crisis of the July Monarchy', *European History Quarterly*, 19 (1989), pp. 469–94.

25 H. de Balzac, *Old Goriot*, trans. M. Crawford (London, 1951), pp. 103–6, 125–36, 180–8, 193, 219–23, 241–2. Judging by subsequent works such as *Peau de Chagrin*, Rastignac does indeed appear to have become a successful manipulator of society; see Ridge, *The Hero*, pp. 99–102.

26 See R.A. Peace, 'The Napoleonic theme in Russian literature', in H.T. Mason and W. Doyle, eds, *The Impact of the French Revolution* (Gloucester, 1989), pp. 47–63, R. Jackson, 'Napoleon in Russian literature', *Yale French Studies*, 26 (Fall–Winter 1960–61), pp. 106–18, A. Pushkin, *The Captain's Daughter and Other Short Stories* (New York, 1936), pp. 238, 250, 252, and M. Lermontov, *A Hero of Our Time* (New York, 1958), p. 176.

27 A. Pushkin, *Eugene Onegin* (New York, 1963), p. 175; Lermontov, *A Hero*, pp. 57, 85.

28 Peace, 'The Napoleonic theme', pp. 53–5.

29 See Peace, 'The Napoleonic theme', pp. 55–6, and F. Dostoevsky, *Crime and Punishment* (New York, 1975), pp. 55–6, 218–21.

30 Dostoevsky, *Crime and Punishment*, pp. 58–74, 350–5.

31 The following paragraphs are largely based on M. Marrinan, *Painting Politics for Louis-Philippe* (New Haven, 1988), pp. 141–200, and B.-A. Day-Hickman, *Napoleonic Art: Nationalism and the Spirit of Rebellion in France (1815–1848)* (Newark, N.J., 1999), pp. 111–17, 136–9.

32 See B. Ménager, *Les Napoléon du Peuple* (Paris, 1988), pp. 85–257, and F. Bluche, *Le Bonapartisme* (Paris, 1980), pp. 205–329.

33 See R. Gildea, *The Past in French History* (New Haven, 1994), p. 97.

34 Napoleon III, *Histoire de Jules César* (San Francisco, 1865).

35 For references to Napoleon, I have used the index to *The Complete Works of Friedrich Nietzsche*, ed. O. Levy (New York, 1964), but I

have also drawn upon *The Will to Power*, ed. W. Kaufmann (New York, 1968) and *Thus Spoke Zarathustra*, ed. R.J. Hollingdale (Harmondsworth, 1969).

36 Professor Moriarty is to be found in A. Conan Doyle, 'The final problem', in *The Memoirs of Sherlock Holmes* (Harmondsworth, 1971). See also J. Symons, *Mortal Consequences* (New York, 1977), pp. 63–75, and D. Calleo, 'Coleridge on Napoleon', *Yale French Studies*, 26 (Fall–Winter 1960–61), pp. 83–93.

6

The people's choice?
Napoleon and popular
culture

As in high art, the Napoleon of the people had mythical aspects,
but nineteenth-century popular culture placed more emphasis on
what Bonaparte shared with the common man. Whereas
Romanticism emphasized individual detachment from the rest of
society, Popular Bonapartism portrayed Napoleon as 'of the
people', rather than distinct from them. Given the immense toll
Bonaparte took upon the people, there is seeming paradox in the
adulation his reputation commanded, but it would be false to see
in Popular Bonapartism nothing more than successful propaganda subsequent to Napoleon's fall. Popular Bonapartism was
initially based on a balance sheet of material gain and loss. In the
later stages of the Empire, hardship appeared to be in the ascendant, but the experiences of 1814 and 1815 then transferred
perceived responsibility to Napoleon's enemies. This altered the
balance sheet, elevating the positive experience of the Napoleonic
era while diminishing the negative.

Thereafter Popular Bonapartism steadily grew, and its hallmarks were the Legend of the Empire as a golden era, and the
cult of Napoleon. The latter was manifest in a broad range of
forms, reflective of its mass nature and indicative of the appeal of
charismatic leadership in the early stages of consumer culture.
Such a phenomenon was not new, but the 'reach' of Popular

Bonapartism into the poorest quarters of rural and urban France was striking. Growth continued until Bonapartism became identified with the regime of Louis-Napoleon and associated with defeat. Sedan revived the Ogre and, unlike after 1815, republicans successfully attributed suffering to Bonapartism.

In Europe, Popular Bonapartism did exist outside France, but it was limited by the association of Napoleon with French oppression. When nationalism took on a mass base, it often inherited an anti-Napoleonic character previously apparent mostly among elite groups, although this was not universally the case. Such limitations did not, however, apply to the United States, where the cult could be adapted to emergent American nationalism and consumer culture. Napoleon became the exemplar of what could be achieved through ambition and will, but possession of these attributes was not perceived as being confined to the 'greats'. Thus more than in Europe, Napoleon's career became a symbol of what could be accomplished by the common man.

By the twentieth century, Popular Bonapartism existed mostly as sentiment and was largely detached from party politics. Under these circumstances it might have continued to flourish, but it was then dealt body blows by World War One and the subsequent rise of European dictatorships. This did not necessarily diminish Napoleon's status as genius, but the reputation became a cautionary tale of what ambition could lead to. He remained part of the chain of Great Men, with both its positive and negative connotations, but he no longer represented the people.

Upon his return from Egypt in 1799, and again in 1815 during the Flight of the Eagle, Bonaparte drew large crowds of workers and peasants urging him on. In both cases his following within the army was crucial to his aspirations, and support was greatest among the rank and file drawn from the masses. There was irony in this. Bonaparte did little to improve the army's medical service, and during the Empire the value of army pensions, save for generals, declined from the levels of the early Revolution. Nor did training and provision of arms, clothing and food indicate any great concern for the common soldier.[1]

Yet, the loyalty of Napoleon's troops was notorious. Bonaparte fostered *élan* by cultivating *esprit de corps*, but he also personalized allegiance. The personal attention he gave to promotion and his use of ceremonial tied accomplishment not just to service to the army, but especially to himself. Perhaps more significantly, the expression 'Little Corporal' connoted close proximity to the soldier. A corporal led the basic fighting unit, the *ordinaire*; he was the sole man of rank in it, but he shared in the daily life of the rank and file. Rapport with the common soldier was partly a product of calculation; Napoleon's ability to identify veterans by name came from careful study of regimental lists. But he was constantly among the men, whether at the daily review, suddenly appearing at a camp fire, or riding through the lines before battle.[2]

According to Bonaparte, the soldiers saw in him their 'protector and avenger'; for France generally, the analogous role was that of 'Saviour'. Throughout his rule, Bonaparte consistently attributed his accumulation of power to the necessity of preserving France from the aggression of foreign despots and the intrigues of their French auxiliaries. From the collapse of the Treaty of Amiens to the Continental System, this refrain of defensive necessity served to justify the increasing toll of sacrifice borne by the people. But as the Empire relentlessly expanded, such justification rang increasingly hollow. For a time, rapid victory kept doubt at bay, but intervention in Spain in 1808 began a process wherein questioning of the Emperor's motivation could flourish.

His enemies were Napoleon's best asset. Bonapartism probably reached its nadir in 1813, but invasion began a reversal. Napoleon waged one of his best campaigns in the defence of France in 1814, relentlessly hurling his diminishing forces at invading armies. Allied occupation then brought rape and pillage. This effectively transferred the source of suffering away from Bonaparte. It did not matter that the First Treaty of Paris was lenient; what impressed the general populace was the material extractions of foreign barbarians and the humiliation of having to accommodate them. Bourbon Restoration was founded on the defeat of France, and royalism sought to portray itself as a shield from foreign domination. Occupation was over by the end of the year and there was no indemnity. Perhaps in time the monarchy's attempt to identify itself with the benefits of peace might have overcome association with defeat. But to the image of being a puppet of foreign powers, Bourbon government added doubts over whether it would defend the new, post-1789 France from the pretensions of *ancien régime* France.

The path was thus prepared for a second coming of the

'Saviour'. During his 'Flight', Napoleon emphasized that he would respect the borders determined by the First Treaty of Paris. His purpose was entirely domestic – to rescue France from the clutches of Bourbons, nobles and priests. Although Napoleon initially sought to encourage belief that his return would be accepted by the Allied Powers, the latter quickly made known their determination to be done with him once and for all. Under the circumstances, popular rallying was impressive. Renewed war was inevitable, but from the standpoint of many Frenchmen, this was unquestionably a defensive war. In cities such as Paris, Lyons and Toulouse, bellicose enthusiasm was most apparent among workers, but in the east, Protestant areas of Provence, and parts of the south-west, support was especially pronounced among the peasantry. There is no precise means of assessing public opinion, but two points are clear: Bonapartism already had an extensive mass base, and the regime again fell in 1815 not because of domestic opposition, but because Allied armies were much greater.[3]

After the second fall, royalist writers could recommence their attack upon Imperial propaganda. In addition to the memoirs and 'serious' literature of the period, there were innumerable pamphlets and *libelles* designed to counteract the legend and cult. All possible personal vices were attributed to the Corsican tyrant, and the public was repeatedly reminded of the costs in conscription, taxation and lives lost or ruined. While exaggerated, such accounts had a real basis in very recent experience. Yet, the Black Legend failed to check the growth of the cult, and Napoleon remained wildly popular in the poorest quarters of Paris and Lyons.[4]

There were many reasons why anti-Napoleonism failed. Even royalist hacks recognized that the onslaught was excessive, so unconditional that many readers were inclined to supply the obviously missing ripostes. Although liberals initially contributed, anti-Napoleonism came to be associated with royalism and its effectiveness declined as the regime plunged into increasing unpopularity. Bourbon attempts to gain martyrdom status, especially through the many expiatory ceremonies honouring figures such as Marie-Antoinette, implicitly condemned the French, whereas Napoleon's 'martyrdom' made foreign powers the villains of the piece.

There were also material reasons for looking back at the Empire as a 'golden age'. Napoleon had benefited by a long run of good harvests, and urban and rural workers had experienced steady improvement in real incomes from roughly 1800 to 1810. Employment levels had been high, and the state had made a point of advertising its role of providing a living through public works. In bad times, Napoleon had not been hesitant to risk association with the Revolution through price-fixing and free provision of Rumford soup (an 'economical' concoction based on peas and barley). The regime had also assured that there would be no going back on the sale of lands nationalized during the Revolution. Matters varied by region, but in general initial sales went to wealthy buyers. Thereafter, however, many of the lands were resold in smaller parcels so that many small proprietors and their families had a direct interest in the continued legality of initial expropriation. No exact figure can be proffered, but, especially when inheritance is taken into account, millions must have been directly interested in a question which hovered throughout the Restoration.[5]

Inclination to view the Imperial past fondly was fostered by hardship in the early Second Restoration. Waterloo ushered in the White Terror of July 1815 to September 1816, during which royalists exacted retribution against 'traitors' who had rallied to Napoleon. This time the Coalition Powers were far less lenient with a nation that had welcomed the tyrant back. Territorial losses in the Second Treaty of Paris were not great, but even the Duke of Richelieu, leader of the Bourbon government, found an indemnity of 700 million *francs* humiliating. An occupying force of 150,000 troops would be provisioned by the French and reduced only as indemnity payments were made. Incidents of looting and rape again added to grievances, and a deep economic depression set in, producing subsistence crises until the summer of 1818. Political conspiracies were interwoven with economic grievances and the name Napoleon became a frequent rallying cry in the many grain riots and revolts that marked the period.[6]

During the White Terror, the Bourbon government made a concerted attempt to suppress reminders of the preceding regime, and shouts of 'Long live the Emperor!' became a criminal offence. In Paris, representations of the Imperial eagle were erased from the façade of the Louvre, and prefects directed a holocaust of Imperial icons in the departments. Busts of the Emperor were melted down, to be replaced in town halls by busts of Louis XVIII. But none of this was likely to expunge memory, at least in the short term, and Popular Bonapartism became first and foremost an expression of grievance against a repressive regime and the harsh material conditions attributed to it.[7]

Government officials were eager to neutralize agents who allegedly orchestrated Popular Bonapartism. They targeted individuals whose past actions made them suspect, and in particular they harassed elements of the former Imperial Army. They were not entirely wrong in doing so; until 1823 there were many conspiracies in which Bonapartism played a part. But what made Popular Bonapartism volatile had little to do with political organization; the combustive material lay in general sentiment. To be able to display a button with an eagle on it became a means of braving oppression. There will always be individuals who wish to draw attention to themselves by such means, but in Restoration France desire to express identification with Napoleon was such that a profitable market in memorabilia soon emerged. Some of the individuals who sold cheap plaster busts of Napoleon doubtless were committed Bonapartists, but economic incentives were also at play. In fact, much of the produce was initially manufactured in the Germanic states and Switzerland.

There has been extensive discussion of the role of the half-pay officer in spreading the Napoleonic cult. There were roughly 20,000 *demi-soldes* in 1816; they were ordered to reside in their department of origin and report periodically to local authorities while awaiting recall. Unless officials were willing to look the other way, they could not take employment, and hence they were often to be found in cafés, filling idle hours with conversation and reminiscence. According to Jean Vidalenc, what the majority most wanted was improvement in their material conditions and return to full service. Officials reported that only a small minority, perhaps 500 to 1000, were politically active as Bonapartists. Yet, while the author's findings do help to put a legend into sharper focus, one should not draw too much by way of general conclusion from them.[8]

The *demi-solde* was but part of a much broader group of men who had served in the Napoleonic armies. There were roughly 142,000 pensioned veterans in 1818, but to qualify for a pension one had to have sustained disabling wounds or served for an extended period of time. For most decommissioned soldiers there were only discharge bonuses. By 1816 the former Imperial Army, which had numbered above 500,000 in 1814, had been reduced to roughly 150,000 men, although it would be restored to roughly 240,000 beginning in March 1818. Many veterans were probably initially pleased to gain their release, but this did not necessarily make them proof against nostalgia. Such men had served in an institution lionized by Napoleon. In the Restoration parliament, Liberal Opposition deputies made a point of championing the army and its past victories, never missing an opportunity to chide governments for neglect of impoverished veterans. Similar themes were developed in the pamphlets of Paul-Louis Courier and the writings of Chatelain. More important still were the poems and songs of Paul-Emile Débraux and Pierre-Jean Béranger; these celebrated the veteran while castigating royalists for refusal to recognize past glory. Here were the origins for subsequent Romantic portraits of the suffering veteran, dreaming of better days.[9]

Veterans possessed cachet. Not all of them were respected or liked, and not all shared in Napoleon worship, but collectively they were a powerful agent of sentimental Bonapartism. Identification with the Little Corporal was a tempting means of establishing prominence in a local watering hole. There was always something fabulous about Napoleonic exploits, from the battle of the Pyramids to the retreat from Moscow. Who was better placed to carry the epic into the realm of village folklore? How was a craven draft-dodger to compare with a veteran experienced in fighting Cossacks? Lionization of the Napoleonic veteran in the village café long preceded Géricault's *The Swiss Sentry at the Louvre* (1819), but the sentiments were much the same. The veteran had served France yet been cast aside, enduring a fate much like his former leader.[10]

Such associations were too powerful for anti-Napoleonists to overcome. Announcement of the Emperor's death in July 1821 produced a spate of pamphlets which continued well into 1822. Georges Lote describes these writings as a literature of circumstance and the authors as 'humble citizens'. It is perhaps more helpful to locate the pamphlets as lying somewhere between elite and Popular Bonapartism; many revealed classical education, but they were characterized also by the images of Popular Bonapartism – the Little Corporal, 'modestly attired', right hand tucked into the waistcoat, gazing over the field of battle.

The pamphlets also indicate how very little has been added to the legend and cult by literary 'debate without end'. Point for point, the pamphlets rebut the charges of the Black Legend with equal intransigence. In doing so, they combine all the essential ingredients of both elite and Popular Bonapartism, suggesting that both flowed from the same source of Napoleonic propaganda and only diverged subsequently. As Lote points out, sentimental Bonapartism owed nothing of substance to Romanticism, and even the writings of Saint Helena added little. Napoleon was a gift of Providence, beyond ordinary mortals. He had fallen due to the whims of fate and base treachery. He possessed all the virtues, to which the veneration of his soldiers attested. The people loved him because he defended them and was one of their own.

What was new flowed from circumstance. Napoleon had been made a martyr, and the greatest of his agonies was the withholding of his wife and son:

> You, illustrious Marie
> You, daughter of the Caesars,
> You who charmed my life
> Amidst its hazards,
>
> You to whom my heart calls
> To close my eyes,
> From your faithful husband
> Receive my farewell.

The reported cause of his death was suspicious; poisoning was more probable than 'hereditary' cancer. Nevertheless death brought apotheosis; as Napoleon returned to the Gods, his ideals and followers would continue the battle for progress.[11]

Sentimental Bonapartism took an extraordinary number of forms. In a recent study, Bernard Ménager has analysed reported arrests for seditious shouts, but such sources reveal only the tip of an iceberg. As Ménager notes, authorities became less 'trigger happy' as the regime slowly gained stability. Moreover, many arrests during the White Terror went unrecorded; numerous individuals were incarcerated without charges ever being lodged. Nevertheless, Ménager's analysis does identify the pattern of Restoration Bonapartism. Cries of 'Long live the Emperor!' increased whenever the regime was perceived to be in political difficulty or during times of dearth. Volume was highest in the early years of the Second Restoration, tapering off from 1818 until the rebellions of the early 1820s. Napoleon's death and the

Bourbon regime's victory in Spain in late 1823 then brought another decline, until the political and economic crises of 1827–30 stimulated a recrudescence.[12]

Regimes bent on controlling opinion through repression are especially susceptible to rumour. Government agents frequently lamented the credulity of the people, but the incessant waves of rumour did reveal several points. Credulity reflected the fabulous nature of the Flight of the Eagle; having returned in 1815, why should the 'Saviour' not do so again? Thus it did not matter whether rumours held that Napoleon had returned at the head of American, Turkish, Polish, Austrian or Spanish forces; such tales spread rapidly. More significantly, such rumours were intermixed with social fears: the Bourbons were about to restore feudal dues and Church tithes. Hence the Bonapartism of the people was the Revolutionary variant of the Hundred Days. In the period preceding 1830, rumour focused on Napoleon's heir: 'Little Napoleon is engaged to the daughter of the Great Sultan. Once the marriage is concluded, he will be on the French throne because it doesn't belong to the King anymore.' Fuelling rumour were visible signs of rebellion. False proclamations from Napoleon, Marie-Louise or exiled officers foretold imminent return. At Paris the underground *Cris du Peuple* specialized in false citations from American journals alleging that Napoleon had escaped. Placards in the countryside predicted dire retribution upon royalists; often they were simply scribbled notes, but they were part of a process of persistently rekindling memory.[13]

Initially the icons of Popular Bonapartism consisted of objects from the Napoleonic period with insignia on them (buttons or medals), army issue (an Imperial sabre or shako), or easily obtainable items such as bouquets of violets, emblematic of the Hundred Days. However, even in 1816 one could find Napoleonic bric-à-brac – prints, wooden statues of Napoleon or the Vendôme Column, tobacco containers in the form of the cocked hat and the like – in Parisian markets, or carried throughout the countryside by itinerant peddlers. As repression eased from 1817 onwards, trade expanded; by 1820 shopkeepers were slipping such items into their wares, although this could bring a visit from the police. After Napoleon's death, prefects and judges became increasingly disposed to ignore the growing profusion of memorabilia, and although the Polignac government of August 1829 brought a crackdown, this merely slowed growth. At

Epinal, the Pellerin printing firm was denied permission to produce prints depicting Napoleon, although many such items were already circulating. Pellerin would have to be content with profiting by scenes of Napoleonic battles until the Revolution of 1830.

The Bourbon Restoration wound up trying simply to control the more populist elements of Bonapartism amidst demand that was socially diverse. For the wealthy there were luxury items: jewellery, porcelain, crystal glass with cameo inlay, silverware, bronze statues, lamps, furniture and expensive prints made from steel engraving. While there was no hard and fast rule, Imperial imagery predominated in such effects. For the less wealthy there were braces, kerchiefs, fans, playing cards, snuff boxes with Bonaparte's image revealed upon opening, canes with the Imperial eagle for a handle, pipes, pitchers, plates, bottles and Imperial elixirs. Here Imperial and the more popular Little Corporal images were both apparent. For the most humble there were paper cut-out soldiers and, especially, wood-block broadsheets – posters with a caption or brief text that cost a *sou*, roughly a penny. After removal of Bourbon constraints, the Pellerin printers could add depictions of the Great Man to their series of battle scenes and the floodgates opened. Beginning with a run of 30,000 prints in late 1830, production hit a peak of 875,000 in 1842, and the Pellerin firm was just one of several specializing in this market. This was almost entirely the domain of the Little Corporal.[14]

In an oral culture, authorities were particularly concerned by verse, and here the impact of Débraux and Béranger was vast. Both celebrated the veteran's nostalgia for the past, linking it to popular discontent. In Débraux's 'Ode to the Column' of 1818, one hears:

> Ah, one is proud to be French
> When one looks at the Vendôme column,
> On his rock at Saint Helena,
> Honour to his country still in mourning.
> The Little Corporal will return.
> Long live the grey frock-coat.

In his 'Memories of the People' of 1828, Béranger describes the sorrow of a peasant woman upon hearing news of Napoleon's death after she had received a 'visitation':

I serve him bread and wine.
He dries his clothes, then
Slowly falls asleep in front of the fire.
Upon awakening and seeing my tears
He says to me: Remain hopeful!

In urban centres military songs celebrating Napoleon held pride
of place among singing societies at cabarets. Elsewhere, almanacs
circulated verse, sung to some popular air, to be heard in the
streets and market place.[15]

Perhaps the greatest arena of battle was the theatre.
Authorities could censor plays, harass acting troupes, and close
theatres after riots fought between royalists and their adversaries.
But brawls remained common and bore testimony to the declining fortunes of the regime throughout the 1820s. What was one
to do? The public would seize upon lines of even the most
innocuous of plays to express its sentiments. Nor were words
necessary; miming the already stereotyped movements, gestures
and poses of Napoleon was sufficient. Mimicry left little doubt as
to whom Talma was really playing in de Jouy's *Sylla* in 1821.
Audiences who flocked to see Mademoiselle George did so partly
to admire her beauty, but officials had little doubt that aesthetic
and ideological values were intertwined in audience appreciation;
she had been Napoleon's mistress.

The lid came off in 1830. Between 1835 and 1841 some
ninety-seven plays based on Napoleon or the Empire were performed in Paris. For the actors Chevalier, Edmond and Gobert
this was indeed a return to a golden age; Gobert brought tears
to the eyes of George, but then again, he had been coached by
Constant, the Emperor's old *valet de chambre*. For actors such
as Provost and Delaistre, who played Hudson Lowe, rewards
were of another order; while the former was pleased to be
shunned at cafés, the latter hired a bodyguard. L.-H. Lecomte
lists 596 plays based on Napoleon written between 1797 and
1899, but Jules Deschamps is doubtless correct in calling this
catalogue far from complete. Moreover, this takes no account
of popular street theatre performed extemporaneously.
Similarly, how is one to classify the performance of jugglers
parading effigies of Napoleon while crowds shouted 'Bravo!' at
Montbéliard? The life of Napoleon as source of entertainment
and edification became ubiquitous under the July Monarchy,
helping to explain why on 19 December 1840 some 200,000

visitors filed through the Invalides to pay their respect to a shrine.[16]

Napoleon was the great martial artist, but what did victory accomplish? More important to Popular Bonapartism than glory was protection; Napoleon was great because he defended the people. This was the persistent message from Saint Helena: 'I always wanted peace', but 'Europe never ceased making war on France . . ., so that we had to overthrow or be overthrown'. Far from being an ogre, Napoleon had waged war with the approval of the masses. He could hardly have done otherwise: 'I had been raised to power by public opinion and I could be overthrown again by it'.

Napoleon could represent the people because he was one of them, understanding their needs and sharing their attributes: 'I am a man of the people, for I come from the people myself'. From our contemporary perspective, the images of Popular Bonapartism may seem incongruous. Pictures of ragged workers collectively embracing the Great Man on Horseback are not so very astonishing; such populism is routinely exploited by leaders. But Napoleon's 'common touch' went well beyond the ordinary, and the people felt they knew their Napoleon. Pictures of Bonaparte at the plough, replete in grey frock-coat and cocked hat, suggested familiarity with common labour. Even if guided by genius, the essence of Napoleonic success lay in relentless toil, and this was a message well attuned to the struggling commoner. Why change attire? He was the same in whatever field.[17]

The Napoleon of the people was the Little Corporal. According to Barbara Day-Hickman, the leading artisan of the Pellerin printing firm, François Georgin, 'eschewed the majestic image of the French emperor characteristic of imperial art in favour of the less imposing but more appealing portrait of Napoleon as a soldier and friend to the common people'. Georgin often copied works from the likes of David or Gros, but he made a point of toning down classical imagery and repeatedly substituted the Little Corporal for the Emperor in the original. Representations of royal majesty and hierarchy were removed in favour of an egalitarian Napoleon mixing comfortably with common soldiers, artisans and peasants and commiserating with their misfortunes. Georgin's Napoleon astonishes a former soldier by recalling his rank, regiment and previous service,

Illustration 6.1 Untitled engraving by Lacour for the 1835 edition of *Le Mémorial de Sainte-Hélène* published by Lequien *fils* of Paris.

shares his soldiers' potatoes roasted at the campfire, or grants a pension to an indigent peasant woman.[18]

The Christological character of Napoleon worship was given a boost by the 'martyrdom' of Saint Helena. Bonaparte was well aware of the value of such association: 'If Jesus Christ had not died on the cross, He would never have been worshipped as God'. And he would have been pleased to learn of a popular ballad recorded by the folklorist Charles Nisard:

> Jesus through his power
> Redeemed the pagan lost in sin.
> Napoleon saved France, but
> Like Jesus he was betrayed.
>
> Following his punishment
> Jesus died on a cross.
> Napoleon on St Helena
> Suffered like Jesus.

It was this messianic strain that gave meaning to François Rude's *The Awakening of Napoleon* and made the statue a point of pilgrimage for thousands.[19]

The very modes of popular culture contributed. In the early nineteenth century the artefacts of rural popular culture still consisted mostly of devotional tracts, prints and icons. It was therefore something of a gamble when the Pellerin firm shifted emphasis away from religious materials to celebration of the Little Corporal, although prints of Saint Napoleon, patron of warriors, had bridged this divide during the Restoration. Georgin applied religious symbolism to the Napoleonic saga, but more important was that peasants bought their prints or statuettes from the same itinerant peddlers who sold them devotional icons. Thus Napoleonic broadsheets were to be found in peasant cottages hanging alongside images of Christ and Mary. They also shared the same talismanic character; Napoleon could intercede with God and ward off evil spirits.[20]

Common folk often peppered Christian tradition with more than a pinch of paganism. Peasant association of Bonaparte with the supernatural was frequently commented upon by contemporaries, but it was Balzac who gave the most lasting account in *The Country Doctor*, published in 1833. Balzac identifies the principal apostles of Popular Bonapartism in the countryside as follows: 'The name of Napoleon alone had penetrated here; it is here a religion, thanks to two or three soldiers of the country returned to their firesides, and who, in the long evenings, relate to these simple people fabulous adventures of this man and his armies'. Subsequently Balzac provides an example of tale spinning wherein Bonaparte is invulnerable to bullets, impervious to the plague and untouched by the Russian winter. A former soldier repeatedly asks his peasant audience 'Is this natural?'. The answer is 'no'; Letizia had entered into a pact with God and Napoleon had divine powers. Association with Christ had, however, begun long before, apparent in the Imperial catechism and celebration of Saint Napoleon Day. Martyrdom simply completed a popular picture.[21]

Such were the materials that Louis-Napoleon exploited until Sedan finally gave French republicans opportunity to uproot Popular Bonapartism. France was not, however, the only country where Popular Bonapartism had been manifest prior to 1870. In the twentieth century, several proponents of the cult made sweeping claims about the extent of Napoleon's following, finding instances of Bonapartism from Patagonia to the Maori of New Zealand. Though obviously inflated, there is something to assertions that tales of Napoleon made him a 'global' figure in terms of celebrity. Even so, the evidence for claims of a universal following was highly anecdotal, deriving mostly from accounts of French travellers abroad.[22]

Certainly the Napoleonic saga exercised great fascination. In Poland, where Napoleon was associated with aspirations for independence, Bonapartism did have wide appeal, but it and nationalism were mostly the domain of elite and middle-class groups. Evidence, particularly in the accounts of British travellers, of the cult in Belgium is more substantial. On the whole, Belgium had prospered under the Empire, and fond memories of Napoleon were intertwined with resentment against Dutch rule imposed by the Vienna Settlement. Championing of Napoleon to smite Restoration reaction could also be found in the Germanic states. But was this the equivalent of Popular Bonapartism in France? Outside France, nationalism could cut both ways. In the absence of an indigenous hero/liberator, Napoleon could be made to serve, but as nationalism slowly took root among the masses, a host of local heroes arose – Bismarck in Germany, Garibaldi in Italy and the Kossuths in Hungary. Moreover, attempts to associate Napoleon with national self-determination

were problematic; it was much easier to convince the French that
Napoleon had been their defender against invading hordes.[23]

In certain regards, the cult of Napoleon among 'Anglo-Saxons'
was more significant. For a writer such as Hazlitt, Bonaparte was
a weapon to be used against the Establishment: Napoleon was
the champion of the rights of the common man. British
Radicalism's aversion to Wellington could produce sympathy,
and this helps to explain why Hudson Lowe became a *bête noire*
in London theatres. By the 1830s, British playwrights were
exhibiting symptoms of the cult, and Napoleon had become as
much a hero as villain of pantomimes, melodrama and ballads.
Gomersal became the equivalent of the French actors Chevalier,
Edmond and Gobert, and he was but one of many who could
have repeated the verse: 'Napoleon! There's magic in the sound.'
By 1845 John Sainsbury had opened his Napoleonic museum in
London. Yet when all was said and done, Napoleon was not a
symbol of domestic reform, and he certainly was not a hero of
nationalism. The cult of Napoleon resulted from the romance of
a ripping yarn.[24]

These tendencies were especially pronounced in the United
States, where we find a level of Popular Bonapartism second only
to that of France. Here, however, Bonapartism posed little threat
to nationalism and could be readily accommodated to it.
America was the land of opportunity, where an able immigrant,
through ability, hard work and enterprise, could triumph. Was
there not something Napoleonic in such imagery?

Interest in Napoleonic exploits began early, manifest in a
statue exhibited at the New York City waxworks in 1797, and as
the career unfolded, it gave rise to campaign histories and biographies. From its origins, discussion was highly partisan and,
judging by editorials on the Emperor's death, the conclusions
drawn were mixed. Napoleon was a man of humble origins, but
extraordinary talents. His abilities were, however, tainted by
inordinate ambition and warmongering. Some of the effects of
his rule, the humbling of despots and legal reform, were good,
but Napoleon himself was a tyrant, lacking the virtue of
Washington. The latter sentiments were shared by the young
republic's luminaries such as Jefferson, Madison and John
Adams, but the editor of the *Salem Gazette* lamented that
Napoleon's crimes were often overlooked in favour of his
victories.

Such reservations soon gave way. Sympathy for the exile had

grown from Waterloo onwards, fostered by a host of Bonapartist refugees. Comments in the *Memorial* such as 'In America you may be on a footing of equality with everyone; you may, if you please, mingle with the crowd without inconvenience, retaining your own manners' certainly did not hurt the reputation, and the spell woven at Saint Helena began to alter the opinion even of Jefferson. Subsequent generations of leading dignitaries either fell under the Napoleonic sway or exploited it. Andrew Jackson owned a bust of the Emperor, and Henry Clay informed the Senate that Napoleon was 'the superior spirit of the age'. Towards the end of the century, in the presidential campaign of 1896, William McKinley fought the populism of William Jennings Bryan with distribution of prints in which McKinley was portrayed wearing a cocked hat and frock-coat. Winning was the idea.[25]

From 1830 onwards, the cult spread like wildfire in popular revues, where sketches such as 'Checkers with Napoleon' and 'The advice of Napoleon to young America' appeared. Imaginary dialogues with Washington and Franklin were perhaps more edifying, but one could garner all of the Emperor's thoughts on fashion in *Godey's Ladies' Book*. Perhaps the latter was a relief from John Stevens Cabot Abbott's biography of Napoleon serialized in *Harper's Review* in the 1850s. Napoleon mania began at the theatre with a play on Waterloo at New York in 1820. Thereafter the number of plays steadily increased, hitting a peak in the 1830s, but continuing until the Civil War. The actors Placide and Charles Kemble Mason rivalled each other in their resemblance to the great man. Composers found in the Empire a frequent source of inspiration for primarily martial pieces such as *Bonaparte's Farewell*, and this was accompanied by a vogue of popular songs such as *Bonaparte's Lament*. By 1859 there were fifteen towns or hamlets named Napoleon or Bonaparte. Bric-à-brac abounded, but perhaps the most valued item was the funeral mask that Antommarchi gave New Orleans. Cuttings from the weeping willows next to Napoleon's tomb at Saint Helena found their way to Copp's Hill cemetary in Boston, and North Carolina could boast an itinerant, but *faux*, Marshal Ney.

Perhaps more ominous was the place Bonaparte found in education. He was cited as a reminder of what could come of learning science and history, or of parsing Latin, and primers informed readers that Napoleon always arose early and was a diligent student. Aimed at the same audience were works such as

Henry Watson's *The Campfires of Napoleon*. Given almost universal recognition that Napoleon was the greatest of all commanders, it was not so very surprising that Harvard students annually chose him as the greatest man in history. Perhaps they had read J.T. Headley's *Napoleon and his Marshals*, which went through fifty editions in the fifteen years following its initial publication in 1846. A similar line of thought led one biographer to label General Grant 'the Napoleon of America', and a second to foist a similar association upon the Cheyenne Dull Knife.[26]

According to Lee Kennett, the cult had two main motifs. The first saw in Napoleon the contemporary embodiment of the chivalric warrior; given the absence of a strong military tradition, Americans adopted Bonaparte. Thus the cult diminished after the Civil War, when he could be replaced by Grant and Lee. Yet decline did not mean an end to the cult. According to Albert Guérard, writing in the 1920s, it continued due to Napoleon's association with the prestige of the soldier. Napoleon was the soldier *par excellence*; unlike Frederick the Great, he was not a prince, nor was he a patrician like Caesar. A French observer, however, viewed matters in more sinister terms: the cult of Napoleon was tied to a latent militarism initially encouraged by the Monroe Doctrine and revivified by the Spanish-American War. At base, worship of Napoleon was tied to American expansionism.[27]

The second motif proved more enduring. Napoleon was the consummate self-made man. Hence references to him were frequent in William Weeks's *Getting on in the World* and I.W. Tilley's *Masters of the Situation, or some Secrets of Success and Power*. Several authors have linked the cult to the businessman's desire for 'gigantic material success' through 'relentless personal aggrandizement'. Not only was Napoleon an efficient manager with a penchant for advertisement, he was also a great risk-taker, constantly looking for new markets rather than settling for small-thinking consolidation. He thus was a hero for the Wall Street millionaire, the captain of industry, the robber baron and the trust-builder. Kennett locates such ambition particularly in the American bourgeoisie, but Howard Mumford Jones and Daniel Aaron take a more convincing line in following Ralph Waldo Emerson's assertion that Napoleon appealed to 'the aspirations of multitudes of little Napoleons, who read his life into their own histories'.

In his lecture on Napoleon in *Representative Men*, published in

1850, Emerson distinguished between 'conservatives' who wished to maintain what they already possessed, and 'democrats' who had their fortune yet to make. The former were 'timid, selfish, illiberal, hating innovation', while the latter were 'selfish also, encroaching, bold, self-relying'. Napoleon was the idol of the latter group, embodying what one could be and do: 'by birth a citizen, who, by very intelligible merits, arrived at such a commanding position, that he could indulge all those tastes which the common man possesses'. Ultimately, Napoleon represented the acquisitive principle as a sign of worldly success. Here we find a clue as to why Bonaparte continues to haunt commercial advertisements; what could be more central to modern mass culture?[28]

If Sedan lodged an ultimately mortal blow to Bonapartism as a political party, it was less lethal to Napoleon's reputation. The cult had revived in France by the 1890s, and it continued relatively unabated in America. But the popular element of Bonapartism was thereafter irreparably damaged by World War One and the subsequent emergence of European dictatorships.

The most evocative image of the Great War is that of the common soldier ordered over the top into the murderous 'No Man's Land' by callous commanders. Restoration images of the soldier/farmer had in fact depicted Imperial veterans stumbling across corpses unearthed by the plough. Absent, however, was the sentiment that such sacrifice had been futile. Matters were different after World War One, when the great hero was the Unknown Soldier. Measured against the sacrifices of the Unknown Soldier and his Napoleonic counterpart, how great were Bonaparte's claims to martyrdom at Saint Helena?[29]

The ramifications for Napoleon's reputation can be traced in the *Revue des etudes napoléoniennes*, a journal, founded in 1912, which mixed academic study with a good deal of 'boosterism'. With state funding, in 1921 the *Revue* organized centennial commemorations of the death of Napoleon. These were mostly conducted in Paris, but ceremonies were also held in Mainz, Rome and Warsaw. By 1926, however, the journal had run into financial difficulties and it suspended publication until 1930. By the latter date it had become the organ of the 'Friends of Napoleon', vaguely defined as all those who 'maintained the memory and the cult of the immortal epoch of the tricolour'.

Under the direction of Edouard Driault, the *Revue* fought the good fight. World War One was the outcome of reactionary despots having blocked Napoleon from giving Europe a federal organization which would have ensured international peace. Thus Europe had lived in a nightmare until the Treaty of Versailles put an end to German pretensions. When the spirit of the Unknown Soldier rose to the heavens, it took its rightful place alongside Napoleon. It was time to restore the Little Corporal to the Vendôme Column in honour of the man who, eighteen hundred years after Christ, had established the reign of equality on earth.[30]

Napoleon as apostle of peace, however, remained a 'tough sell'. There was a defensive tone to the *Revue*, apparent in Albert Meynier's calculation of the number of casualties in the Napoleonic Wars so as to compare them favourably to the losses of the Great War. In 1931, the *Revue* included an extended article by Jules Deschamps on the cult in Belgium, drawn from his *Sur la Légende de Napoléon*, published in the same year. Deschamps was partly reacting against Albert Guérard's hostile *Reflections on the Napoleonic Legend*. But he also took aim at an article published in 1925 in the *Mercure de France* in which Camille Vallaux opined that Napoleon had as much blood on his hands as the Kaiser, and that 'speeches, a parade, and canon fire at the Invalides' on 5 May 1921 had fostered an image of the French as warmongers. Deschamps rejected the image of Napoleon as Ogre, but in his *Sur la Légende* he then stepped into a second front for the cult. Deschamps (like Driault) argued that Bonaparte had fulfilled a need for order after a period of anarchy. In doing so, he drew an analogy to the stability provided by contemporary dictatorships, and his emphasis on the role of great leaders in overcoming the parliamentary chattering classes had a fascist ring to it. Deschamps had thus countered the Ogre by playing into the hand of the Tyrant.[31]

As we discussed in Chapter 4, the rise of interwar dictatorships, World War Two and the Cold War provided contexts wherein the Ogre and Tyrant images flourished. Yet, the field was far from uncontested by more positive images – Napoleon as harbinger of progress, or as artisan of the modern state. What was largely lost, however, was Popular Bonapartism's view of Napoleon as a man of the people. This becomes evident if we turn to the most popular of twentieth-century media, the cinema. Even a rapid survey of Napoleon in film reveals two obvious points. The visual stereotypes of Popular Bonapartism continue;

more often than not, we see the Little Corporal in his traditional attire and poses. But Napoleon in film is the detached individual of nineteenth-century elite culture. Whether he is glorified, vilified or belittled, he is not 'of the people'.

Abel Gance's 1927 masterpiece *Napoléon* is an ode to patriotism, but Bonaparte's relation to the Revolution is the principal theme. Napoleon is the heir of the Revolution and, more particularly, its saviour. Allegory to Christ's passion is unmistakable as Bonaparte witnesses crowd savagery on the night of 10 August 1792; he will provide the leadership, order and direction necessary to save the Revolution from the anarchism unleashed by demagoguery. Anti-parliamentary overtones are very strong; Napoleon disdains speech-makers and his strength lies in silent, forceful action.

From the opening scenes of the snowball fight at Brienne onwards, it is the Little Corporal of cocked hat and frock-coat that we see, but Bonaparte is singular and detached. There are scenes of affection with his family, and he is depicted as an innocent in relations with Josephine. But he is first and foremost the man of destiny – on a mission, conquering the elements, and with no time to waste on crowd adoration. He gives energy, discipline and enthusiasm to his troops, transforming them from impoverished ruffians into the nucleus of the Grand Army. Repeatedly the Eagle gazes down upon the scene; he sees everything and he imposes his will upon all obstacles. Amidst carnage after the siege of Toulon, his presence gives consolation to dying soldiers who reach out to him from the mud. But while he suffers, Napoleon is invulnerable and ultimately alone.

Patriotism took an increasingly militant tone in film immediately prior to, and during, World War Two. In this context, depiction of Napoleon pivoted on which nationalist myths were being propagated. Two films, *The Firefly* and *That Hamilton Woman*, illustrate these points. Moreover, they share a common feature. Neither portrays Napoleon directly; yet, the plot of each hinges upon him. There is, however, no need to illustrate Napoleon's character; the films can simply rely upon audience recognition of the Black Legend.

Directed by Robert Z. Leonard, *The Firefly* was released in 1937, amidst the Spanish Civil War. The film stars Jeanette MacDonald as Nina Maria, an alluring singer and dancer who serves Ferdinand VII as a spy by gathering information from besotted French officers. In the opening scenes, Ferdinand is proclaimed King to popular rejoicing at Madrid in 1808. Immediately thereafter, however, Napoleon's baneful presence is felt through the agency of General Savary, who carries the Emperor's invitation to Ferdinand to take part in a conference at Bayonne to resolve the Spanish succession dispute. Ferdinand, honourable and kind, agrees. Others are suspicious; according to Nina Maria's spymaster, 'Napoleon wants to get control of Europe. The only thing that stands in his way is Ferdinand and his popularity.' Nina Maria is thus despatched to Bayonne to uncover what the Emperor is conniving at, but she falls in love with a French counter-espionage agent who betrays her. Thus she fails to send her warning that Ferdinand is scheduled for arrest.

Thereafter follow forced abdication and appointment of Joseph as ruler, but the good people turn their back on Napoleon's brother as he enters Madrid. Riots, repression and civil war ensue, until the 'people's war' is transformed by the arrival of Wellington, who turns partisans into regular troops. Victory brings liberation, symbolized by images of the common man smashing the chains of enslavement. In all of this, Napoleon appears but once and in the most fleeting fashion, but his character is represented by his duplicitous agents, and he stands for enslavement of the popular will. Here, then, we have Napoleon the forerunner of contemporary military dictators, against whom the people must defend themselves.

On New Year's eve, the hero (played by Laurence Olivier) of *That Hamilton Woman* summarizes the eighteenth century as a series of 'greats': 'Marlborough went to war and Washington crossed the Delaware. Louis XVI and Marie-Antoinette. The last of the Stuarts, Peter the Great, Voltaire, Clive of India, Bonaparte.' To which Lady Hamilton (played by Vivien Leigh) adds 'Nelson'. Alexander Korda's film presents a tale of two lovers caught between duty and passion, but looming ominously in the background is Napoleon the warmonger. Winston Churchill was very keen that Korda's film should be made to arouse pro-British sentiments among American audiences in 1941, and, much as in Oman's *Napoleon at the Channel*, historical parallel abounds.

Though he dies in the process, Nelson does his duty, saving Britain from the clutches of Bonaparte. He had warned all along of the dangers of the Treaty of Amiens: 'You are celebrating a peace with Napoleon Bonaparte. . . . but, gentlemen, you will never make peace with Napoleon. He doesn't mean peace today;

he just wants to gain a little time to rearm himself at sea and make new alliances with Italy and Spain.' Should anyone have missed the point, Nelson's dialogue continues: 'Napoleon can never be master of the world until he has smashed us up, and believe me gentlemen, he intends to be master of the world. You cannot make peace with dictators; you have to destroy them.' In the light of Hitler, the Napoleonic Ogre and Tyrant shine.

Sacha Guitry's *Napoléon*, released in 1955, is rather more sophisticated, and less obviously related to contemporary politics, than the films previously discussed. It does, however, have a message, achieved largely by setting Talleyrand as principal narrator of the 'facts' of Napoleon's career. Plot consists of alternating scenes of conquest – martial, political and romantic – but Talleyrand's ironic commentary serves to deflate any exalted sentiments associated with 'great moments'. Characterization of Bonaparte presents an interesting mix of both the cult and the Black Legend. Napoleon is brilliant, inspiring and relentless, but there is more than a little of the charlatan about him. After Bonaparte's avowal of eternal love to Désirée Clary, Talleyrand comments 'this flower lasted no longer than the life of a rose', and the action and its protagonist move on. In the famous contretemps wherein Bonaparte confronts Josephine with her infidelities, he is depicted as far from losing his head while listening from behind the bedroom door to his wife crying; his first question is about the debts she has incurred. In the morning after, Bourrienne finds the two in bed; Bonaparte's laconic explanation is 'that's how it is', but his mind is on another conquest – the coup of Brumaire. The central passion here is attainment of power, perhaps a comment by Guitry on the nature of the Fourth Republic.

Almost entirely absent is the Napoleon of the people. Bonaparte does refer to the sovereignty of the people when it suits him, but Talleyrand's aside that France sought 'a saviour' and found 'a master' is much closer to the spirit of the tale. There is pathos in the final sequences wherein Napoleon becomes the martyr of Saint Helena (with Orson Welles as a glowering Hudson Lowe), and a final apotheosis shows the 'Little Corporal' as the people see him. But the latter is a vision of the heart, and certainly not the film itself. Napoleon is not of the people; he is 'one of the greatest men the world has ever known, an extraordinary being who nevertheless resembled a man'. Although Talleyrand describes Napoleon's modest attire as a mystery, it is one of the means by which he cultivates image, and thereby manipulates the people.

There is little of the dry irony of a Talleyrand to be found in Sergei Bondarchuk's mammoth 1964 production of *War and Peace*. Napoleon is not a principal character, but his role is an essential one – to disrupt the lives of the many Russians presented. It is only with the Moscow campaign that sustained portrayal begins, and then Napoleon emerges within the conventions of the Black Legend: he is completely self-absorbed in pursuit of his destiny. Particularly striking is a surreal depiction of Bonaparte among the corpses of Borodino. With Church bells tolling and the field still smoking, Napoleon rocks back and forth atop his white horse, brooding. Against this backdrop, one hears Tolstoy: 'Not for that hour and day alone were the mind and conscience of this man shut off from the real world around him'. Although he, 'more than any other human being', was responsible for what was happening, he never could in the least 'understand goodness, or truth, or beauty or even the significance of his own actions'. Subsequently confounded by Russian patriotism, Napoleon races away from his retreating followers. The counterpoint to scenes of devastation is narration of a bulletin: 'No matter where I go, you my soldiers, shall carry our mission forward. Our destiny is not to defend our borders, but to conquer other nations.' Allusion to Hitler is obvious, but more germane here is the image of Ogre – a destroyer of life indifferent to the decimation of his own men.

In the 1970 film version of *Waterloo* produced by Dino de Laurentiis and directed by Bondarchuk, Napoleon is again the God of War. Much of the film is based on contrasting portraits of Napoleon, played by Rod Steiger, and Wellington, played by Christopher Plummer. Beneath Wellington's aristocratic morgue, we find courage, fair play and sincere concern for his men. Napoleon is another kettle of fish. While he 'does war honour', his ability does not make him a 'gentleman'. Wellington represents something beyond himself – England and *noblesse oblige* – while Napoleon is utterly consumed by his own fate. Napoleon does possess virtues: he is courageous, a fighter to the end, and vastly superior to those who surround him. But he will leave nothing behind other than the fame of having extended 'the limits of glory'. The consequences of such glory are apparent in the laying out of corpses after the firestorm of battle. While Wellington remarks, 'Next to a battle lost, the saddest thing is a battle won', Napoleon concludes 'We must leave this place of dead flesh'. At points Bonaparte does come close to remorse, but there is never any doubt as to whether such reflections could hinder ambition. His comment after Quatre-Bras is: 'The field of glory is never a pretty sight. Nevertheless 16,000 Prussians dead, that's good news to slap on the walls of Paris.'

There are many historical echoes in the film – Napoleon's demagoguery at Grenoble is strongly suggestive of Hitler. 'I am France and France is me', he tells the crowd. In private, however, his message is that what is important is 'my brains, my ambitions, my desires, my hopes, my imagination, and above all else, my will'. More than a touch of egocentric madness is suggested as he struggles to impose his will and mind over a dying body. Thus alongside the Ogre we have a study in tyranny highly reminiscent of Alan Bullock's biography of Hitler. Despite the film's studious depiction of frock-coat, cocked hat, white charger, and hands folded behind the back, there is nothing of the Napoleon of the people here.

In all of the above films, Napoleon is presented as a subject for serious reflection, but, of course, elements of the reputation lend themselves to comedy. Directed by Terry Gilliam, with a screenplay by Michael Palin, *Time Bandits*, released in 1982, is a reminder of the longevity of the belittlement theme. Part child's fantasy and part science fiction, the movie depicts the adventures of six robber-dwarves and a young boy who voyage through time while evading the Supreme Being, from whom they have stolen a map of existence. In the first historical episode, the dwarves set about plundering Bonaparte during the First Italian campaign. 'He's rich', they note, when the boy expresses incredulity. Napoleon has just taken Castiglione, but while his men are busy conducting executions, he is seated, enraptured by a miniature Punch and Judy show and uninterested in the mayor's desire to surrender. Played by Palin, Bonaparte wants a repeat of the puppet show because 'That's what I like, little things hitting each other'.

Naturally Bonaparte is pleased when the dwarves perform something of a dance/donnybrook to the tune of 'Me and my Shadow', and he makes them 'Generals, for a bit'. Thereafter Napoleon drinks himself into a stupor while listing the heights of great men: 'Alexander the Great was five feet exactly. Isn't that incredible? Alexander the Great, whose empire stretched from India to Hungary, one inch shorter than me!' Cromwell, 'the only

man with any purpose in British history', was 'not a big man at
all'; Charlemagne, 'a dumpy little five footer', was 'a good chap'.
Most of the dwarves manage to stay awake until the future
Emperor snores; then they steal all his loot. Need one say more?
  Apparently director Stephen Herek thought so; at any event,
Bill and Ted's Excellent Adventure would seem to attest to the
influence of Monty Python on contemporary comedy. In this
1989 film, two California 'dudes' travel back in time to 'bag'
famous leaders by way of preparing a high-school history report.
The one figure shared with *Time Bandits* is the 'short, dead dude'
Napoleon, played by Terry Camerelli. Upon first viewing their
arrival at Austerlitz in a time-travelling phone booth, Napoleon's
immediate reaction is to order his men to 'Blow it up!', but Bill
and Ted manage to kidnap and transport him back to California.
They leave him with Ted's younger brother Deacon as baby-
sitter, and thus we are treated to Napoleon eating an enormous
bowl of ice cream (which gains him a 'Ziggy Piggy' sticker by
way of reward), cheating while keeping score in a bowling alley,
and meeting his California Waterloo – a giant water-slide which
he takes to after initial hesitation, pushing children aside rather
than waiting in queue at the top. All in all, then, as well as a
'vertically challenged' great man, we also have a spoilt, wilful
and ill-mannered child, not so very different from Gillray's
caricatures.

Given fairly universal scepticism over 'Great Men' in contemporary western culture, the decline of the Napoleon of the people is
hardly surprising. Very few heroes have not been found wanting
in an age disposed to prove that 'greats' were no better than the
rest of us if one only shines a light on private as well as public
conduct. In Napoleon's case, however, little historical revisionism
has been required; the Black Legend developed in parallel to the
cult. Yet, the Black Legend could not overcome the cult until the
historical circumstances of the twentieth century gave it decisive
advantage. In this regard, historical parallel with Hitler was not
the crucial element; in time, perception of similarities has
declined as scrutiny emphasizes differences. What was more
devastating for Popular Bonapartism was mass slaughter in the
two world wars; attempts to reconcile Napoleon and the
Unknown Soldier founder on the rock of self-sacrifice. If
Napoleon retains a place within French patriotism, this is not
generally conducive to universal hero worship, and, while he may

be seen as a builder of the modern state or even European integration, neither of these are readily linked to the aspirations of the common people. The image of visionary may retain some credibility, but Napoleon's willingness to sacrifice others makes it very difficult to associate his 'vision' with altruism. Too many such sacrifices have been asked.

Nevertheless, Napoleon does retain exceptional resonance in the popular imagination, and this is not simply a matter of warmongering and tyranny. Central to his reputation are the characteristics of talent, will, ambition and material reward. The key here is that these attributes have been universalized in mass consumer culture, with its emphasis on pursuit of self-interest and material acquisition. The sympathetic appeal of the Napoleonic saga becomes much greater if we view it simply in terms of individual ambition and set aside ideals of public service as little more than rhetoric. Napoleon was singularly talented and not truly of the people, but there are many aspiring Napoleons among the people.

Notes

1 See I. Woloch, *The French Veteran from the Revolution to the Restoration* (Chapel Hill, N.C., 1979), pp. 195–294, and, for a comprehensive indictment, J. Morvan, *Le Soldat Impérial* (Paris, 1904).

2 See J. Lynn, 'Towards an army of honour: the moral evolution of the French army, 1789–1815', *French Historical Studies*, 16 (Spring 1989), pp. 152–82, and M. Herz, 'From the "Little Corporal" to "Mongénéral": a comparison of two myths', *Yale French Studies*, 26 (Fall–Winter 1960–1), pp. 37–44.

3 See R.S. Alexander, *Bonapartism and Revolutionary Tradition in France* (Cambridge, 1991), pp. 1–126, 155–72, 188–203.

4 See J. Tulard, *L'Anti-Napoléon* (Paris, 1965), pp. 9–214.

5 See Tulard, *L'Anti-Napoléon*, pp. 215–22, and the same author's *Napoleon: The Myth of the Saviour* (London, 1985), pp. 186–92, wherein are summarized some of the findings of his *La vie quotidienne des Français sous Napoléon* (Paris, 1978).

6 On the early years of the Restoration, see G. de Bertier de Sauvigny, *The Restoration* (Philadelphia, 1966), pp. 3–157.

7 For general background, see J. Lucas-Dubreton, *Le Culte de Napoléon 1815–1848* (Paris, 1960), pp. 9–131, F. Bluche, *Le Bonapartisme* (Paris, 1908), pp. 123–204, and A. Guérard, *Reflections on the Napoleonic Legend* (London, 1924), pp. 114–45.

8 See J. Vidalenc, *Les Demi-Soldes* (Paris, 1955) and, for a useful summary, Woloch, *The French Veteran*, pp. 295–302.

9 See N.M. Athanassoglou-Kallmyer, 'Sad Cincinnatus: "Le Soldat Laboreur" as an image of the Napoleonic veteran after the Empire', *Arts Magazine*, 60 (May 1986), pp. 65–77.

10 See B.-A. Day-Hickman, *Napoleonic Art: Nationalism and the Spirit of Rebellion in France (1815–1848)* (Newark, N.J., 1999), pp. 26–32, and Lucas-Dubreton, *Le Culte*, pp. 136–45.

11 G. Lote, 'La mort de Napoléon et l'opinion bonapartiste en 1821', *Revue des études napoléoniennes*, 21 (July 1930), pp. 19–58; the verse is to be found on p. 38.

12 See B. Ménager, *Les Napoléon du Peuple* (Paris, 1988), pp. 15–83, and Day-Hickman, *Napoleonic Art*, p. 32.

13 See Day-Hickman, *Napoleonic Art*, pp. 32–3, and Lucas-Dubreton, *Le Culte*, pp. 118–19.

14 See Day-Hickman, *Napoleonic Art*, pp. 18–23, 33–47, Lucas-Dubreton, *Le Culte*, pp. 129–30, 183–4, 242, and J. Grand-Carteret, 'La Légende Napoléonienne par l'image vue sous un jour nouveau', *Revue des études napoléoniennes* (January–February 1923), pp. 28–46.

15 See J. Deschamps, *Sur la Légende de Napoléon* (Paris, 1931), pp. 83–97, Lucas-Dubreton, *Le Culte*, pp. 122–4, 222, 238–9, and Day-Hickman, *Napoleonic Art*, pp. 28–32, where the translations of Débraux and Béranger can be found.

16 See Deschamps, *Sur la Légende*, pp. 110–18, Day-Hickman, *Napoleonic Art*, p. 33, Lucas-Dubreton, *Le Culte*, pp. 119–24, 185–6, 240–1, 286–9, and A.-J. Tudesq, *L'élection présidentielle de Louis-Napoléon Bonaparte* (Paris, 1965), pp. 16–21.

17 Quotes in the above two paragraphs are taken from P. Gonnard, *The Exile of St Helena* (London, 1909), pp. 121–3, 132, 146. See also Athanassoglou-Kallmyer, 'Sad Cincinnatus', pp. 72–4.

18 See Day-Hickman, *Napoleonic Art*, pp. 52–83, and L. Humm Cormier *et al.*, *All the Banners Wave* (Providence, R.I., 1982), pp. 8–13, 27–32.

19 See Gonnard, *The Exile*, p. 9, and Day-Hickman, *Napoleonic Art*, pp. 103–4 and 140–2.

20 Day-Hickman, *Napoleonic Art*, pp. 92–110. See also M. Lyons, 'What did the peasants read? Written and printed culture in rural France, 1815–1914', *European History Quarterly*, 7: 2 (1997), pp. 165–97.

21 H. de Balzac, *The Country Doctor* (London, 1899), pp. 51, 220–49; see also Lucas-Dubreton, *Le Culte*, pp. 191–2, 288–9.

22 See Deschamps, *Sur la Légende*, pp. 31–4, 65–94, 118–23, and Lucas-Dubreton, *Le Culte*, pp. 187–90.

23 See Deschamps, *Sur la Légende*, pp. 171–218, and W. Zajewski, 'Le Culte de Napoléon à Dantzig', *Revue d'histoire moderne et contemporaine*, 23 (1976), pp. 556–72.

24 Deschamps, *Sur la Légende*, pp. 221–4, and Lucas-Dubreton, *Le Culte*, pp. 187–8.

25 See H. Mumford Jones and D. Aaron, 'Notes on the Napoleonic legend in America', *Franco-American Review*, 43 (January 1937), pp. 10–15, D. Horward and W. Rogers, 'The American press and the

death of Napoleon', *Journalism Quarterly*, 2 (Winter 1966), pp. 715–21, J.S. Reeves, *The Napoleonic Exiles in America* (Baltimore, 1905), L. Kennet, 'Le Culte de Napoléon aux Etats-Unis jusqu'à la Guerre de Sécession', *Revue de l'Institut Napoléon*, 124 (1972), pp. 145–56, and Deschamps, *Sur la Légende*, pp. 80–1.

26 See Kennet, 'Le Culte', pp. 148–54, Mumford Jones and Aaron, 'Notes on the Napoleonic legend', pp. 16–18, H. Dieck, *The most complete and authentic history of the life and public services of General Grant, 'The Napoleon of America'* (Cincinnati, 1885), and E. Brininstool, *Dull Knife (a Cheyenne Napoleon)* (Hollywood, 1935).

27 See C. Vallaux, 'La Légende Napoléonienne aux Etats-Unis', *Mercure de France*, 15 January 1925, pp. 289–307.

28 See R. Emerson, *Representative Men*, in W.E. Williams and D.E. Wilson, eds, *The Collected Works of Ralph Waldo Emerson*, IV (Cambridge, Mass., 1987), pp. 129–48, Kennett, 'Le Culte', pp. 155–6, Mumford Jones and Aaron, 'Notes on the Napoleonic legend', pp. 22–6, and Guérard, *Reflections*, pp. 101–13.

29 See Athanassoglou-Kallmyer, 'Sad Cincinnatus', pp. 64–70.

30 See E. Driault, 'Après un siècle de légende et d'histoire', *Revue des études napoléoniennes*, 31 (1930), pp. 87–100.

31 See E. Driault, 'Napoléon, le génie de l'ordre', *Revue des études napoléoniennes*, 30 (1930), pp. 8–25, A Meynier, 'Levées et pertes d'hommes sous le Consulat et l'Empire', *Revue des études napoléoniennes*, 30 (1930), pp. 26–51, Deschamps, *Sur la Légende*, pp. 13–16, 130–9, and Vallaux, 'La Légende', pp. 289–90, 307.

|7|

The Great Man meets the twentieth century

Whether they were 'for or against', most nineteenth-century writers assumed that Napoleon had shaped the course of history, and they were prone to attribute causation simply to his will. However, challenges to the 'Great Man' school were developing, and they would gain ascendancy in the twentieth century. Broadly speaking, these challenges took two main forms. The first consisted of analyses which viewed Napoleon as a 'type'; he was categorized and this reduced his uniqueness. The second consisted of approaches emphasizing long-term developments as the agents of historical change. The *longue durée* might apply to material conditions, intellectual movements or cultural developments, but one way or another, emphasis upon it tended to reduce the significance of individual agency.

These approaches were not entirely new, but it is especially in works written after the Great War that one can see their impact on Napoleonic literature. On the whole, discussion shifted away from the influence of Napoleon's will to the limits that long-term developments placed upon it. In this context, authors frequently discussed whether Napoleon was representative of some greater force, and hence its agent, or futilely running against the sands of time. At points there was a good deal of determinism apparent in such writing, and nothing could be more wounding to Napoleon's reputation.

Yet, despite such challenges, Napoleon retains his place as a crucial figure in modern history. The upshot of analysis of his relation to the *longue durée* has been to emphasize his role in creation of structures which proved enduring, especially his shaping of the modern state. The image of state builder thus comes to the fore in the reputation, but it is in fact an old one, apparent in the association of figures such as Mehemet Ali and Kemal Atatürk with Napoleon. In effect, then, twentieth-century history has tended to cut out the more extravagant claims of the 'Great Man' school, but in doing so it has clarified what remains the most convincing of those claims.

Although definition of what constitutes 'history' has long been contentious, a characteristic of the discipline has been to incorporate methods from other fields of study. This has been especially apparent in biography, where one often encounters the theories of the psychologists Sigmund Freud and Karl Jung. But it has also been the case in general studies of society and politics, wherein the influence of the sociologist Max Weber has been great. All three of these writers had something interesting to say about Napoleon, but more significant was the way in which they set an example for categorizing him as a 'type'.

In Freud's formal writings, reference to Napoleon is largely incidental. At one point Freud analyses how his own sense of achievement is troubled by a 'father complex', and he links this to a comment made by Napoleon to Joseph during his coronation as Emperor. Perhaps most striking is the way that Napoleon's life can be plumbed for references: Bonaparte as a master of remembering names, his ability to sleep at will, or a Napoleonic aphorism, 'anatomy is destiny', cited twice in discussion of sexual instincts. 'The life' was evidently very familiar to Freud, and, presumably, to his readers also.

More suggestive is a letter to Thomas Mann in which Freud ponders the biblical Joseph as a 'mythical prototype' for Bonaparte's career. Napoleon is the second son of a Corsican family, wherein 'the privilege of the eldest is guarded with particularly sacred awe'. He sets about displacing brother Joseph as family patriarch and, having done so, then overcompensates. He becomes excessively indulgent of Joseph and marries a surrogate – Josephine. When, for political considerations, he divorces Josephine, he forsakes his myth, and by way of atonement the 'great destroyer' sets about 'his self-destruction'. Hence the fall of the Empire. At first glance, Freud's interpretation of Napoleon's life would appear to grant him enormous agency in affecting the lives of others. Yet Bonaparte himself is described as the puppet of a subconscious urge to fulfil the pattern of a mythical prototype. One should not be unfair; Freud was merely jotting down thoughts in a private letter. But Freud's musings have often inspired others.[1]

Among the latter was Carl Jung, who carries us into the realm of the collective psyche, where Napoleon lurks as an embodiment of a potent archetype. Napoleon has an inner voice which leads him to judge all matters for himself, breaking conventions in the process of fully developing his personality. All individuals do so to some extent, but in great personalities the tendency is more pronounced, and because he follows the direction of his inner psyche, he is potentially powerful. His historical significance, however, lies in his being a variant of a psychic archetype – the mana personality, a master of the will, to which a culture collectively responds. When the collective psyche responds to him, he becomes an expression of psychic force far more potent than 'happenings of a physical or biological order'. The results of such phenomena can be disastrous: 'Instead of being at the mercy of wild beasts, earthquakes, landslides and inundations, modern man is battered by the elemental forces of his own psyche'. Ultimately it is the mind that matters: 'To quite a terrifying degree we are threatened by wars and revolutions which are nothing other than psychic epidemics'. But it is not the individual mind of Napoleon that counts, it is the power of psychic archetypes.[2]

Rather than recite the many works in which Freudian and Jungian psychology can be found, we will settle here for outlining how psychological theories affect Napoleonic biography. Much attention has been paid to Napoleon's childhood and his relations with his parents and siblings. Overweening ambition is frequently attributed to inattentive parents; perhaps history would have taken another course had Napoleon not been the sole child of Letizia put out to a wet nurse. Napoleon's sense of rivalry with Joseph was undoubtedly acute, and for some authors his assertiveness was a portent of relations with European monarchs. He always needed to prove himself, and his incessant wars stemmed from an insecurity complex.

Bonaparte's adolescence proves a rich vein, and here his sexual relations are heavily mined. Dimensions come into play for theorizing along the lines of Freud's 'anatomy is destiny' aphorism, and recently a historian has assured us that evidence indicates that Napoleon's penis was 'average'. A relationship between sex and power, however, does appear very obvious in Napoleon's case; Josephine's adultery was less a source of personal affliction than a matter of public image requiring assertion of mastery. Marriage to Marie-Louise was a traditional act of dynastic foreign relations, but the key to the marriage's success was that she fulfilled her maternal obligations. Thus it is tempting to tie Bonaparte's personal relations to the patriarchal nature of his Civil Code. The legislation concerning adultery was bigoted, and seems to reflect Napoleon's own serial adultery. Was this further evidence of an insecurity complex, or was it just a matter that he could do pretty much as he wanted? Adultery was not exactly rare among monarchs.

Often accompanying such investigations are discussions of the impact of social customs upon character formation. Imperial Europe was not the product of some grand vision, but rather an extension of clan rivalry waged between Napoleon and Pozzo di Borgo. Alternatively, perhaps the lawless nature of Corsican society predisposed Bonaparte towards the imposition of order so manifest in his rule. Why was he so fond of designing uniforms? Moreover, his origins give rise to questions concerning the role of a 'foreigner' in shaping France's destiny. Did his position as 'outsider' allow him to view the needs of France objectively because he was not tied to any particular faction? Was he French or European because of his reading of Enlightenment authors, or was he freed of such categorization by Romantic individualism? Did his 'mana personality' link him to that other 'outsider' – Adolf Hitler? Perhaps the essential formative influence was the military? But then again, discipline went out the window in 1812 as Romantic ambition gained ascendancy over rational planning. Perhaps role playing, begun in childhood, drove Napoleon from beginning to end?[3]

If nothing else, such ruminations illustrate Napoleon's celebrity. At one level, intense scrutiny would seem to invest enormous importance in him, but identifying Napoleon as a 'type' has a levelling effect which runs against the grain of the 'Great Man' school. To be classified as having an 'anal retentive' preoccupation with order hardly qualifies one as unique. Still, such categorization does render Napoleon comprehensible in strictly human terms, shedding the deification and demonizing of much nineteenth-century literature.

Classification of Napoleon as a 'type' can also be seen in the writings of Max Weber. In *Economy and Society* (1968), a compilation of works written mostly in the early 1900s, Weber cites Napoleon as an example of charismatic authority. Napoleon's power rests upon the confidence he inspires among his followers, whose support is based on faith in his 'historical mission'. Yet, while charisma is sufficient to establish his regime, it is insufficient to produce lasting authority. Hence, Napoleon transforms his rule through 'strict disciplinary organization', using the army, reform of the state, and legal codes for the purpose. In his creation of an impersonal, authoritarian state Napoleon is modern; yet, when all is said and done, he is but one of a long line of charismatic leaders, sharing characteristics with many. He is a recognizable 'type', closely linked to Caesar in that his initial support is based in the army and the irrational faith of the populace.

Weber's work has been highly influential among academics in the twentieth century. Many authors had preceded Weber in linking Napoleon to Caesarism, but it is Weber's description of the charismatic leader that appears most frequently in the previously discussed literature on 'Men on Horseback' and dictatorship. Weber's emphasis on personal charisma and the quasi-religious faith of the followers would, however, contrast sharply with historical approaches that insisted upon the primacy of material conditions.[4]

The collapse of the 'Great Man' school after the Great War to some extent was the culmination of challenges initially posed much earlier. History as a chronicle of kings and battles had long given way to more encompassing approaches by the time that, say, Jules Michelet gained his reputation in the first half of the nineteenth century. Michelet transferred heroic qualities usually attributed to individuals to the 'people' as he traced the development of the French nation through the Middle Ages to the Revolution. When, after the fall of the Second Empire, he turned his attention to the Napoleonic era, he disparaged Bonaparte as a betrayer of the people. Perhaps his invective inadvertently paid tribute to the significance of the tyrant, but in Michelet we can see a trend towards focusing on social groups as the vectors of progress, rather than 'Great Men'.[5]

Where this might lead became apparent in Leo Tolstoy's novel *War and Peace* (1869). Tolstoy's epic is underpinned by a determinist philosophy which holds that individual aspirations are but illusions amidst the sweep of broader forces. The author's dismissal of the 'Great Man' theme is caustic: 'To historians who believe . . . that French armies marched into Russia at the will of one man – Napoleon, the argument that Russia remained a power because Napoleon had a bad cold on 26 August may seem logical and convincing'. Like Michelet, Tolstoy's great hero is the (Russian) people, and he embodies this force in General Kutuzov, whose wisdom lies in avoiding action while circumstance unfolds. On the other hand, Bonaparte's belief that he can control events is likened to a child 'holding on to the straps inside a carriage and imagining that he is driving it'. Napoleon is hostage to the tides of mass movements; from 1792 France rolls eastward, until in 1812 she confronts a Russian counter-force which surges westwards.

Both the main male protagonists of the novel, Pierre Bezuhov and Prince Andrey Bolkonsky, share the delusion that Napoleon's career was a product of his own will. But while Pierre concludes that Napoleon is the Antichrist, it is Andrey, wounded on the battlefield, who has the true revelation: 'at that moment Napoleon seemed to him such a small, insignificant creature compared with what was passing now between his own soul and that lofty limitless firmament with the clouds flying over it'. Andrey's thoughts return to the 'quiet home life and peaceful happiness of Bald Hills', a clear mark of Tolstoyan approval. In his emphasis on the significance of the family life of ordinary mortals, Tolstoy was a forerunner of twentieth-century 'history from the bottom up', but one can see the seeds of this development in Michelet.[6]

Other challenges were less frontal, but no less significant. Alexis de Tocqueville, a contemporary of Michelet, did not write a work specifically on Napoleon, but two of his principal themes had great resonance for later scholars: the emergence of democracy, and concentration of power in the central government. Neither of these could be attributed simply to an individual, and indeed Tocqueville traced their origins well back into pre-Revolutionary times. For Tocqueville, the great danger lay in destruction of pluralism; as intermediary bodies were swept aside by democratic egalitarianism, absolute power was simply transferred to the unitary state. Where Napoleon might fit into this pattern is obvious, but the key is that he would be but one contributor to developments which occurred over the course of several centuries.[7]

Two other leading nineteenth-century writers also merit particular mention. François Guizot identified progress with the rise of the middle class, a process which he traced back to the Middle Ages. The approach of Karl Marx was similar in that he also attributed 'progress' to a social group, but Marx's great hero was the proletariat. Marx agreed that the middle class or bourgeoisie had been the principal agent of change since the Middle Ages, but he saw the Revolution of 1789 as ushering in a new period of struggle in which the proletariat would overcome the bourgeoisie. Thus Marx not only interpreted the past, he also predicted the future. He based his arguments on his philosophy of 'historical materialism', which posits that social and political relations are inevitably determined by ownership of the means of production. From this perspective, ideology is simply an expression of material interests.[8]

From roughly the Great War until the 1970s, Marxist history became increasingly prevalent among French historians, reaching a status very close to orthodoxy. For the Revolutionary–Napoleonic period, its two leading exponents were Georges Lefebvre and Albert Soboul.[9]

Of the two, Lefebvre was less trammelled by dogma. The broad outlines of his *Napoleon* (originally published as *Napoléon* in 1935) did conform to Marxist essentials, but, like Marx in his early writings, Lefebvre did not view Bonaparte as simply a tool of the bourgeoisie. The material interests of the bourgeoisie were secured by Consular reforms – the Concordat and educational restructuring entrenched social order, and the Napoleonic codes enshrined the principle of private property. Napoleon, however, then sought to push beyond the interests of the bourgeoisie. Imperial warmongering was mostly a consequence of his Romantic ego, and his attempt to fuse old and new elites alienated a bourgeoisie still attached to civil equality. Moreover, his increasing despotism revived longing for liberty. Hence, in the end, the bourgeoisie deserted the Empire, abetting the triumph of the Allied Powers. Napoleon's dream of global conquest had run aground against bourgeois material interests.

Yet there is a certain ambiguity at the core of the work. Lefebvre's argument that Napoleon's legacy proved enduring only in so much as it was in accord with the bourgeois Revolution did place limits upon Napoleon's agency. But the author also carefully avoided depiction of Napoleon's fall as inevitable. Social, spiritual and economic forces opposed to Napoleon's genius might 'have been overthrown or at least kept in check if the *Grande Armée* had not been suddenly destroyed'. In his conclusion, Lefebvre rejected determinism directly: 'Alexander's will-power might well have failed at Moscow, and the allied army might have been destroyed at Lützen'. One senses here that the historian in Lefebvre had drawn back from bald assertion that historical materialism would have inevitably overcome the will of the individual under discussion.[10]

Lefebvre's 'successor' Soboul put forward the basic tenets of Marxist interpretation more bluntly. Having introduced the coup of Brumaire in *Le Directoire et le Consulat* (1972), Soboul wastes little time in asserting that if Bonaparte is to govern, he must assume the social heritage of the Revolution. In a section entitled 'The social foundations or the force of circumstance', the author then elaborates; Bonaparte must respond to the aspirations of the Revolutionary bourgeoisie, and while he can put his mark on history, he cannot alter its course. Warmongering does pave the way for despotism, but the Emperor cannot efface 'the indelible mark of the origins of his power nor escape the limits assigned by history'. Soboul rehearsed similar arguments in a more direct assault on the 'Great Man' school in *Le Premier Empire* (1973). Bonaparte could succeed only in so much as he served the social interests of the times; history is a matter of men, not a man, however great. The proper perspective is from the bottom up; Napoleon's triumphs were determined by the *longue durée* in the form of a favourable conjuncture of demographic and economic growth. It was such forces that determined history, not the hazards of events such as Desaix arriving in the nick of time at Marengo.[11]

Soboul's use of the expression *la longue durée* reflected a second propitious conjuncture – Marxist interpretation was complemented by the foundation of the Annales school of history by Marc Bloch and Lucien Febvre in 1929. The great contribution of the Annales was to give social history more depth, principally through investigation of the long-term structures that shape everyday life: economic development and population trends, the impact of geography and climate, and the relation of such factors to attitudes and values. Although Annales writers were not necessarily Marxist, their detailed studies of material conditions did provide Marxists with much grist for their mill. The Annales also reinforced a tendency towards analysis rather than narrative, intentionally turning away from events. Given how central Napoleon was to the latter, this naturally reduced discussion of him.[12]

Louis Bergeron's *France under Napoleon* (originally published as *L'épisode napoléonien* in 1972) illustrates several of the characteristics of Annales scholarship. The book is part of a series, and foreign policy is considered in another volume by a different author, but this only partly explains why narrative is almost wholly absent. Even in assigning special importance to an 'event' (the coup of Brumaire), the author adds that 'such will not be our practice'; focus upon long-term developments eschews the history of events. At points, Bergeron calls into question the significance of the Napoleonic 'episode' itself. The state's impact on the life of the masses was limited; population growth continued, but it was levelling off in a long-term trend which would continue into the twentieth century. Economic development largely stagnated. There was no fundamental transformation in the rural economy and seaports were stifled by loss of overseas markets. An increasingly conservative elite demonstrated little entrepreneurial dynamism, so that there was no industrial takeoff. Viewed from such perspectives, 'France changed very little from 1800 to 1815'. Thus, the 'importance of the period and of the man are unavoidably reduced when seen in the light of long gradual movements, deep tendencies, or elements of resistance'.

Superficially this might appear an attempt to write Napoleon out of history, but Bergeron's approach is more complex than the above quotes suggest. For example, he concludes that Napoleon's attempt at elite fusion did in fact work in the long run. Formation of the 'notables' as a ruling class constituted a basic change in social structure. More striking, however, was the change Napoleon rendered in the political system. Unlike Lefebvre and Soboul, Bergeron grants that Napoleon's personal dictatorship marked a new departure, quite different from the previous dictatorships of the Revolution and heralding the advent of the police state. The Napoleonic state was novel in its political forms and 'new style for the exercise of power', and Napoleon had created a state system of 'unequalled modernity'.

Bergeron's work thus goes a long way towards delimiting Napoleon's impact. Partly this results from the author's not having to take international states systems or Napoleon the 'Great Commander' into account, but deepening analysis of the day-today life of the average soul does serve to curb some of the excesses of the 'Great Man' school. Even so, Bergeron does grant Napoleon significant agency in terms of his creation of new structures and systems. In particular, the author points to formation of the modern state, a theme which would steadily rise to the fore in subsequent scholarship.[13]

Despite its prominence, Marxist interpretation had many critics, and war was waged on many academic fronts. Among the combatants, of particular concern for this chapter are historians who have argued that ideas are at least as important as material conditions. At one level, this is the very reverse of Marxism, but the history of ideas also poses challenges to Napoleon's reputation because it too emphasizes the *longue durée*. Intellectual history places causal agency in systems of ideas which develop gradually until they are strong enough to overthrow older ones. As a new system confronts a traditional one, individuals can play a role in being the first to express new ideas, but it is the ideas that provoke change. Individuals can also play a part in the struggle to implement new ideas through political, social or legal systems, but this simply affects when an ideology overthrows its rival.

In the history of ideas, the Revolutionary–Napoleonic era is generally interpreted as an attempt to apply the ideals of the Enlightenment. In this context, Napoleon is often viewed as an 'enlightened despot', although usage of the term can differ in meaning. The term itself is more frequently applied to eighteenth-century rulers such as Frederick and Catherine the Great, monarchs who professed to govern according to reason and for the general welfare of their subjects. In doing so, they responded to the call of Enlightenment *philosophes* through reforms establishing religious toleration, reducing or limiting serfdom, improving education, rationalizing administration, codifying law, or stimulating economic activity. But they did not accept limits to their own powers, and, indeed, in pursuing territorial aggrandizement they often ignored the more humanitarian impulse of the *philosophes*.[14]

The temptation to place Napoleon in such a category is obvious. He strangled liberty, but on the whole his reforms were similar to those of his eighteenth-century predecessors, who also had been no partisans of representative government or democracy. If the essence of the 'Age of Reason' lay in rationalization, Napoleon certainly had strong claims to such a tradition. Much pivots, however, on the qualifier 'enlightened'; few historians question his despotism, but many drop the qualifier. One way or another, discussion circles around whether Napoleon was representative of the prevailing ideas of his times.

When Leo Gershoy published *The French Revolution and Napoleon* (1933), trends in France had begun to cross the Atlantic, and the author sought to find an accommodation between ideas and material conditions as causal factors. He granted that to 'make avowedly propagandist literature responsible for the great upheaval that came at the end of the century is to assign to ideas a force that more properly belongs to outmoded institutions and intolerable conditions'. But he added that to 'deny the influence of the intellectual movement which grew in intensity and gained increasing acceptance toward the end of the Old Régime is equally false'. For Gershoy, the 'truth' lay 'somewhere between these two extremes'.

Gershoy avoided labelling Bonaparte an enlightened despot, seeing him instead as a 'Man on Horseback' who 'had no other conception of government than that of a nation yielding prompt obedience to his commands'. Napoleon had a 'logical administrative mind', but for 'mankind in general and idealists in particular he entertained a deep feeling of contempt'. He could not continue the Revolution because he was 'hostile to the idea of liberty', and there was nothing novel about his substitution of 'the idea of authority' for that of liberty; Bonapartism was a variant of Caesarism.[15]

The rise of contemporary dictatorships had stimulated a very different interpretation when Geoffrey Bruun published his *Europe and the French Imperium* (1938). Bruun saw the liberal Revolution of 1789 as a deviation from Enlightenment thought. The programme of the *philosophes* had not been a 'seedtime of political democracy'; rather, it was 'the era of the princely despots'. The thinkers of the age had been absorbed by 'the idea of enlightened autocracy' and had 'conscientiously . . . laid down the intellectual foundations of Caesarism'. The true heir of the *philosophes*, Bonaparte, was in line with the enlightened despots in 'pursuing the same basic program of administrative consolidation', behind 'a facade of humanitarian pretexts'. In creating a state of 'unparalleled efficiency and vigor', Napoleon 'obeyed the most powerful political tradition of the age'.

We are very far here from historical materialism, but the

distance from Gershoy is also vast. Not only is Napoleon more representative of the 'heritage of philosophy' than the Revolution, he is also a consequence of it, implementing the 'ideal' of a 'more rational order of society', and reflecting the *philosophes'* faith in natural law. His destruction of liberty should not, however, be attributed to his 'arrogant genius'; it was a product of the predominant ideas of the Age of Reason.[16]

Different again was Felix Markham's *Napoleon and the Awakening of Europe* (1954). Especially arresting in this work is how the author shifts ground from the history of ideas to that of 'Great Men' in a manner similar to that of Lefebvre reaching beyond the confines of class conflict. Napoleon is 'steeped in the ideas of the Enlightenment' and he does share 'Voltairian scepticism'. But he also possesses the 'romantic sensibility of Rousseau' overlaid by 'devouring egoism'. His 'romantic ambition' leads him well beyond 'the limited ambition of the enlightened despots', and 'Moscow and St Helena, as well as Austerlitz and the Empire, seem to be implicit in his very character'. Napoleon 'was the greatest man of action whose life is known to historians in intimate detail', but he was not simply the representative of any set of ideas.[17]

Robert Holtman's *The Napoleonic Revolution* (1967) offers a synthesis of the trends previously discussed. Like Bruun, he views Napoleon in the light of the rationalizing enlightened despots, but he also sees, like Gershoy, the Revolution as an attempt to apply the ideas of the *philosophes*. Napoleon inherits both traditions and much of his rule is based on consolidation of the Revolution, although he must stray from the latter in pursuit of autocracy. Holtman meticulously assesses the aspects of the eighteenth-century background which 'explain Napoleon's actions or had a continuing influence on him', but in identifying Bonaparte's innovations, he leaves wide scope for individual impact. A certain bow to the Annales is apparent in recognition that France's material strength provided Bonaparte with his opportunity, and the author accepts that much of the programme was designed to appeal to Lefebvre's Revolutionary bourgeoisie. But Markham's 'Great Man' is also accommodated in a conclusion which finds a balance between individual will and the *longue durée*. Forces independent of Napoleon's will, economic and intellectual, were at work and to some extent they circumscribed him. Yet, 'Napoleon was a motive force in the making of history'; he was 'far from being a mere creature of historical determinism', and his 'hallmark was enduringly stamped on France, on Europe, and beyond'.[18]

By the late 1970s, Marxist influence was declining rapidly, and the 1980s would bring the emergence of cultural history as a new prevailing trend. Of particular note in the latter regard are studies of political culture which trace the rise of public opinion as a great agent of change. Such works concentrate on the dissemination of new ideals by groups such as journalists and lawyers, rather than just the Enlightenment *philosophes*, and they also analyse the growing audience of such vectors. In these regards, cultural history has certain ties to intellectual history, but it distinguishes itself by the emphasis it places on the means by which ideals are transmitted. To uncover the inculcation of new values, authors often employ discourse analysis, deconstructing literary and visual expression.[19]

The focus of such work has been on the eighteenth century, but in *Revolutionary France 1770–1880* (first published in a French edition in 1988), François Furet has provided an example of how Napoleon can be viewed in terms of political culture. Furet pays careful attention to text and visual symbols, and the chapter on Napoleon gives detailed analysis of the imagery of the Imperial coronation. Some mention is made of material conditions, but these are generally given short shrift. Even the economic flaws of the Continental Blockade are less important than the failure of 'French Europe' to rally sufficiently to 'support the ideological and social model of the Revolution'.

Furet interprets Napoleonic rule as a final phase of the Revolution, and one can detect a certain parallel with Lefebvre. During the Consulate Bonaparte achieves his most enduring accomplishments through the reforms that constituted his contract with the French, 'whom he understood so well'. To retain power, he must address bourgeois desire to secure their Revolutionary gains, but his contract consists essentially of implementation of the ideals of rationalization and social equality. For these objectives, the French are willing to sacrifice liberty.

But there is something more at play than Bonaparte's ability to interpret public opinion: his will. Furet underlines the influence of Bonaparte's Corsican origins when discussing the Napoleonic codes, although he balances this by adding that several articles of civil law reflected a 'shift towards conservatism, notably as regards the family'. While the codes adjusted law to the contemporary 'state of mind and morals', women were the 'principal losers'. Moreover, from 1804 onwards, Napoleon's 'Carolingian adventure' shapes history. Imperialism partly springs from Revolutionary messianism, but it also results from Napoleon's desire to put his stamp on Europe. Ultimately Napoleon exhausts France, producing liberal royalism, but this is a consequence of individual decisions and, indeed, events; the amount of narrative in the second half of Furet's chapter is striking when one considers his *Annales* origins.[20]

In his observations on the Napoleonic codes, Furet reflects the conclusions of women's history. Not all works in women's history can be categorized as cultural history, but emphasis upon political culture has been pronounced in several major studies wherein, in so much as his role is considered, Napoleon emerges as a gender tyrant. The question here for our consideration is whether he is viewed as an individual bigot or simply the representative of male tyranny generally.[21]

In *Women and the Public Sphere in the Age of the French Revolution* (1988), Joan Landes argues that the period of 1750 to 1850 was characterized by creation of a public sphere 'constructed against women, not just without them'. During the *ancien régime*, power had been exercised essentially in private as an extension of the authority of the King. In this system women had held at least some influence through their role in formation of the patronage chains that dominated court life, or through more direct sway over individual male holders of power. However, republican discourse had come to associate private politics and women as sources of corruption. Thus it was no coincidence that institution of the Republic in 1792 accelerated a drive both to render politics transparent by making it public and to confine women to the domestic sphere of hearth and home.

Napoleon himself plays no part in Landes's interpretation, but the Napoleonic Civil Code is seen as the capstone in the process of excluding women. The Civil Code 'reinforced the authority of husbands and fathers at the expense of wives and children' and deprived 'women of the right to perform as civil witnesses, to plead in court in their own name, or to own property without the husband's consent'. It 'excluded women from the definition of citizenship even as it proclaimed the rights of all citizens'. Napoleon, thus, was an agent of gender tyranny, but this was deeply rooted long before he came along.[22]

Lynn Hunt's *The Family Romance of the French Revolution* (1992) leads to a similar conclusion where Napoleon is concerned. The author's starting point is Freud's concept of the family romance: a fantasy of replacing the authority of one's parents with some substitute. Hunt however shifts this fantasy from the individual psyche to the collective, to examine how 'family romances, both conscious and unconscious, helped organize the political experience of the Revolution'. Association of family and polity was of course ubiquitous (it is timeless) in cultural representation, but the author is able to trace a pattern in literature and the visual arts wherein the *ancien régime* father (King) is slain by his children and his authority replaced by a band of equal brothers. The latter then fall out among themselves, preparing the way for a more thoroughgoing patriarch than Louis XVI ever was – Napoleon. As with Landes, Bonaparte is not discussed as an individual, but his regime and Civil Code are presented as the culmination of a process of implementing male tyranny.[23]

Landes and Hunt are representative of a general view that the Revolutionary–Napoleonic era was regressive in the broad sweep of women's history. Not all historians agree, and R.B. Rose has raised questions about what he sees as unduly pessimistic interpretation. In defending the 'classic Revolution' (from 1789 to 1794), Rose, however, readily concedes that the Napoleonic regime was a product of the *ancien régime* recovering amidst reaction against the 'true' Revolution. Thus, there is a certain consensus over the meaning of Brumaire, and it has solid foundations. Napoleon's view that the role of women was to produce children is notorious, and the Civil Code and educational system illustrated how narrowly based was the alleged meritocracy symbolized by the Legion of Honour. Yet, it is also true that women's history has yet to focus much attention on the Napoleonic period.[24]

There is much to be said for Furet's observation that Bonaparte's Corsican values placed him comfortably in a broader stream of neo-classical republicanism which fostered patriarchy. However, Bonaparte's personal interventions in the framing of the Civil Code were less straightforward than might be expected. He did, for example, insist upon retention of divorce, although the grounds for it were narrowed and practice declined substantially thereafter. Rod Phillips has concluded that there is little evidence that Bonaparte was motivated by thoughts of a possible break with Josephine, and Samantha Hartley finds that Napoleon's role in the framing of the legislation was to seek a compromise between the liberal principles of the Revolution and gathering social conservatism. Enlightenment secularism was retained in family law and under Bonaparte there was to be no transfer of authority back to the Catholic Church. Moreover, Napoleon was insistent that divorce should be made available throughout the Empire even when this was bound to produce trouble, although Spain was an exception to the rule.[25]

One can also wonder how 'public sphere' theory actually applies to the Napoleonic system, given the downgrading of representative institutions. Did this constitute a recovery of the 'private sphere' of politics in which women had formerly played a significant part? Or was the republican notion that women's virtue would inevitably be lost through participation in the public sphere so strong that women simply retired from all things political in 1794? An essay on 'Upper-class French women after 1789' by Barbara Corrado Pope would seem to suggest the latter, but informative as it is, it only scratches the surface of a very broad topic. The salon life of the Directory would certainly suggest otherwise, and this was, after all, a milieu in which Napoleon pursued power, although he did not necessarily approve of it. Why was it that the Empire made a policy of spreading salons abroad?[26]

Such questions do not necessarily contradict current conventions as to Napoleon's role in women's history, but they do suggest that much remains to be pondered. For the time being, Napoleon emerges very much as a gender tyrant, but he does so more as a product of long-term forces than his own volition.

In an article published in 1963, Franklin Ford asked to what extent the Revolutionary–Napoleonic era constituted a watershed. He then identified five categories of change: reorganization of government administration, revolution in the 'demands, the implications, the very sociology of war', increased public involvement in politics, 'revolutionary change' in the arts, and change in social structure. In terms of these categories, historians have subsequently associated Napoleon mostly with change in government and warfare.[27]

The theme of state building has been pronounced in works published in the 1990s. Isser Woloch's *The New Regime* (1994), for example, bears a certain relation to Tocqueville's *The Old Regime*. But Woloch's approach consists of identifying civic values, tracing the extent to which they were implemented by state reform, and identifying what was to prove enduring in transformation of the civic order between 1789 and the 1820s. Given this framework, the Napoleonic state emerges more as an enterprise in implementing or curtailing Revolutionary initiatives than in beginning new ones. Napoleon does inculcate certain values, apparent in his forcing broad acceptance of the obligation of conscription. But his part in the more liberal elements of the Revolutionary heritage, such as providing universal primary education or welfare, is much less positive. If one takes the aspirations of the liberal and Jacobin Revolution as a bench mark, then Napoleon's creative role tends to be reduced. But then again, much of his work lay elsewhere.[28]

Where that work lay can be seen in an article published by Howard Brown in 1997. Prior to the Revolution, provision of civil order had largely been left to local communities, with the central state intervening only during moments of crisis, usually by sending in the army. Thereafter, however, endemic struggle between revolutionary and counter-revolutionary forces produced anarchy, with large swathes of France subjected to the violence of brigand bands against which local police and justice systems proved impotent. In this scenario, longing for order supplanted liberal values. By late 1797 the Directory was responding with initiatives similar to *ancien régime* practices; these essentially amounted to reliance on the army not just for provision of order, but for justice too.

Bonaparte thus inherited policies by which he benefited; provision of order was crucial to rallying support. However, after breaking the back of civil disorder, Bonaparte then established the 'security state', which 'emphasizes surveillance and regulatory control in maintaining public order, rather than the use of coercive force to restore it'. Provision of order, achieved by exceptional measures often setting aside the due process of law, could then be regularized through the reforms of the Consulate – administrative reorganization, the Concordat, legal codes and the rest. But the key was that the state became proactive rather than reactive, and this would remain permanent. Brown distinguishes between the 'security state' and the 'police state', though he notes that several of the exceptional measures analysed by Michael Sibalis, including reversion to a form of the notorious *ancien régime lettres de cachet*, constituted parts of an 'embryonic police state'. Where the line between these two forms of the state is drawn remains grey, however, and presents a potentially fruitful line for future scholarship.[29]

State building also receives detailed consideration in Martyn Lyons's *Napoleon Bonaparte and the Legacy of the French Revolution* (1994) and Geoffrey Ellis's *Napoleon* (1997). Neither study is a 'straight' biography concentrating simply on Napoleon's life, and as works of synthesis they combine elements of the various approaches previously discussed. Thus they present examples of the twentieth-century project of defining Napoleon's relation to the broader forces shaping history.

The theoretical underpinnings of Lyons's work are similar to those of Lefebvre. Rejecting accounts that saw in Napoleon 'the power of individual will and energy over circumstance', Lyons argues that 'Napoleon's individual trajectory cannot be understood outside the historical forces which helped to direct it'. On the positive side of the ledger, his Consular reforms constituted 'lasting contributions', making him 'the founder of the modern state'. During the Consulate, Bonaparte acted in accord with the 'bourgeois Revolution of 1789–99', but when he veered onto his Imperial course, he left behind the 'needs of France and of its revolutionary history'. Perpetual warfare conflicted with the material interests of France and its bourgeoisie. Dictatorship was not a problem, provided that it was founded on social promotion of 'propertied wealth, personal talent and service to the state'. But Napoleon's regressive steps against the principle of equality brought decline. Transition in 1804 to hereditary Empire, establishment of imperial nobility in 1808 and marriage to a Habsburg in 1810 corroded support, so that when the European Powers finally united, one defeat was sufficient to topple the Empire, despite France's 'wealth and demographic resources'.

Resemblance to Lefebvre is thus more than passing; yet, there is a shift in emphasis. Lefebvre had explicitly rejected determinism, leaving a very major 'what if?' surrounding Napoleon's military decisions in 1812 and 1813. Lyons, however, reflects the emphasis that historical writing has subsequently placed on the *longue durée*. He is especially adept at integrating the finding of Annales-school research, although he rejects the contention that the period was merely an 'episode'. His discussion of women's history fits comfortably with the image of Napoleon as agent of gender bigotry, and a chapter on 'Art, propaganda and the cult of personality' provides the close analysis of signs and symbols associated with cultural history. However, ideas and values are always related back to the material interests to which the charismatic leader must appeal.[30]

Geoffrey Ellis's *Napoleon* also places Napoleonic agency within the confines of long-term structural developments. Napoleon's 'real legacy to France' lay 'almost entirely in the sphere of his civil rule'. His 'institutional legacy had its origins not in the heyday of the Empire, but in the earlier years, and more especially in those of the Consulate'. Older fascination with Napoleon's 'posturings as a new Caesar or Charlemagne' missed the point; his significance lay in legal codes and administrative reform. From the latter perspective, he can be seen as 'the emperor of the bourgeoisie', provided that one recognizes that the term 'bourgeois' encompasses a new landowning elite of notables rather than industrial capitalists. He was also a 'prophet of the modern state' in that he bequeathed a 'stronger and more efficient structure of State centralism than anything that had gone before'.

Like Lyons, Ellis sees little by way of enduring impact in the Imperial venture. Arguing that Napoleon's 'real legacy' had little to do with European integration, the author emphasizes the 'France first' element of Imperial policies. This topic, however, takes us into the concerns of the next chapter, and so we will leave it for the moment by simply noting that Ellis frames his discussion within the bounds of Napoleon's purpose, underlining the significance of 'unintended results'. Such an approach tends to reinforce Napoleon's significance, although it calls into question the success of his will.

Although Ellis thus assigns Napoleon's legacy to French state building, he does give extensive consideration to Napoleon's ego. More than in Lyons's work, Ellis incorporates the concerns that have become standard to biography. Thus *Napoleon* takes account of the insights of authors such as Dorothy Carrington and Harold Parker concerning the import of Bonaparte's Corsican origins, familial relations and classical or Romantic cultural influences. Here too we can see the trend to put Napoleon in his proper place: he was an extraordinary composite of various traits, but none of these was unique to him, and when all is said and done, he was a product of environment (in the broad sense of the term) and genes.[31]

The image of state builder is an old one, and it is a telltale sign that the expression 'the Napoleon of . . .' refers to other state builders almost as frequently as to 'Men on Horseback'. Often the difference is a matter of emphasis, but we can clarify the distinction by looking briefly at Ali Pasha, Mehemet Ali and Kemal Atatürk. All three were to some extent 'Men on Horseback', but only Mehemet Ali and Atatürk are linked to Napoleon by state building. Ali Pasha's relation to Napoleon is, in fact, closer to that of figures such as Santa Anna.

Recently, K.E. Fleming has published a study of Ali Pasha entitled *The Muslim Bonaparte*, adopting an association first made famous by Lord Byron. For contemporaries, there were striking similarities between the two men. From 1787 to 1820, Ali Pasha was the Ottoman-appointed governor of Ioannina, which encompassed most of what is today mainland Greece. He had taken power as a bandit chief, and his authority had then been formally recognized by the Ottoman Porte. Ali Pasha became known for strict enforcement of law and order, embarked on an ambitious public works programme, and encouraged the development of trade, generally to his personal benefit. In foreign relations, he acted as a powerful regional leader independent of the Porte, and he cultivated this through association with Bonaparte. Ali had a pronounced taste for Imperial decor, but while he borrowed the symbols of France, this was partly to demonstrate his own independence, especially where the British were concerned.

Despite his accomplishments, Ali Pasha never gained the reputation of 'state builder'. Europeans portrayed him as an Oriental despot, ignoring Ali's cultivation of the image of western modernizer while focusing on alleged cruelty and sexual depravity. Ali at times played to such stereotypes for his own purposes, but more important was that he was depicted as an example of why contemporary Greece bore such little resemblance to European notions of classical antiquity. Thus he became a symbol of the barbarity that Philhellenism was struggling against. Although his rule in certain regards fostered the formation of modern Greece, for instance through promotion of demotic Greek, Ali nonetheless came to stand for what was overthrown by the Greek independence movement. Unlike Bonaparte, he left behind no state system explicitly associated with the formation of modern Greece.[32]

The difference becomes more evident if we turn to Mehemet Ali. From a narrow perspective, Mehemet Ali looks simply like a more successful version of Ali Pasha. They both were governors who sought to gain independence during periods of weak Ottoman central authority. Mehemet Ali liked to point out that he was born in the same year as Napoleon, and perhaps it was the same guiding star that brought him to Egypt in 1801 as part of an Albanian detachment in a Turkish expeditionary force. Following the French and British evacuations of 1802, he gradually gained ascendancy in Egypt through elimination of Mameluke rivals. After he had effectively seized power, the Porte formally accepted him as pasha in 1806. Thereafter, however, Ali went on to conquer the Sudan in the 1820s, and seize Syria and Palestine in the early 1830s, so that he was in a position to threaten the sultanate itself. It was only European intervention in the 1840s that ended expansion, forcing Ali to surrender Syria and Palestine in return for Ottoman agreement that the governorship of Egypt would be hereditary. He thus succeeded where Napoleon had failed, founding a dynasty which lasted until the 1950s.[33]

Ali's career thus provided plenty of material for the image of warmonger. His decision to address Louis-Philippe as 'Emperor' was, of course, designed to promote French sympathy for the 'Oriental Napoleon', but this association was with Napoleon the conqueror. Moreover, he was guided entirely by pursuit of power, and it was towards this end that his domestic reforms were directed. Yet, Ali's role in the transformation of Egyptian state and society was profound.[34]

His first concern was the army, and his employment of veteran officers of the Grand Army for reform of military organization, training and supply only heightened association with Napoleon. He undertook extensive public works, developed industry while making it and foreign trade a state monopoly, and completely revamped the tax system, using it partly for land redistribution and creation of a new elite. His methods of governing featured the Napoleonic hallmarks of rationalization in administrative structures, centralization of power from the top down, and replacement of representative bodies by appointed officials. To improve his army and bureaucracy, he created schools to train his new elite, and from the 1820s onwards large batches of Egyptian students were sent to France to further this aim. His insistence on public order included the principle of religious toleration, and although Islamic Religious Courts remained the only judicial system during his rule, Mehemet Ali initiated studies of French law codes which would lead to reform under his successors.

None of this was designed to promote national sovereignty and, inadvertently, Mehemet Ali did open the door to European imperialism. Yet, there is little to disagree with in P.G. Vatikiotis's conclusion that: 'the consequences of the Pasha's pursuit of power and dominion constituted the essential foundations of the development of modern Egypt – both as a state and a society'. More recently, Arthur Goldschmidt has also concluded that, although Ali was not an Egyptian nationalist, he 'was the founder of the modern Egyptian state'. The key is that he had brought about lasting change to political and social structure.[35]

Kemal Atatürk presents us with a contrasting variant in that his modernizing impulse was closely linked to Turkish patriotism. There were three sources to his rise to power. The first lay in his military career. He initially gained fame in the defence of Turkey from Allied forces at Gallipoli in 1915, and his status as war hero was later confirmed by his command of the army that liberated Turkey of Greek forces in 1921–22. The second source of power lay in Kemal's organization of various resistance groups into a nationalist movement in 1919–20, and subsequently the People's Party, founded in August 1923. The third source lay in the general crisis besetting Turkey in the aftermath of World War One. Defeat led to Allied occupation, dismemberment of much of what remained of the Ottoman Empire, harsh conditions in the Treaty of Sèvres, and possible loss of much of Anatolia to a Greek invasion. Despite these external threats, the conservative Ottoman regime was reluctant to unleash nationalist sentiment as a counter-force, and hence the nationalist movement led by Kemal was one of both liberation and revolution.[36]

Jacob Landau's prediction in 1984 that Atatürk's reputation would rest more on his role as 'builder and modernizer' than on his feats as 'strategist and field commander' appears sound. Under Kemal's guidance, Turkey became a presidential republic with a constitution. Despite brief experiments with multi-party democracy, Turkey remained a one-party state under Kemal, who was President from 1923 until his death in 1938. The state could be ruthless when threatened by opposition, but it was progressive in granting women the vote and the right to sit in parliament. Perhaps the most striking feature of the revolution was its separation of Church and state. This was accomplished gradually, but the two leading measures lay in abolition of the Caliphate and replacement of Islamic law by legal codes adopted mostly from Switzerland. In addition, the constitution specifically forbade formation of political parties along religious lines, while the state promoted secular education. Many of the regime's most sensitive reforms lay in cultural matters, often running against Islamic custom and tradition. The most visible symbol lay in the banning of the fez, although the state backed away from similar measures regarding the veil. Equally significant were adoption of the Gregorian calendar and Sunday as a holiday, insistence on the 24-hour clock for measuring time, and introduction of the Latin alphabet.[37]

One can go too far in evaluating the impact of a single leader, and much of contemporary scholarship is directed towards assessing to what extent precedents for the Kemalist revolution are to be found in the earlier periods of Ottoman history. Kemal himself had many able backers, and to a certain extent he represented a well-established part of the elite; the revolution was from the 'top down' rather than the reverse. Not all the reforms proved successful, and their impact away from urban centres was often negligible. Moreover, as with any regime, the Turkish state remains a work in progress, struggling to establish multi-party democracy while retaining the ban on religiously based parties.

Still, there can be no doubt as to the fundamental nature of the Kemalist revolution. Nor is there much question as to the importance of Kemal's charismatic leadership. In these regards Kemal's reputation is akin to the Napoleonic image of state builder, but it differs in significant regards. Kemal himself was an admirer, but a discriminating one. He liked to quote Bonaparte, but his conclusion from extensive reading was that Napoleon had let himself be carried along by events, failing to establish and follow a suitable programme. Worse still, in pursuing conquest, Napoleon had sacrificed the interests of France. In contrast, Kemal negotiated peace with neighbouring states so that attention could be focused on domestic renewal. Thus, while Atatürk and Bonaparte may be linked favourably as state builders, or unfavourably as dictatorial Men on Horseback, the image of warmonger belongs to Napoleon alone. To Kemal the latter was evidence of egoism overriding patriotism. But for others, Napoleonic conquest could be seen as the prelude to state building on a greater than national scale.[38]

Historical approaches that viewed Napoleon as a 'type' or emphasized the importance of the *longue durée* held the potential to damage Napoleon's reputation severely. The reputation is based less on whether Napoleon was a force for good or evil, than that he was a force. In questioning his uniqueness and his agency, trends in historical writing challenged his significance and shattered many of the assumptions of the 'Great Man' school. There was a world over which Napoleon had little influence, and there were basic constraints to the imposition of his will. Yet the ultimate impact of such approaches has been to clarify what was significant about Napoleon by clearing away excessive claims. Even if categorizing him as a 'type' renders him less unique, he remains an extraordinary specimen all the same. Moreover, his achievements become all the more arresting when he is viewed as a human being rather than the agent of divine or satanic will. Similarly, better understanding of the limits of what any individual could accomplish tends to make what Napoleon achieved appear all the more remarkable.

Whether his fostering of elite fusion was integral to the emergence of the 'notables' as a ruling class can be questioned, but his role in creating the modern French state is subject to little doubt. His work was one of synthesis, bringing together elements of Revolutionary and *ancien régime* government. What was crucial, however, was not the originality of the component parts, but rather that the system worked. Under Napoleon, the state took on a far more active role in regulating social order on a permanent basis, and this created lasting expectations of what the state should do.

The question of whether Napoleon was simply the representative of broader forces tends to pivot on how one defines such forces. Determinism assumes that what subsequently emerged must have been the defining force of an era, and that it was largely unitary. Historians, however, often disagree as to the nature of that force. While one historian sees the liberal Revolution as the culmination of the Enlightenment, another sees the autocratic Napoleon as the true heir. Perhaps the Enlightenment held a variety of elements from which Napoleon could choose? Similarly, the argument that Napoleon was an agent of the bourgeoisie during the Consulate looks far from convincing after decades of debate over whether the Revolution was bourgeois, and unresolved dispute as to how one can actually define the bourgeoisie. Was the bourgeoisie so very triumphant and so homogeneous that Napoleon could not play divide and rule? Finally, one can note that the very notion of public opinion is not without its problems. Unified public opinion is a very rare historical phenomenon; far more familiar is a welter of often conflicting opinions and a great deal of indifference. Within this welter there were many options from which Napoleon could pick and choose.

None of which is to say that Napoleon's will was untrammelled. But he did have plenty of opportunity to make choices, and better understanding of his options only increases interest in the decisions he made.

Notes

1 See the index of *The Standard Edition of the Complete Psychological Works of Sigmund Freud*, ed. J. Strachey (London, 1966–74), and *Letters of Sigmund Freud*, ed. E.L. Freud (New York, 1960), pp. 432–4.

2 See C.G. Jung, *The Symbolic Life* (Princeton, N.J., 1976), pp. 221–2, *Two Essays on Analytical Psychology* (Cleveland, 1967), pp. 242–53, and *The Development of Personality* (Princeton, N.J., 1954), pp. 176–83.

3 Frank McLynn discusses Napoleon's penis in *Napoleon* (London, 1998), p. 278. Among many studies of character formation, see N. Young, *The Growth of Napoleon, a Study of Environment* (London, 1910), D. Carrington, *Napoleon and his Parents: On the Threshold of History* (Harmondsworth, 1984), D. Seward, *Napoleon's Family* (London, 1986), H. Parker, 'The formation of Napoleon's personality: an exploratory essay', in H. Parker, ed., *Problems in European History* (Durham, N.C., 1979), pp. 72–88, the same author's 'Napoleon and the values of the French army: the early phases', *Proceedings of the Annual Meeting of the Western Society for French History*, 18 (1991), pp. 233–42, and 'Why did Napoleon invade Russia?', *Consortium on Revolutionary Europe 1750–1850, Proceedings 1989* (1990), pp. 80–96, P. Paterson Jones, ed., *Napoleon: An Intimate Account of the Years of Supremacy 1800–1814* (San Francisco, 1992), and F. Richardson, *Napoleon: Bisexual Emperor* (New York, 1973).

4 M. Weber, *Economy and Society*, ed. G. Ross and C. Wittich (New York, 1968), I, pp. 212–301, 373; II, pp. 529, 692, 865–6; III, pp. 1, 149, 1155, 1451.

5 See H.A.C. Collingham, *The July Monarchy* (London, 1988), pp. 258–64, and P. Geyl, *Napoleon: For and Against* (London, 1986), pp. 125–6. The essence of Michelet's approach can be seen in J. Michelet, *The People*, trans. John P. McKay (Chicago, 1973); his attack on the tyrant can be seen in *Oeuvres Complètes*, ed. Paul Viallaneix, XXI (Paris, 1982).

6 Much of the above comes from R.A. Peace, 'The Napoleonic theme in Russian literature', in H.T. Mason and W. Doyle, eds, *The Impact of the French Revolution* (Gloucester, 1989), pp. 55–62, but see also

R. Jackson, 'Napoleon in Russian literature', *Yale French Studies*, 26 (Fall–Winter 1960–61), pp. 114–18.

7 For A. de Tocqueville's two masterpieces, see *The Old Régime and the French Revolution* (Garden City, N.Y., 1955), and *Democracy in America*, 2 vols (New York, 1961).

8 For background, see D. Johnson, *Guizot* (London, 1963), and F. Furet, *Marx and the French Revolution* (Chicago, 1988).

9 See W. Doyle, *Origins of the French Revolution* (Oxford, 1999), pp. 5–34.

10 G. Lefebvre, *Napoleon* (New York, 1969), I, pp. ix–x; II, pp. 195, 263, 368–70.

11 A. Soboul, *Le Directoire et le Consulat* (Paris, 1972), pp. 84–123, and *Le Premier Empire* (Paris, 1973), pp. 8–14. The same points are made in Soboul's 'Le héros, la légende et l'histoire', *La Pensée*, 143 (1969), pp. 37–61, wherein he interprets the Legend as an exercise in masking the extent to which Napoleon had run against the forces unleashed by the Revolution.

12 To examine Annales school approaches and preoccupations, see R. Forster and O. Ranum, eds, *Rural Society in France* (Baltimore, 1977).

13 See L. Bergeron, *France under Napoleon* (Princeton, N.J., 1981), pp. ix–xiv, 3–4, 13–20, 23–31, 62–72, 108–90.

14 See L. Gershoy, *The French Revolution and Napoleon* (New York, 1964), pp. 84–90.

15 Gershoy, *The French Revolution*, pp. 58, 347–60, 373, 381, 405, 441, 454.

16 G. Bruun, *Europe and the French Imperium 1799–1814* (New York, 1938), particularly pp. xv–xvi, 1–14.

17 See F.M.H. Markham, *Napoleon and the Awakening of Europe* (London, 1966), pp. 3, 16, 54–63, 94, 123, 173–5. Napoleon's very Black agency is also much to the fore in A. Cobban, *A History of Modern France*, II (Harmondsworth, 1961), pp. 9–70.

18 See R. Holtman, *The Napoleonic Revolution* (Baton Rouge, La., 1978), particularly pp. 15–25, 211–12.

19 See Doyle, *Origins*, pp. 35–41.

20 F. Furet, *Revolutionary France 1780–1880* (Oxford, 1996), pp. 211–66.

21 Furet, *Revolutionary France*, pp. 230–3.

22 J. Landes, *Women and the Public Sphere* (Ithaca, N.Y., 1988), especially pp. 1–13, 145–6, 170.

23 L. Hunt, *The Family Romance of the French Revolution* (Berkeley, Calif., 1992).

24 The 'pessimistic' view can be seen in a couple of recent general surveys: O. Hufton, *The Prospect Before Her* (New York, 1996), pp. 490–1, 509–13, and S. Groag Bell and K. Offen, *Women, the Family, and Freedom* (Stanford, 1983), p. 22. See also the discussion in R.B. Rose, 'Feminism, women and the French Revolution', *Historical Reflections*, 21:1 (1995), pp. 187–205. The point concerning the imits to Napoleonic meritocracy is made in D.M.G. Sutherland, *France 1789–1815* (London, 1985), pp. 366–9, 374–6.

25 See R. Phillips, *Putting Asunder* (Cambridge, 1988), pp. 185–8, and S. Hartley, 'Not a "women's issue": divorce and the family as a political background for secularizers and Catholics from 1792 to 1816' (M.A. dissertation, University of Victoria, 1999), pp. 55–74.
26 See B. Corrado Pope, 'Revolution and retreat: upper-class French women after 1789', in C.R. Berkin and C.M. Lovett, eds, *Women, War, and Revolution* (New York, 1980), pp. 215–36.
27 F.L. Ford, 'The Revolutionary–Napoleonic era: how much of a watershed?', *American Historical Review*, 69:1 (October 1963), pp. 18–29. The author's arguments were subsequently developed in his *Europe 1780–1830* (London, 1970).
28 See I. Woloch, *The New Regime* (New York, 1994).
29 See H. Brown, 'From organic society to security state: the war on brigandage in France, 1797–1802', *Journal of Modern History*, 69 (December 1997), pp. 661–95, and M. Sibalis, 'Prisoners by *Mesure de Haute Police* under Napoleon I: reviving the *lettres de cachet*', *Proceedings of the Annual Meeting of the Western Society for French History*, 18 (1991), pp. 261–9.
30 M. Lyons, *Napoleon Bonaparte and the Legacy of the French Revolution* (London, 1994), especially pp. 294–300.
31 G. Ellis, *Napoleon* (London, 1997), especially pp. 231–7.
32 K.E. Fleming, *The Muslim Bonaparte: Diplomacy and Orientalism in Ali Pasha's Greece* (Princeton, N.J., 1999).
33 These passages are based on P.J. Vatikiotis, *The Modern History of Egypt* (London, 1969), pp. 49–73, J.C.B. Richmond, *Egypt 1798–1952* (London, 1977), pp. 31–69, A. Goldschmidt, *Modern Egypt* (Boulder, Colo., 1988), pp. 13–22, H. Dodwell, *The Founder of Modern Egypt* (Cambridge, 1931), and A. Silvera, 'The first Egyptian student mission to France under Muhammad Ali', in E. Kedourie and S.G. Haim, eds, *Modern Egypt* (London, 1980), pp. 1–22.
34 See R. Flower, *Napoleon to Nasser* (London, 1972), p. 74, and Collingham, *The July Monarchy*, pp. 221–39.
35 Vatikiotis, *Egypt*, p. 73, and Goldschmidt, *Modern Egypt*, p. 22.
36 These paragraphs are based largely on B. Lewis, *The Emergence of Modern Turkey* (Oxford, 1968), pp. 239–93, A. Kazancigal and E. Ozbudun, eds, *Atatürk: Founder of a Modern State* (London, 1981), and J.M. Landau, ed., *Atatürk and the Modernization of Turkey* (Boulder, Colo., 1984).
37 See the introduction to Landau, ed., *Atatürk*.
38 See H.C. Armstrong, *Grey Wolf* (London, 1935), p. 68, and Lord Kinross, *Atatürk* (London, 1964), pp. 18, 477–8.

|8|

Napoleon and Europe: conqueror or unifier?

In the nineteenth and much of the twentieth centuries, analysis of foreign policy played a major part in shaping Napoleon's reputation. Even a rapid glance at Pieter Geyl's *For and Against* reveals how extensive such examination was. After World War Two, there was a tapering off in diplomatic history, but in the past two decades there has been a significant revival. No claim can be made to represent all of this literature in this chapter, especially if we include studies of the Napoleonic Empire as part of the consideration. Some of the most revealing research on the Empire has been conducted in national, regional or local studies, but the volume is so vast that we must rely on the syntheses of authors who take all of Europe into account. Given these points, the objective of what follows is simply to trace the impact of recent analyses of the relation between Napoleon and Europe on the reputation of Napoleon.[1]

Within the literature generally, the major themes can be summarized as a set of interrelated questions. First, did inter-state relations undergo systemic change during the Napoleonic era? If there were significant departures, what were these and to what extent was Napoleon responsible for them? What was the character of Napoleon's foreign policy, and what were his objectives? The latter question entails discussion of the nature of his Empire. Was the Empire designed as anything more than a conquering machine? If more than plunder was involved, what were the other elements and how did they relate to the conquering impulse? Interpretation of Napoleon is often affected by contemporary context, and in recent years the Napoleonic 'enterprise' has come to be viewed from the perspective of post-World War Two European integration. Was Napoleon trying to create a homogenous European state?

Objectives are one thing; results are often another. For example, it could well be that Napoleon had no real intention of creating a unified Europe, and yet fostered integration through the implementation of systems that ultimately spread a common heritage previously lacking. On the other hand, it has long been held that Napoleonic rule facilitated the rise of nationalism, which would harden divisions. Perhaps the Empire, intentionally or unintentionally, promoted two antagonistic forces?

Two rival images predominate in discussion of these questions. The image of Conqueror prevails among authors who view the Empire with a sceptical eye. That Napoleon conquered is simply a matter of fact, but it is upon the question of plunder that the potency of the image rests. The contrasting image is that of Unifier, with its implication that Napoleon was building more than a spoils system. Initially the image of Unifier was closely tied to Napoleon's intentions, but as historians focus on the long term, increasingly the question turns less on individual will than on impact. In an age preoccupied by European integration, Napoleon emerges as a Unifier through his promotion of the modern state outside France, but his role as Conqueror refuses simply to wither away.

Three relatively recent studies have placed Napoleon within the perspective of the *longue durée* of inter-state relations, and while each grants him great significance, they all reinforce the least favourable images of the reputation.

In the preface to *The Rise of the Great Powers 1648–1815* (1983), Derek McKay and H.M. Scott note that diplomatic history 'has been rather out of fashion in recent years', and thereafter they provide a survey to address this lacuna. From the Seven Years War (1756–63) to the Revolution, France is a Power in decline. This can be seen in French inability to influence developments in eastern Europe, where erstwhile allies Poland and the Ottoman Empire are subject to the depredations of Austria, Russia and Prussia. Similarly, in the west, the French can do little to aid the Dutch Patriot movement as Prussian intervention restores William V in 1787. France is also in decline as a maritime rival to Britain. Expelled from mainland North America, and with their base in India largely destroyed by 1763, the French do gain revenge by abetting American independence, but France acquires little territorially and war with Britain exacerbates deepening financial crisis.[2]

The French Revolution then transforms the European states system. Particularly on the French side, ideological motivation plays a part in the origins of the wars in 1792–93, but from the onset the French also demonstrate expansionist inclinations not so very different from *ancien régime* diplomacy. Campo Formio, negotiated by Bonaparte in 1797, however, marks a watershed as the limited Revolutionary objective of acquiring 'natural frontiers' gives way to a much broader agenda. After Brumaire, Napoleon's policies partly follow lines dictated by the situation he inherits, but he exacerbates destabilizing factors. Bonaparte relies on military victory to resolve problems and has little respect for diplomatic conventions as major Powers find themselves humiliated and stripped of substantial possessions. Resultant resentment means that each victory inevitably leads to further conflict.[3]

Napoleon is not depicted as a monster, but neither is he portrayed as someone with whom others could deal. As a *parvenu*, he seeks to impose his dynastic pretensions through creation of satellite monarchies. The satellites do make a contribution to the Empire, through levies of men and money, but this provokes antagonism, making the Empire volatile. Even the enthroned siblings raise difficulties, especially due to the toll taken upon their subjects by the Continental System. By 1810 the Emperor is pondering a European-wide government, but the danger of fraying relations with Russia necessitates laying aside such schemes. In the end, the other Powers will not reconcile themselves to Napoleon, but he provokes this by increasingly ruthless conduct from roughly 1807 onwards. Even in 1813–14, his refusal to compromise shores up Allied unity.

The long-term result of the Revolutionary–Napoleonic wars is to confirm the emergence of new Powers, a process which can be traced back to 1648. France is no longer a dominant continental Power and her decline as a maritime Power has also greatly accelerated. Britain, Russia and Prussia consolidate major acquisitions in the Vienna Settlement, and Austria regains her Great Power status, although her apparent strength is superficial. The upshot is a rough balance among a pentarchy of Powers who will impose their will upon the rest of Europe until 1870–71.

Napoleon's role has been to help bring about this formulation, and his pursuit of total victory has taught the other Powers the necessity of settling disputes among themselves through negotiation, rather than automatic recourse to war.[4]

Paul Kennedy's *The Rise and Fall of the Great Powers* (1989) covers the period 1500–2000. Like McKay and Scott, the author places the Napoleonic wars in the contexts of volatile relations dating back to the mid-eighteenth century, and, more particularly, Franco-British rivalry entailing seven major wars between 1689 and 1815. The Napoleonic wars thus represent a culmination, but they do have particular features. More than diplomatic considerations, Kennedy stresses differences in the economic systems of Britain and France. Britain's ability to sustain prolonged conflict rests on naval supremacy, rapid economic growth stimulated by overseas commerce and industrial revolution, and increasing sophistication in public and private finance. Against this, the Napoleonic system is essentially one of plunder. The Continental Blockade is designed to attack Albion where she is most sensitive (in commerce and finance), but it is the forced requisitions, indemnities and conscription imposed upon continentals that keeps the Grand Army rolling.

The French system fails the test; it collapses due to the antagonism it produces among the conquered, overextension attributable to Napoleonic hubris, and British ability to subsidize enemies of the Empire. At the Vienna Congress a new equilibrium among the Powers is established, with a system of containment checking the rise of any future Napoleons. At sea, however, the very reverse is true; Britain enjoys 'a near-monopoly' of naval power complemented by her economic and financial superiority. Napoleon's historical role, thus, has been to advance Britain's position as mistress of the seas and master of world trade.[5]

Paul W. Schroeder's *The Transformation of European Politics 1763–1848* (1994) follows lines roughly akin to those of McKay and Scott, while providing a wealth of new detail, especially concerning developments in central and eastern Europe. For the author, the key to the Revolutionary–Napoleonic era is that certain states learn, by hard experience, that their policies must be guided by more than short-sighted pursuit of immediate interests. This entails willingness to compromise, and formulation of policy based on understanding the interests of other states. From this perspective, Schroeder is more critical of British policies than Kennedy, but the British do grasp the essential lesson in the end. Thus they contribute to creation of the post-Napoleonic Congress System that brings European inter-state relations a period of relative stability.

Napoleon's role is that of bad example, and in Schroeder's account we find the Black Legend resurrected with a vengeance. In his perpetual deceit Bonaparte is a charlatan; in his incessant warmongering he is part habitual gambler, part *condottiere* and part Mafia godfather. Repeatedly he eschews opportunities to contribute to the formulation of some sort of states system that might yield durable peace, and with each treaty he is already preparing for future war. While he is an opportunist, he is not an able statesman because he knows no means other than coercion, so that he is completely inept when, late in the Empire, he needs to compromise. Although he liked to emulate Alexander, Caesar and Charlemagne, the only convincing analogy is to Hitler.

The Empire is colonial in nature, designed to subjugate the rest of Europe to French interests. Some good effects may have come of the Napoleonic rationalizing impulse, but these were largely vitiated by the first principle of the Empire – plunder for future warmongering. Far from leading to some sort of federal or integrated Europe, Napoleon's colonial system had no 'underlying purpose at all'. He conquered for the sake of conquering, addicted to victory long after it was necessary to stabilize his rule. There was no end or defined purpose to his policies and no durable peace or stable states system could have resulted as long as he reigned.[6]

The wars of the Napoleonic period have been studied in three recently published works. Each provides discussion of military strategy and tactics, and all three combine these concerns with analysis of inter-state relations, domestic politics, change in the nature of the state, and economic developments. Thus they represent a trend towards 'total history' also apparent in diplomatic history. Here again, it is the darker side of the reputation that tends to advance, although not quite as boldly or baldly as in Schroeder's account.

In *The Wars of Napoleon* (1995), Charles Esdaille draws conclusions which at times are similar to those of Kennedy and Schroeder. The period 'put an end to the ambitions entertained by successive French rulers since the days of Louis XIV', and confirmed Britain's triumph in her rivalry with France. Napoleon bore much responsibility for decline in that he personally was the

main cause of incessant warfare. Battle was not a product of
clashing British and French imperialism; Britain acted in defence
of her security, placed in peril by Bonaparte's attempt to expel her
influence from the continent. British expansion overseas was a
consequence of Napoleonic aggression, and the British repeatedly offered colonial concessions in pursuit of a European settlement. Napoleon, however, would never accept.[7]

While the image of Warmonger is consistent in Esdaille's
portrait, that of Conqueror is somewhat qualified. Esdaille grants
that the ethos of the Empire was reformist, designed to transform
'European society root and branch'. Bonaparte inherited the idea
of a French civilizing mission, and he was 'genuinely possessed by
the notion of French excellence'. Hence a pronounced drive for
uniformity. The key lay in application of the Napoleonic Code,
implicit in which was Revolutionary assault upon the old order,
but reform could also be seen in the revamping of political,
administrative and fiscal structures, and the imposition of
religious toleration.[8]

What is crucial for the author, however, is that reform was a
means towards enhancing the efficiency of the state, and thus 'its
ability to serve Napoleon'. Moreover, 'reform was always a
weapon of exploitation whose employment was necessitated by
the demands of his perpetual wars'. It thereby served the purposes of a brutal spoils system based on conscription, taxation,
requisition, outright plunder, and a Continental System designed
to make the rest of Europe an agricultural colony for France.
Had the Empire lasted, the result would have been a subjugated
Europe, not an integrated one for the benefit of all.[9]

In analysing the impact of the Empire, Esdaille emphasizes that
much of the reform programme failed. Despite his tutelage, many
of Napoleon's imposed rulers proved reluctant. They needed to
cultivate local elites, and were alarmed by the danger of provoking popular resistance based on attachment to old traditions
(especially popular religion) and dislike of the demanding
modern state. Nor is the author much impressed by the
emulation that Napoleon allegedly inspired among other rulers.
Little by way of basic social or political transformation occurred
as continental regimes limited reform to the purposes of enhancing dynastic prestige and military power. In essence, reforms
constituted 'the last, and frequently not very impressive, gasp of
enlightened absolutism' and they were put to largely reactionary
purposes.[10]

Two authors writing in Arnold's Modern Wars series have reached similar conclusions, but diverge from Esdaille in several notable regards. In *The French Revolutionary Wars 1787–1802* (1996), T.C.W. Blanning emphasizes the role of inter-state relations in shaping the course of the Revolution. Foreign policy failures contributed to the de-legitimization of the *ancien régime* in France, but with their frequent resort to popular violence Revolutionary governments failed to secure sufficient consensus to establish their own legitimacy. This produced endemic instability and only the army possessed sufficient coercive power to re-establish order. Meanwhile, the eruption of total war in 1792 led to the organization of state and society for the purpose of waging war.

What emerges from Blanning's perspective is the extent to which the structures of Napoleonic rule were already in place long before Brumaire. Despite its rhetoric of carrying liberty abroad, the Revolution had already turned to conquest by the summer of 1793, and by the First Italian campaign the Directory had become dependent upon war to resolve its financial problems. Also established was the instrument of the satellite state: 'a device for maximizing international control with a minimum of metropolitan effort'. Ideology provided satellites with 'the fine raiment of principle', but the bottom line was French material interest. Such a system, however, had basic weaknesses; plunder, chauvinism and especially anticlericalism soon unleashed massive resistance. When the other Powers finally set aside their own rivalries and learned to tap into popular resistance, the basic flaws would be exposed. Like Schroeder, Blanning sees Napoleon's principal role as that of scourge – an individual who, because he has no basic policy other than waging war, forces the other Powers to learn hard lessons.[11]

In *The Napoleonic Wars 1803–1815* (1997), David Gates puts forward an argument similar to Schroeder's thesis, but more specific in chronology. It is after the victories of 1805–7 that Napoleon habitually resorts to war in pursuit of 'a total victory over the whole of Europe'. Gates does not necessarily imply that this constituted having no policy at all, but he does argue that Napoleon's 'political and military strategies' had diverged, perhaps due to declining acumen as exhaustion set in. By 1814 he had become such an obstacle to peace that Europe could not leave his power unbroken.

Yet the image of Conqueror is less prominent in this work. For one thing, Napoleon has company. All the Powers, especially the British, play their part in causing wars and leave Napoleon few options. France is not the only state bent on empire, and the British are not shy when it comes to imposing their interests upon neutrals. The British are determined to open South America to their trade by undermining Spanish and Portuguese control, and Napoleon's Egyptian expedition provides them with what is mostly an excuse for extending penetration of India. Like Kennedy, Gates notes Suvarov's reservations over bringing complete collapse to the French Empire, because it fosters British hegemony. Metternich held similar concerns over abetting Russian and Prussian aspirations in central and eastern Europe in 1813–14, but ultimately his proposals for compromise were meaningless because neither Russian nor Prussian monarchs would have accepted them.

While the Conqueror is certainly present, the Unifier also lurks in the emphasis the author places on Napoleon's penchant for modernization. Gates acknowledges the element of French primacy in Napoleonic policy, but argues that conquest was meant to bring fundamental change, not just despoliation. Napoleon 'was eager to transform Spain into a modern state which would be both politically and socially compatible with France and her other vassals. This would entail the kind of reforms already exported to Germany and Italy.' It was Napoleon who granted the first German constitution (in Westphalia), many French reforms were beneficial, particularly in the Rhineland, and it was in response to Napoleon that his rivals set about remodelling their own states. They did so, however, to entrench established hierarchy and, of course, preserve dynasty. With the sole exception of Spain, popular resistance never truly threatened the Empire, and virtually everywhere revolt had little to do with nationalism. Then again, the concept of the nation at arms gave monarchs and their elites legitimate cause for alarm.

In the latter conclusions Gates echoes Esdaille, but he also takes Esdaille to task for 'a lack of empathy' concerning Napoleonic reform. All empires have exploitation as their essence, 'through the classic methods of military conquest and political and economic subjugation'. From this perspective, the 'only remarkable thing about Napoleon's empire is that . . . it applied colonialism to the heart of the developed world'. Gates perhaps has Britain particularly in mind, although one could extend the point to Prussia, Austria and Russia. More germane to our concern, however, is the reflection that integration may have been an objective rather than simply a means, although it was undermined by failure to consolidate.[12]

When Napoleon the Conqueror is viewed in isolation, the result is to heighten the sinister side of the reputation. When he is viewed as one among many conquerors, perspective alters. This is especially the case when study takes a global perspective.

A central theme of Paul Fregosi's *Dreams of Empire: Napoleon and the First World War, 1792–1815* (1989) is Napoleon's desire to conquer overseas. Bonaparte's expedition to Egypt was meant to be a springboard to India; purchase of Louisiana was a step towards recreation of New France in North America; and the Emperor even hankered after Australia. Napoleon wished to emulate Alexander the Great rather than Charlemagne, and it was only British thwarting of his 'oriental complex' that confined him to Europe; even the road to Moscow led to India.

But while Napoleon dreams, it is the British who build lasting empire, acting on what is essentially the same impulse: colonial expansion was consistently 'one of Britain's major, if unacknowledged, war aims'. At various points, this was apparent in Europe. British actions at Toulon in 1793 were part of a long tradition of 'nibbling at Europe'. British intentions were less to aid French royalists than to establish a naval base to complement Gibraltar. Similar plans were made to exploit Paoli's antipathy towards French republicans, and the same motivation lay behind British refusal to turn Malta over to Russia.[13]

Fregosi insists that British imperialism was not simply a defensive response to struggle with France, and he provides extensive evidence to support his point. Picking off colonies in the West Indies and the Far East did serve to clamp down on piratical corsairs, but permanent possession was the ultimate objective. Assaults on Uruguay and Argentina in 1806–7, and plans of attack on Mexico and Venezuela, pointed to British desire to penetrate South America prior to Napoleon's intervention in Spain. Were the Turks wrong in suspecting British intentions in the expedition to Alexandria in 1807?

British conduct of foreign policy differed little from that of Napoleon. After Amiens, both sides, 'with equal bad faith . . . set about rebuilding their war machines'. In their machinations over India, 'Franco-British treachery was . . . mutual'. 'Fair play' was set aside when it came to neutrals such as Denmark and

America, and in the attempt to destroy the Turkish navy at the Dardanelles in 1807. At the heart of the imperial impulse lay plunder, whether at Buenos Aires or in Ireland, where the British army 'was a collection of drunken, incompetent and corrupt ruffians who bullied, abused, plundered and slaughtered the peasant population with utter impunity'. Thus Fregosi's work provides ample material for Gate's unwillingness to attribute sole culpability for the wars to Napoleon; there was more than one vampire hovering over the globe.[14]

In *Collision of Empires* (1992) A.D. Harvey views Revolutionary–Napoleonic conflict as the first of three world wars in which Britain participated from 1793 onwards. He stresses the absence of clear war aims in British foreign policy, which fostered suspicion among continentals of British opportunism, and added to resentment of the power Albion gained by virtue of her wealth. Such antagonism flared throughout the period, but it reached its peak after the bombardment of Copenhagen in 1807, in which 2000 civilian inhabitants died. Napoleon sought to exploit Anglophobia through the Continental Blockade and System, but he overplayed his hand in Portugal and Spain, releasing Britain from isolation. This led to his fall, while Britain acquired 'a position of world leadership'.[15]

The chief exception to general British muddling in Harvey's account is Wellington, whose organization of resources and imposition of discipline are contrasted with the conduct of French armies, and the 'more ambitious but theoretically unsound strategy of Napoleon'. In so much as he appears, Bonaparte emerges as an able propagandist, but yesterday's man. He does not understand the financial underpinnings of British power and, indeed, 'the bias of his mind was always towards the past'; what was modern in the Empire 'had been inherited from the Revolution'. Ultimately his combination of mercantilism and plunder was defeated by British warfare based on the sound 'principles of the market economy'.[16]

In contrast to Fregosi, Harvey concentrates upon the European theatre. This approach yields extensive material concerning the antagonism the British generated, say by Hood's conduct of the siege of Toulon (which alienated the Spanish under Godoy) or the bullying of neutral Denmark. Yet, while the author at times refers to British colonialism, this subject lies largely outside the principal concerns of the work, especially from 1800 onwards. Hence little is said concerning expansion of control in India and the West Indies, or penetration of South America. It is in the latter spheres, however, that British policy looks most Napoleonic and illiberal.

In sum, then, the Revolutionary–Napoleonic era did provoke major change in European inter-state relations, leading to the Congress system of semi-permanent consultation among the leading Powers. Through his pursuit of total victory, Napoleon had underlined for others the importance of diplomacy based on negotiation rather than automatic resort to war. Yet, in the long term, the period of 1789–1815 simply consummated a development which can be traced back to 1648 – the emergence of a rough balance among five Powers. Within these patterns there were states on the rise or in decline. France was the most obvious of the latter; she was no longer capable of dominating the continent. Prussia and Russia were obvious 'winners' at Vienna, generally at the expense of smaller former states. Austria had also made significant acquisitions, but her position was declining relative to the other victors. The greatest of emerging Powers was Britain, due to the combination of overseas acquisitions, naval supremacy, and an economy which had already entered into industrial revolution.

Napoleon's role had not, however, been simply to frighten other leaders into acting in concert; he had also exhausted France in his incessant search for victory and failure to consolidate territorial gains. The extent to which opportunities for peace actually existed remains a matter for debate, and certainly he was not unique among rulers in his aggression. On the other hand, he was very quick to seek solutions through warfare, and it is difficult to see much by way of Napoleonic long-term policy other than personal ambition stoked by territorial aggrandizement.

Thus the image of Conqueror emerges very strongly indeed, especially among authors who see the Empire as little more than a spoils system. Whether this marked a turning away from the Revolution depends on whether one grants the Revolution an ideological basis, or whether one sees the 'war of peoples upon kings' as merely a piece of rhetoric. To ponder whether the Empire consisted of anything more than plunder, however, we need to turn to studies specifically on it. Much of the battle between the images of Conqueror versus Unifier lies therein.

In the preface to *Napoleon's Satellite Kingdoms* (1965), Owen Connelly drew attention to the absence of a synthesis on 'the puppet states'. He then sought to fill the gap between general histories of the Grand Empire and specialized regional studies with a work on the five satellite monarchies created by Napoleon between May 1805 and June 1808. Although the present chapter is generally confined to works published after 1980, *Satellite Kingdoms* was relatively unique until recently, and hence it provides a logical starting point.[17]

Connelly's book includes extensive accounts of the rulers and principal officials of the monarchies, but it is particularly in the author's examination of the nature and scope of change brought by the new regimes that our interest lies. Taken as a whole, the reforming impulse was impressive – whether in creation of new political, administrative or judicial structures, financial reorganization, introduction of French law, public works projects, educational initiatives or military reform. Inevitably the pace of change varied according to the character of the ruler, indigenous opposition, and the extent to which French practices differed from traditional ones, but everywhere the same impulse could be seen.

Napoleon liked uniformity and, more importantly, was the main vector of social revolution, harassing his satellite monarchs when they hesitated, and pushing aside their reservations when he felt inclined to do so. For this reason, Polish nobles were extremely reluctant to support creation of a satellite Kingdom of Poland; they 'feared the advent of a "revolutionary" Napoleonic government'. Moreover, by 1810 Napoleon was planning to create a unified European government through direct annexation of satellites to France. Such was the fate of Holland and part of Westphalia, and full integration would have resulted had the Empire not collapsed. Napoleon's defeat then 'destroyed all semblance of European unity and left a power balance which Russia (or the Soviet Union) has played to her advantage ever since'.[18]

Napoleon was 'more than a conqueror'. He had a plan for an integrated Europe with centralized control, and it was because he thought in terms of the Empire as a whole that he so often clashed with his satellite rulers. Whereas many historians have expressed sympathy for Louis's attempt to spare Holland the rigours of the Continental System, Connelly takes the opposite position: 'if one . . . regards the whole empire as Napoleon did, that is, as a structure which would bring peace, efficient government, and progress to all of Europe – in the long run – then the empire becomes worthy of great sacrifice'. Conversely, Jerome gains praise: 'From the domestic viewpoint the reign had produced fiscal disaster. From the imperial viewpoint Westphalia had served outstandingly. Jerome met every requirement established by Napoleon – to the very end.'[19]

Implicit in Connelly's interpretation is the argument that the drive for 'total victory' was a necessary step towards creating a new unified Europe. Towards this end Napoleon was able to attract a diverse range of men of 'practical bent and modern outlook', willing to set aside national loyalties and work for this larger vision. They 'saw themselves as functionaries of a European government, at home anywhere in Europe. They were Europeans the like of whom would not be seen for a century', as nationalism arose to muffle 'the voices of most who saw Europe whole'.[20]

The Empire was not based on plunder – France gave more in men and money than it took from its satellites. The satellites 'contributed largely by supporting French troops within their borders, [and] much of the money they supplied was spent locally . . . to the benefit of native merchants and producers'. Moreover, because of the cost of the war in Spain, 'the French taxpayer's burden was increased by the holding of the satellite kingdoms'. Even Napoleon's more brutal actions resulted from a guiding objective: he 'wanted Spanish rebellion ruthlessly crushed so that Spain, under an efficient, progressive government, could better serve both her people and the empire'. If commoners rebelled, this was because they were motivated by an 'anachronistic nationalism' based on traditionalism and failure to comprehend progressive change.[21]

Of more recent studies, Stuart Woolf's *Napoleon's Integration of Europe* (1991) is in some ways closest in spirit to Connelly's book, but it differs in crucial regards. Whereas Connelly's study was written amidst the Cold War, Woolf's work reflects the 1990s preoccupations of European union, although this does not necessarily imply a 'pro-European' standpoint. Further differences naturally result from Woolf's analysis of national or regional studies written between 1965 and 1990. Moreover, in Woolf's approach one can see the impress of structuralism: 'history does not just consist of great men, nor are the years of Napoleonic domination explicable in terms of his battlefields'.

Woolf's principal concern is to understand 'the attempt by the political class that had emerged from the Revolution to extend their ideals of progress and civilization to every region of Europe touched by French armies'. Partly as a consequence of the Enlightenment, the French elite had developed a view of itself as a harbinger of progress, and believed that its values could be applied everywhere to the benefit of all. Progress was linear, with all peoples advancing along the same path, but at different rates. While chauvinism was deeply engrained in it, such a vision was also informed by a certain cosmopolitan idealism. It did not see the elimination of 'inferior races' as a part of progress, though it did intend to transform foreign peoples and direct them to a better material life.[22]

The Revolution gave opportunity to the French to apply their 'civilizing mission', but it also brought a shedding of certain ideals. By Brumaire, liberty based on representative government and self-determination had long since given way; what remained was belief in the state as the vector of progress. The rationalized French model of government and administration would be applied, yielding civil order and stability after at least a decade of upheaval. Although they would not be the sole beneficiaries, European elites would respond to the benefits of the model and collaborate in implementing it.

Particularly revealing is Woolf's identification of stages of imperialism wherein certain experienced professionals began the process shortly after conquest, preparing the ground for subsequent fuller assimilation by a combination of French and non-French administrators. Dividing the process into stages enhances the impression of system. So too does consideration of the bureaucratic penchant for gathering statistics so as to plan better the development of most walks of life through efficient taxation, extensive public works, expanded education, rudimentary public welfare, and, of course, endless regulation. The same impression arises from analysis of the training of a new European administrative elite. Thus, there was a plan within the Empire, and its implementation was gathering pace even as the political-military situation fell apart in 1812–14.

Yet, Woolf's portrait of the Empire also underlines elements of disorganization and what emerges is not one clearly organized system, but a variety of initiatives which were often uncoordinated and at times contradictory. Crucial here is that such inconsistencies can be traced back to the Emperor himself.

Napoleon was an advocate of uniformity and he was often aggressive when his agents would have preferred a more gradual approach. However, Napoleon was also the main source of contradictions that undermined application of the reform model. Although professionalism was apparent throughout the various wings of government, it was weakened by equally prominent elite patronage. Recreation of nobility, especially the carving out of fiefdoms from princely domains, often imposed crippling financial restrictions on satellite states. Warmongering placed excessive burdens on local elites and commoners alike, undermining collaboration and occasionally placing civil administrators in opposition to demanding military officers. Imposition of the Continental Blockade and System took an enormous toll, not due just to disruption of commerce by exclusion of British trade, but also because of preference given to French interests.

Thus, while the Empire did contain an integrating vision, Napoleon shared only partly in it, and he was directly tied to policies that undermined successful application of the new model. The model did have benefits, especially concerning improved efficiency, and hence parts of it would be adopted by Restoration governments. But it would then become a tool for reinforcing international divisions. Also divisive was that the Empire had not promoted social integration. The spreading of salons and learned societies may have provided certain elements with a cosmopolitan culture, but this tended to reinforce divisions between elites and the general populace. Moreover, proponents of the model often ran roughshod over local traditions, customs and liberties. Especially in their attitudes to 'irrational' popular religion, reformers stirred up a hornet's nest of resistance which undermined attempts to provide stability.

Geoffrey Ellis's interpretation of the Empire differs greatly from those of Connelly and Woolf. In *The Napoleonic Empire* (1991) Ellis, like Woolf, draws attention to historical trends away from 'studies in the cult of personality, or from the deeds of war and conquest, to the longer-term underlying structures and mentalities of the Napoleonic Empire'. Yet, Napoleon emerges as integral to the ethos of an Empire which reflected his nature as warlord.[23]

Ellis's analysis of the Empire parallels the manner in which Napoleon built it – starting with his restructuring of the Revolution in France, and then extending outwards to the lands he conquered or bullied into submission. The Revolution had bequeathed Bonaparte certain assets which he reformulated during the Consulate, but he also inherited a losing position overseas, necessitating that his policies be 'Europocentric'. Varying circumstance and the limits of time meant that reforms initiated in France could only be applied piecemeal abroad. Moreover, the Empire was not the product of a master plan; Napoleon's 'grand design' evolved according to 'pragmatic opportunism'. Aggrandizement was, however, consistently fuelled by personal ambition 'inflated by the military dynamic of successive conquests'.

Napoleon's policy for Europe consisted of creating 'military vassals', and the Empire was to be the 'servile provider of the Grand Army'. Towards consolidating his dynasty, he sought to create a new, loyal elite. For this purpose, Napoleon developed a new system of honours and titles, and he gave the titles a material base, using lands confiscated outside France for this purpose. Despoliation was not new, but Napoleon redirected it. The lion's share of awards went to military men, but the spoils system was also designed to foster attachment among local notables through provision of state appointment, land gifts and pensions. Thus there was a direct tie between recreation of social hierarchy in France and Imperial treatment of annexed lands and subject states.

The Empire's social policies cut against the alleged modernizing tendency of Imperial reform. Dynastic placements, fiscal levies and land gifts were inconsistent with export of Napoleon's egalitarian legal codes, and while feudalism was abolished in principle, it survived in practice. In a survey of local studies, Ellis finds two consistent themes: 'continuity within the evolving social and professional elites of the annexed territories, and the often conservative results of French policy there'. There was an exception: implementation of more professional bureaucratic structures; yet, even this constituted rationalization rather than modernization. At base, Napoleon was closest to the warrior kings of the past, and his Empire reflected this.[24]

Ellis's interpretation, thus, differs radically from Connelly's older view. Napoleon's 'good government' was severely compromised by his dynastic policies, so that the reform element was significantly diminished. How Ellis's work relates to that of Woolf is more complex, but the essential lines can be gleaned from Ellis's *Napoleon* (1996). In the latter, Ellis agrees that

Bonaparte's ambitions were essentially European, especially as he was land-locked by British naval supremacy, but questions whether he had any plan for an Empire wherein the constituent parts would be truly integrated. To gain support he would provide civil order, and to bind the elite he would offer rewards for service. But, quoting Woolf's conclusion, Ellis emphasizes a central point: 'the pressure for the integration of elites that was an intrinsic part of the Napoleonic philosophy of administration widened the social gap between the propertied and property-less'. In social terms, the Empire did not bring modernization and it fostered division.

There are, however, certain areas of broad agreement in the political sphere. Citing Woolf's 'case for viewing Napoleon's civil state as in some sense an administrative "model" of forward-looking centralism and uniformity which could be exported to all lands brought under his rule', Ellis modifies his previous image of the warlord: 'Napoleon was both behind and ahead of his time, the last of the enlightened despots, and a prophet of the modern state'. Yet, Ellis is much less inclined to draw a distinction between Napoleon and Woolf's 'political class' in evaluating the real meaning of the Empire. Moreover, Ellis is also very sceptical over the integration argument when it comes to economic policy. The Continental System was ruthlessly exploitive and it was a direct product of Napoleon's will: the 'notion of a wider European common market, or *Zollverein*, offended all his basic instincts'. If Napoleon had offered 'the subject and allied states genuine reciprocity of trade in the huge Imperial market, in other words if he had given them a real incentive to cut their ties with Britain, who knows how differently it [the Empire] might have ended?'[25]

After reading Michael Broers's *Europe under Napoleon 1799–1815* (1996), one might be inclined to ask whether the fall of the Empire really mattered to subsequent European history. Once again the 'Great Man' approach is eschewed, in favour of viewing 'the era through the eyes of those on the ground'. The latter objective is met through extensive discussion of both those who sought to establish the Empire and those who resisted it. All the same, while Frankenstein's monster (the modern state) is the chief subject, the Doctor (Napoleon) haunts each page.[26]

The image of insatiable Conqueror is strikingly absent from Broers's account. Napoleon is not blinded by ambition and at points he wishes peace in order to consolidate acquisitions. Rapid expansion partly results from reaction to the aggression of others. Formation of the Third Coalition provokes the Austrian campaign of 1805; Prussia is largely responsible for the war of 1806; Alexander is spoiling for a fight in 1812; and both the intervention in Iberia and campaign of 1812 spring from the objective of forcing Britain into peace through application of the Continental Blockade. Victory is essential because without it resistance within the Empire becomes threatening. After his fall, the Vienna Settlement basically reformulates the Napoleonic states system with its creation of relatively large buffer states; the only difference is that the latter are now designed to hem in France rather than Austria and Russia. Where Napoleon most differed from his continental rivals was that he was better when it came to reforms that strengthened the state.

Napoleon was not a 'crazed warlord'; he was the proponent of a system born of the Enlightenment, and he intended to extend it to all of Europe. The system consisted of raising the power and authority of the state above all rivals. Moreover, the state would be ultra-interventionist, bent on reformulating society along what it deemed more rational lines. To secure support it would enhance material prosperity while assuring security through provision of order. It would also seek to acculturate through formal education and the spreading of French Enlightenment values. In short, the essence of the Empire lay in creation of the modern state; while this could not save the Empire, it was the way of the European future.[27]

Like Woolf, Broers rejects the argument that the Empire was socially conservative. On the contrary, the attack on noble and Church privilege accelerated in the final stages of the Empire. Particularly original is Broers's discussion of an inner and outer Empire. Geography plays a part in distinguishing the two, in that most of the outer Empire was distant from the inner heartland. But if one scratches below the surface, what emerges is that the inner Empire consisted of regions where the modern state was relatively accepted. In the outer Empire, attempts to implement the modern state produced loathing. While much of France itself lay within the inner Empire, not all of it did.

Broers places great emphasis on the extent to which the modern state was detested. Dislike of French chauvinism played a part in this, but more fundamental was reaction against an elitist culture which was fundamentally alien to the belief systems of the masses. While some of the actions of the Imperial regime (termination of seigneurialism, emancipation of the Jews, or abolition of the Spanish Inquisition) may have been laudable, application of Enlightenment values caused vast discontent. Antipathy could stem from dynastic loyalties or, especially, reaction against state attempts to subordinate and 'rationalize' religion, but at base it consisted of dislike of massive intervention overturning local tradition and custom. One is left with the impression of a small island of support for modernization amidst a sea of counter-revolution. Broers makes very clear that resistance to, and liberation from, the Empire had little to do with nationalism; it derived from revolt against imposition of the nation-state.

The author's ability to explain the 'mindset' of the Empire of professionals and bureaucrats is striking, but this is not born of sympathy for their project, and in this regard Broers's tone differs from that of Woolf. While the latter takes pains to underline the negative aspects of cultural chauvinism, Broers raises basic questions about the very nature of the system, regardless of its French origins. Both authors view the model as a forerunner of the nation-state and, more recently, emerging European government. But Broers appears much more reserved over the merits of the modern state generally, especially its destruction of pluralism and particularism or regional identity. As a vector of Enlightenment values, the state is fundamentally oppressive. Such a perspective is not unique in Napoleonic literature, but authors prepared to shed the 'liberal, broadly progressive sensibilities' of the 'Enlightenment project' have been relatively rare in modern times.[28]

Among many of the works previously discussed, especially those of Esdaille, Gates, Woolf and Broers, there are frequent warnings against overestimating nationalism in the Napoleonic period. While Blanning questions the extent of current revisionism, it would appear that a sea change has taken place as authors react against mythologies propagated especially in nineteenth-century historiography. At Saint Helena, Napoleon portrayed himself as a proponent of national self-determination: 'There are in Europe more than 30 million French, 15 million Spanish, 15 million Italians, and 30 million Germans. I would have wished to make each of these peoples a single united body.' Historians naturally questioned this piece of propaganda, but in the main they did see nationalism as a growing force during the era.[29]

In his *The Napoleonic Revolution* (1967), Robert Holtman summarized what was largely the academic consensus in a chapter entitled 'The catalyst of nationalism'. To a very limited extent Napoleon had intentionally fostered nationalism in Italy and Poland to combat *ancien régime* loyalties. Because he had fought against old dynasties, he later came to be viewed 'as the defender of nationalities against reactionary kings' by many liberals. More important, however, were Napoleon's unintentional contributions. By reduction in the number of states, and particularly through destruction of the Holy Roman Empire, Napoleon 'unwittingly promoted a feeling of nationalism' among those who had been thrown together into larger political entities. Most important of all, however, was that Napoleonic conquering produced a common bond among the subjugated, creating 'the same feelings of national unity as in France'.

Holtman also expressed a good deal of qualifying caution. He noted that 'national motivation in the Spaniards' fight against Napoleon' should not be exaggerated. Dynastic loyalty, religious sentiments and defence of local material interests were also present. Revolt led by Andreas Hofer in the Tyrol illustrated 'class and group differences' rather than nationalism, and while the Austrian government encouraged this rebellion, the regime itself was 'dynastic and feudal'. Reforms in Prussia did constitute the prerequisites to 'modernization in Prussia', but their intention was 'to benefit the treasury, the king and the nobility'. They had 'none of the egalitarian spirit' of French Revolutionary reforms.[30]

Viewed from the perspective of Holtman's writing, recent works tilt the balance of interpretation in favour of caution. Mass nationalism, even in the wars of liberation, was very little in evidence. Resistance to the Empire sprang from sentiments which had little to do with notions of national sovereignty or 'a feeling of community among the governed'. Even in the upper echelons of society, nationalism was confined to a small number of intellectuals largely excluded from power. Baron Stein, for whom Prussian reform was based on notions of national sovereignty, was exceptional and he would be easily cast aside by the time of the Vienna Settlement.

On the other hand, Napoleon did provide materials which could be used to build nationalism after 1815. Partly this was a matter of image construction, and the images were diverse because nationalism itself was far from uniform. As noted, liberals could present Bonaparte as defender of the peoples of Europe. Conversely, the Black Legend could be cast as the stimulus to national awakening. In a competing variant to these constructions, emphasis could be placed on the role of dynasties or elites in rallying subjects to defence of shared customs, traditions and heritage from the Jacobin on Horseback.[31]

Parallel, but not entirely identical, to the development of nationalism was that of the modern state. Obviously the two were convergent, yet one suspects that analysis of the relation between the two poses a 'chicken or egg' question. Did nationalism prepare the ground for the emergence of the modern state by providing willingness to accept new burdens as part of citizenship? Or did the modern state create nationalism as a means to tapping into greater resources? Regardless of origins, it is obvious that the relationship was symbiotic and that the two became progressively intertwined.[32]

What was Napoleon's role in this? Even taking Ellis's salutary reminders of the archaic Conqueror element into account, the arguments of Woolf and Broers concerning Napoleon's extension of the modern state beyond French borders are very strong. Relatively little systematic consideration has been given to measuring Napoleon's European impact from the perspective of subsequent periods, but a valuable departure can be found in *Napoleon's Legacy* (1999), a volume of essays edited by David Laven and Lucy Riall. In their introduction, the editors identify the principal themes that emerge from the essays, and, on the whole, Napoleon's most significant legacy lies in his introduction of the modern state. This is not to say that other European states had not previously attempted reform, but such efforts had largely withered in the face of reaction, whereas Napoleon's regime was clearly more effective in implementing lasting change.[33]

Reaction to the Napoleonic model varied dramatically according to where one looks. It was associated with the ideals of the Revolution, and hence viewed with suspicion by Restoration rulers. Moreover, rulers were under social constraints, having previously allied with the nobility and clergy in combating French influence. Added to this was the outcome of previous warring – many regimes were deeply in debt and the Napoleonic state was expensive to run.

Yet, there was something intrinsically attractive in the model – enhancement of state power. If restored regimes eschewed adopting the model and its personnel wholesale, almost all of them retained certain elements. In the Duchy of Parma, most of the Kingdom of Italy's administrative apparatus was maintained, and the most effective of Napoleonic institutions were kept in the Papal States. In the Duchy of Modena, Grand Duchy of Tuscany and in Piedmont, sustained efforts were made to return to the *ancien régime*, but the Two Sicilies witnessed a 'posthumous conquest of Napoleon' wherein his model was newly applied. Outside Italy, similar variety was the norm. Czar Alexander left Napoleon's political institutions, legal system and army 'largely intact' in Poland. Ferdinand of Spain retained aspects of Napoleonic rule in fiscal matters and organization of the army. Most rulers, whether in Piedmont or Prussia, found the *gendarmerie* useful, and while much of Restoration Europe did witness an aligning of 'Crown and altar', below the surface in Spain, Italy and Prussia one can detect the state steadily growing as the senior partner.

Restoration rulers, however, overlooked an important part of the Napoleonic model: the appearance of public consent. Napoleon adorned his regime with at least the rhetoric and imagery of popular sovereignty, and retained institutions which, although they held little power, did give the impression of consultation. In failing to apply this part of the formula, restored regimes undermined their credibility through association with 'the absolutist past', even as adoption of the Napoleonic model enhanced their ability to provide efficient 'police states'. This was to prove their Achilles' heel, giving opportunity to elements disgruntled by the Restoration settlement. All of this augurs well for enhanced appreciation of Napoleon's European legacy. Yet, in its emphasis upon growing state authority, it tends to understate a complementary element which can also be traced through the Enlightenment, Revolution and Napoleonic model. The latter lay in expectations. The Napoleonic state elevated itself not just in terms of ability to control, but also in terms of what it could supply. From this perspective, one can see why it antagonized particularist sensibilities – not simply because it usurped authority, but because it proposed to do more. Despite, from our perspective, the relatively limited resources at its disposal, there were few seeming limits to what the Napoleonic state thought it could do. Napoleon can be viewed as an embodiment of central government conquering society through elimination of rivals, but we should not underestimate the carrot that accompanied the stick. The revolution in expectations which the Napoleonic state propagated was one of Napoleon's most promising, and threatening, legacies.

By way of summary, then, what can be said of the impact on Napoleon's reputation of recent studies of his relation to Europe? Given the current state of play in diplomatic history and studies of the Empire, it appears likely that the 'debate without end' will continue. When one views history from the perspective of the other leading European states, Napoleon does indeed appear a Conqueror. He was bent upon establishing his empire, and while he did wish for periods of consolidation through peace, one looks in vain for any evidence that there were limits beyond which he would not expand. British naval and maritime mastery forced a focusing on Europe, but this did not necessarily indicate any permanent limit upon ambition. On the other hand, the rapid growth of the Empire was partly in response to the aggression of other states. If from 1812 Britain and the continental Powers learned that they must make some compromises among themselves, they were forced to this recognition by harsh necessity, and one also looks in vain for any inclination to limit their own expansion permanently. From the standpoint of the less powerful of European states and non-European peoples, Napoleon was indeed a Conqueror, but he was hardly unique, even if he was better at it on the continent.

It is very hard to see in Napoleon nothing but the Conqueror. There was a system at the heart of the Empire which went well beyond despoliation. Did this make Napoleon a Unifier, at least in intention? The doubts expressed by Ellis cannot be pushed aside here; 'France first' was a part of Napoleon's empire and it was tied to his plans of dynastic consolidation within France. He inherited conquering from the Revolution, but he also redirected it in what can be considered an anachronistic fashion. Yet, it is best to see in the Empire two contradictory impulses, both of which harken back to the Emperor himself. Alongside 'France first' came application of the Napoleonic model, which its advocates, including Napoleon, thought would better the lives of the majority in the long run. There certainly was chauvinism in this, but this was hardly unique in imperialism generally, and it was fundamentally different from the Nazi New Order.

Thus evidence concerning the Unifier image points in contrary directions, and the same point can be made regarding impact.

Export of the Napoleonic model did foster the emergence of the modern state in much of Europe, although it was applied to a varying extent and towards ends that were often socially divisive. The model extended the power of central government, and challenged previously limited notions of what the state should do, through means which were roughly similar wherever it was applied. Individual states could use such means for purposes that divided Europe, partly through the dissemination of nationalist mythologies. But differences in the lives of Europeans would be reduced by Napoleonic impact, just as nationalists were setting about emphasizing the importance of those differences.

Once again the protean character of Napoleon's reputation reveals itself. At a time when at least some Europeans are interested in locating a common historical heritage, the Empire can be made to serve this purpose, and the Unifier image is enhanced. Yet it is unlikely that the Conqueror image will ever yield the spotlight entirely. 'France first' played its part in the Empire, and France was not a 'first among equals'. The leading Napoleonic legacy, the modern state, is in itself a divisive phenomenon, whether applied at a national or European level. It may bring uniformity and even unity through shared perception of common interest, but it also entails a conquering of individual and group liberties, in the name of control and fulfilment of expectation.

Notes

1 See P. Geyl, *Napoleon: For and Against* (London, 1986) in its entirety, and G. Ellis, *Napoleon* (London, 1997), pp. 189–230; also useful is the section entitled 'The responsibility for the war of 1803', in F. Kafker and J. Laux, eds, *Napoleon and his Times: Selected Interpretations* (Malabar, Fla., 1989), pp. 91–120. Readers who wish to survey the field more broadly can start with J.A. Meyer, *An Annotated Bibliography of the Napoleonic Era: Recent Publications, 1945–1975* (Westport, Conn., 1987), and C.J. Esdaille, 'The Napoleonic period: some thoughts on recent historiography', *European History Quarterly*, 23: 3 (July 1993), pp. 415–32.

2 The following summary is taken from D. McKay and H.M. Scott, *The Rise of the Great Powers 1648–1815* (London, 1983), pp. 201–344; the quote is on p. xi.

3 Whether ideology played much part in motivation has been questioned by T.C.W. Blanning in *The Origins of the French Revolutionary Wars* (London, 1986).

4 McKay and Scott, *The Rise of the Great Powers*, pp. 303–44.
5 P. Kennedy, *The Rise and Fall of the Great Powers* (London, 1989), pp. 149–80.
6 See P. Schroeder, *The Transformation of European Politics 1763–1848* (Oxford, 1994), pp. 177–559; the quote is to be found on p. 393.
7 C.J. Esdaille, *The Wars of Napoleon* (London, 1995), especially pp. 1–36; the quotes are on pp. 33, 286.
8 Esdaille, *The Wars*, pp. 74–5, 84, 91.
9 Esdaille, *The Wars*, pp. 76–7, 97–8.
10 Esdaille, *The Wars*, pp. 91, 216.
11 See Blanning, *The French Revolutionary Wars*; the quotes are on pp. 169–70.
12 D. Gates, *The Napoleonic Wars 1803–1815* (London, 1997); the quotes are to be found on pp. 2, 69, 105, 160 and 268–9.
13 P. Fregosi, *Dreams of Empire: Napoleon and the First World War, 1792–1815* (London, 1989), pp. 57, 355.
14 Fregosi, *Dreams*, pp. 132, 202, 229–30.
15 A.D. Harvey, *Collision of Empire: Britain in three World Wars, 1793–1945* (London, 1992), p. 200.
16 Harvey, *Collision*, pp. 105 and 162.
17 O. Connelly, *Napoleon's Satellite Kingdoms* (New York, 1965), pp. ix–x.
18 Connelly, *Napoleon's Satellite Kingdoms*, pp. 265–6, 333–9.
19 Connelly, *Napoleon's Satellite Kingdoms*, pp. 144–5, 209.
20 Connelly, *Napoleon's Satellite Kingdoms*, p. 338.
21 Connelly, *Napoleon's Satellite Kingdoms*, pp. 336–46.
22 S. Woolf, *Napoleon's Integration of Europe* (London, 1991), pp. vii–ix. See also S. Woolf, 'French civilization and ethnicity in the Napoleonic Empire', *Past and Present*, 124 (1989), pp. 96–120, and 'The construction of a European world-view in the Revolutionary–Napoleonic Years', *Past and Present*, 137 (1992), pp. 72–101.
23 G. Ellis, *The Napoleonic Empire* (Atlantic Highlands, N.J., 1991), pp. 1–7.
24 Ellis, *Napoleonic Empire*, pp. 49, 54,, 70, 85, 107–13.
25 Ellis, *Napoleon*, pp. 3–7, 51–2, 112; see also G. Ellis, *Napoleon's Continental Blockade: The Case of Alsace* (New York, 1981), especially pp. 1–25 and 104–48.
26 See M. Broers, *Europe under Napoleon 1799–1815* (London, 1996), p. xii.
27 Broers, *Europe under Napoleon*, p. 5.
28 Broers, *Europe under Napoleon*, p. 5.
29 For a recent discussion of literature on nationalism generally, see E. Hobsbawm, *Nations and Nationalism since 1780* (Cambridge, 1990), pp. 1–13. Blanning's reservations are expressed in *The French Revolutionary Wars*, pp. 246–7. The quote of Napoleon comes from R. Holtman, *The Napoleonic Revolution* (Baton Rouge, La., 1978), p. 151.
30 Holtman, *Napoleonic Revolution*, pp. 179–93.

31 See C. Clark, 'The wars of liberation in Prussian memory: reflections on the memorialization of war in early nineteenth-century Germany', *Journal of Modern History*, 68 (September 1996), pp. 550–76.
32 See Hobsbawm, *Nations*, especially pp. 80–100.
33 The following passages are drawn from D. Laven and L. Riall, eds, *Napoleon's Legacy* (London, 2000), especially pp. 1–26.

Conclusion

In the preceding chapters we have discussed many of the central Napoleonic images and associations individually, but what can be said of them as an ensemble, and of the process of reputation construction generally?

One of the striking features of the 'debate without end' is how passionate it has been. Napoleon himself set the tone, but the extravagance of his assertion of greatness was not so very unique, given precedents set by the likes of Louis XIV. There was, however, a notable departure in his propaganda: the combination of claims both to a historical chain of great men and to representation of the contemporary people. In this formula lay the essence of charismatic leadership. It was all the more potent in that Napoleon was not born a king, aristocrat or patrician. One could see many things in David's painting of the Imperial coronation, but it was hard to miss the point that at the heart of all the splendour lay one man's accomplishments. The origins of that man could, in turn, be seen whenever he donned his familiar attire – the cocked hat, grey frock-coat and black boots. Here was a model for future 'Men on Horseback', but for the old elite, Napoleon was a 'Jacobin on Horseback'.

Representation of Napoleon would also be propagated by Imperial style in architecture and decor. During the Napoleonic period, middle-class elements began to participate in the acquisition of decorative art objects, spreading images of the Empire and its founder. Add to this subsequent popular consumption of Napoleonic memorabilia, especially cheap wood-block prints, and one begins to see why opponents of the cult and Legend were so preoccupied by Napoleon. They were surrounded by his image and desperate to dispel what they considered false representation.

On the continent, the Black Legend shared the propensity of the cult and Legend to portray Napoleon as something more than human. This could be seen among 'great' writers, both for and against, whether in the works of Hugo or Vigny. There was, however, nothing new in depicting Bonaparte as demon or demi-god; the same penchant was apparent in Gros's *Bonaparte Visiting the Victims of the Plague at Jaffa* or Goya's *Colossus* during the Napoleonic era. It could also be seen in the pamphlet literature surrounding news of Napoleon's death in 1821. The images and interpretations of elite writers were, in fact, common.

The most significant Romantic contribution to the cult lay in emphasis upon the 'Great Man' part of Napoleonic propaganda. The Romantic hero was a 'loner' detached from society. In the writing of Balzac this led to the proposition that 'Great Men' could not be confined within the bounds of common convention and law; *raison d'état* was thus transferred to the individual. The most direct riposte came from Dostoevsky, who attacked the proposition not on its own secular terms, but by insisting that God could not be removed from the laws governing behaviour. Nietzsche restored Balzac's secular approach to the 'Great Man' theme, seeing in Napoleon an example of individual will imposing itself upon the common herd. Nietzsche's superman is the heir of the 'Great Man', but he is the antidote to, not the representative of, the power of the masses. At this point the dual element of Napoleon's propaganda has been broken.

Matters evolved differently in the 'Anglo-Saxon' world. The belittlement theme in British literature has persisted to the present day, apparent in contemporary cinema. Given that it is often expressed through caricature, it tends as much to exaggeration as the 'Great Man' theme. But in the hands of Scott and Thackeray, the belittlement theme was a forerunner of twentieth-century inclination to remove Napoleon's unworldly associations and plant his feet firmly on the ground. The belittlement theme was, however, by no means predominant in British and American representation of Napoleon. Tennyson's thunderings in 1852 found their equivalent in twentieth-century film and literature when Hitler evoked memories of an earlier threat across the Channel. Depiction of Napoleon as tyrannical, warmongering dictator was often designed to rekindle a 'special relationship' across the Atlantic, but in America it confronted one of the strongest elements of Napoleon's reputation.

The essence of Popular Bonapartism lay in representation of Napoleon as being 'of the people', rather than detached from them. The Napoleon of the people did possess supernatural characteristics, but his main virtue lay in close proximity to the commoner. Popular Bonapartism was, of course, most apparent in France, where Napoleon could readily be portrayed as a protector and patriot, rather than threat and conqueror. But it did spread abroad, even taking revenge on Hudson Lowe in British theatre. It was in America, however, that Popular Bonapartism most rapidly took on its modern character.

Bonapartism evoked little sense of direct threat in America, and in fact Napoleon's reputation could be readily adapted to emerging American identity. In a land of immigrants, thrusting ambition could be seen as a virtue. Napoleon became an icon of what one could accomplish and acquire through hard work and gumption. Hence, he was the darling of self-help manuals and educational primers. The message was 'think big', but the key was that being Napoleonic was not confined to a narrow, established elite. It takes confidence and assertion to set Napoleon as a model for emulation, and neither of these two characteristics has been lacking in American culture.

The Great War and subsequent rise of totalitarian dictatorships damaged the image of Napoleon as protector and representative of the interests of the common man. But core elements of the American version of Popular Bonapartism remain. Napoleon can still be taken as an exemplar of what ambition might hope to accomplish, and, especially, acquire. Herein lies the explanation for the continuing use by advertising media of Napoleon as an icon for consumer culture. But it is also true that Napoleon remains associated with exceptional talent, whether it be put to good or bad use. Conan Doyle's Moriarty and Holmes are linked through association with Napoleonic genius. From this perspective, Napoleon represents the opposite of mediocrity, and while the Romantic view of detached hero returns, such genius can be attributed to the common man. Napoleon is not an obvious model for elite culture's stumbling 'anti-hero', but he serves very well in popular culture's love of the hero and villain.

Complicating matters for anyone who studies Napoleon is that he sought to associate himself with so many important developments. Such claims must be assessed, and assessment has often been influenced by how an author or artist feels about the associated development. De Staël believed passionately in her version of the liberal Revolution, which she desperately wanted to detach from Bonapartism. Michelet's onslaught reflected his desire to separate Napoleon from his own hero – the people of France. Maurras hoped to disassociate Napoleon from patriotism. Conversely, attachment to an ideal or value can force at least limited accommodation of Napoleon's legacy. Even Tocqueville planned in his projected history of the Empire to acknowledge Napoleon's ability to inspire patriotism, although the great liberal doubtless would have found much that was undesirable in Napoleonic rule. The bitterness of Hugo's diatribes against Louis-Napoleon had more than a little to do with the painful necessity of Hugo detaching his republican ideals from the glory Napoleon had brought France. Outside France, Napoleon gained many admirers because he was associated with battle against *ancien régime* privilege, even if he had spread French rule.

Similarly, Napoleon evokes strong response because of associations which he did not promote, but others did. Charges of tyranny and warmongering issued naturally enough among his contemporaries, but it was only later that he became viewed as the prototype of the 'Man on Horseback' and 'modern dictator'. Figures such as Santa Anna consciously promoted analogy. Even when facing possible execution for treason, Santa Anna cited the fate of Napoleon (exile) as a precedent for how to deal with men of his kind. In the build-up to the Nuremberg Trials, Churchill also thought of the solution to the 'Napoleon problem' of 1815 as a possible precedent for dealing with war criminals. The reputation has been much affected by guilt by association.

Because 'Men on Horseback' and brutal dictatorships remain threatening, Napoleon continues to come in for rough handling by contemporary writers such as Seward, Schom, Schroeder and Esdaille. One still encounters invective which, if it is one step removed from that of de Staël, is still remarkably personal in tone. Perhaps this reflects the joy of iconoclasm, or the righteous indignation inspired by false idols. But one wonders whether there is not an element of fear involved, not of a man long dead, but of the fascination Napoleon still exercises. The sentiment of 'never again' underlines such writing, and surely this springs from the popularity Napoleon enjoyed in his own lifetime and thereafter. His ability to inspire perhaps makes Napoleon a continuing danger.

Napoleon's ability to provoke strong reaction thus still fuels the reputation. This is all the more remarkable in that several trends in twentieth-century thought seemed potentially threatening to the contention that Napoleon was uniquely significant. Classification of him as a psychological or sociological type does reduce perception of his originality, although he remains an arresting specimen. On the other hand, viewing him as recognizably human removes some of the more anachronistic aspects of the 'Great Man' school. Some readers probably do identify with gods and demons, but one suspects that Napoleon as an example of the 'insecurity complex' holds greater appeal to contemporary readers. Seemingly insatiable public appetite for news of Napoleon's day-to-day life first became apparent during the exile at Saint Helena. Napoleon was initially surprised; after all, he was no longer performing great deeds. But he duly set about exploiting public fascination, and a steady stream of intimate details has issued ever since. In this regard, he was the first media 'star'. But, as with contemporary variants of the phenomenon, much of public interest lies in discovering that the high and mighty have very common features and foibles.

More threatening to the reputation is the perspective of the *longue durée*, wherein individuals and events are generally viewed as just the froth above the deeper waters of long-term structural developments, material and intellectual. In Tolstoy one encounters a direct attack upon the significance of Napoleon's will, with the implication that no will counts for much in the march of time. Among academic writers the tendency has been to emphasize the limits which long-term forces placed upon Napoleonic agency, but not necessarily to eliminate him entirely as a historical factor. Various arguments have been made that Napoleon was the representative or agent of certain broad forces: the Revolutionary bourgeoisie, enlightened despotism or gender tyranny. In the latter case, we shall have to wait to see how future writing develops, but neither of the first two has held up well over time. When the academic lens focuses, allegedly homogeneous forces tend to fragment; within the bourgeoisie, Enlightenment and public opinion there was a variety of options from which Napoleon could pick and choose. Thus Napoleon's will re-enters the fray. The cumulative impact of approaches emphasizing the *longue durée* has been to clarify where Napoleonic agency actually lay, but this reduction of the number of claims strengthens those that remain. Moreover, emphasis on the force of circumstance can make those who manage to alter it, even slightly, appear all the more extraordinary.

Bonaparte was by no means solely responsible for forging the Napoleonic model of state and society, but he played the part of catalyst in driving others to completion. The individual components of the model were not necessarily new, but the combination of them was, and Napoleon certainly played a decisive role in spreading the model abroad. Perhaps most importantly, for better and worse, the Napoleonic model worked. Its essence lay in increased state intervention, both in creation of the 'security state' and in fulfilment of a modicum of the expectations of provision of public welfare raised by the Revolution. Along with the *gendarme* came the technocrat. State building has, however, long been one of the stronger Napoleonic associations. Stendhal was particularly insistent upon it, and Balzac termed Napoleon the king of the bureaucrats. Moreover, it was the image of state builder that led to portrayal of Mehemet Ali and Kemal Atatürk as Napoleonic figures.

In the current debates over whether application of the Napoleonic model was a forerunner of European integration, one can again sense tempers rising. Partly this results from depth of feeling over integration itself, but there is something rather traditional about dispute whenever it comes to defining Napoleon's legacy. In certain regards, Napoleon can be viewed as a European unifier, partly by intention and partly by unintended impact. There was a certain plan at the heart of the Empire and some of it would be continued long after Napoleon's departure from Europe. It did bear the Enlightenment hallmark of rationalizing, and a fair measure of what we now call 'social engineering'. Authors can admire and despise both these components. But the Empire consisted of more than simple application of the 'model', and while uniformity was one of its components, so too was 'France first'. Would full integration have resulted from victory in the 1812 campaign? Would all Europeans have been treated equally? Or would further conquering have continued to impede implementation of the model while the Emperor sought more spoils for his distinctly militarist elite? We shall never know; one cannot assess an opportunist without knowing what opportunities would have presented themselves. In this case, it seems best to recognize that there was no single 'true' legacy; he was both

Conqueror and Unifier. Here again we find a chameleon of many colours.

Because the reputation contains such diversity, circumstance plays a major role in shaping it. Yet, while the potency of certain images fluctuates, that of others remains relatively constant. As a general rule, the strength of images associated with particular historical developments varies in accord with contemporary pre-occupations. On the other hand, images associated with basic human characteristics or capacities are less subject to variation. We can demonstrate this through consideration of two strong images – those of the Conqueror and the Great Commander.

One might have expected the Conqueror image to have been especially evocative in the immediate aftermath of the Empire, but it was weakened by the antagonism generated by Napoleon's enemies. Amidst Restoration reaction, association of Napoleon with the Revolutionary ideals of liberty and equality soon gained credibility. Napoleon and his followers then added association with national self-determination, and even this seemingly improbable claim held appeal. The Conqueror did not disappear, but he found himself surrounded by a host of contradicting rivals. The advent of Louis-Napoleon and renewed Empire then altered the picture, initially abroad, and subsequently in France. Outside France the Conqueror conjures images of plunder and exploitation; inside France it is linked to massive and futile sacrifice made to one man's ambition. Hence, although the Conqueror reappeared in the late 1860s, it was only after Sedan that he triumphed in France. This time republicans, unlike in 1815–48, strongly emphasized the image. Even so, by the 1890s the Conqueror was again under serious challenge due to Napoleon's association with patriotism. France recalled her 'Saviour'.

World War One and the rise of aggressive dictatorships reinvigorated the Conqueror, and he has remained prominent ever since, although the development of European integration fosters an old rival, the Unifier. The image of Napoleon as visionary of a united Europe sprang from the Napoleonic period itself, and was promoted as a vague form of federalism by Napoleon at Saint Helena and thereafter by Louis-Napoleon. But Nietzsche, in the late nineteenth century, and Driault, in the early twentieth, were swimming upstream in evoking this image in an age of nationalism. It is highly unlikely that the Conqueror will ever disappear, but if he is stripped of the plundering association by emphasis upon a plan for an integrated Europe, he will lose one of his best weapons. A virtue of the 'debate without end' is that such a prospect is highly improbable.

While the Conqueror, thus, has had his ups and downs, the Great Commander has carried on in relatively steady fashion. The Great Commander is not entirely impervious to change and historical revision. In the USA, his lustre diminished when the Civil War brought indigenous rivals to the fore, and his association with *élan* and offensive warfare lost some of its appeal in France after the Great War. Some historians have emphasized the extent to which he 'blundered', although this remains very much a minority position when the entire career is taken into consideration. The Napoleonic record, including its breathtaking expanse, speaks for itself. But the stability of the Great Commander image has more to do with its close proximity to one of the fundamental Napoleonic associations – talent. The weakest allegation of the Black Legend was that Napoleon was untalented, and it was soon dropped. One can contest individual elements of Napoleon's association with talent, but taken as a whole, the place of talent in the reputation has never been seriously challenged.

The Conqueror is also linked to a basic Napoleonic association, but the relation is less immediate. Like the Ogre, the reckless gambler, the *condottiere* and the outsider, the Conqueror connotes selfish ambition. Yet, Napoleon as callous megalomaniac has continuously been challenged by the images of the Little Corporal, the Visionary and the modern Prometheus. If we leave aside whether Napoleon was motivated by egoism or altruism, we come to a more fundamental element of the reputation: his will to alter circumstance. The Conqueror is closely related to Napoleonic will, but the tie is loosened by the claims of the rival images. One can debate over the Conqueror and Visionary, but they are both derivatives of the primary association of Napoleon with will power, about which there are few grounds for dispute.

Will and talent are the bedrock of the reputation, and the closer an image is to either of them, the more durable and stable it is. For most of us, unlike Nietzsche, will and talent are essentially amoral in their connotations; they can be put to either good or bad ends. But they both hold innate interest, especially when they reach extraordinary proportions. When an individual comes to be seen as the embodiment of will and talent, he or she gains enormous fascination. In Napoleon's case, power undoubtedly plays a major part in sustained interest, but the key lies less in that he possessed power, or even in what he did with it, than in how he gained it. From birth, we all pursue power in various forms, and there is something appealing in the notion that will and talent can yield it, despite the obstacles posed by circumstance.

Napoleon's image as the self-made man taps into a universal preoccupation and the Romantics were not wrong in emphasizing the Napoleonic capacity to inspire. Better yet, the reputation remains sufficiently diverse that Napoleonic association with will and talent need not necessarily connote evil ends, although it certainly can. While Napoleon's chameleon-like qualities hinder attempts at definitive interpretation, they also provide ample opportunity for others to see in him what they want to see. In this sense, Napoleon's reputation remains beyond good and evil, and he can be portrayed either as a great hero or great villain. That his claims to greatness continue to provoke such strong responses assures that the reputation remains vibrant, and for Napoleon this is the greatest of all achievements.

Select chronology of the principal events and works discussed

Given the nature of this work, I have thought it best to extend chronology beyond the Napoleonic period, and to include the release of films and publication of major works up to 1945. For a more detailed chronology of the Napoleonic period, see P. Geyl, *Napoleon: For and Against* (London, 1986), and for a 'panoramic' listing of works on Napoleon, see J. Tulard, *Le Mythe de Napoléon* (Paris, 1971).

1769   A 'saviour' is born at Ajaccio on 15 August.

1779   Napoleone Buonaparte enters military school at Brienne.

1787   Ali Pasha becomes governor of Ioannina.

1789   The French Revolution begins. Napoleone returns to Corsica on leave from the army.

1792   France enters into war against the First Coalition in April. The Convention declares France a republic in September.

1793   Louis XVI is executed in January. The Buonaparte family flees Corsica in June. Napoleon enters the public stage with the recapture of Toulon and gains promotion to brigadier-general in December.

1794 The fall of Robespierre marks the end of the Terror and beginning of Thermidor, and Napoleon is temporarily incarcerated in August.

1795 Napoleon introduces the 'whiff of grapeshot' as a means of crowd control in Paris in October.

1796 Napoleon is appointed commander of the Army of Italy and marries Josephine in March. The First Italian campaign begins in April and includes the battle of Arcola (15–17 November).

1797 The Treaty of Campo Formio is signed with Austria in October and Napoleon returns to Paris to rub shoulders with the intelligentsia in the Institute. A statue of Napoleon is exhibited at the New York city waxworks.

1798 The Egyptian campaign and Second Coalition begin in May. Napoleon exploits the battle of the Pyramids (21 July) for propaganda purposes, but Nelson destroys the French fleet at Aboukir Bay (1 August).

1799 Napoleon returns to Paris in October and takes part in the *coup d'état* of Brumaire (18–19 November), which leads to the founding of the Consulate. Napoleon is named First Consul in December.

1800 A plebiscite 'approves' the new regime in January and the fundamental law revamps local government and administration. A Consular order, also in January, reduces the number of Parisian newspapers to thirteen. De Staël publishes *De la littérature* in April. The Second Italian campaign begins in May; it includes the battle of Marengo (14 June). A royalist assassination attempt misses Napoleon in December and enables him to have leading Jacobins deported. Paul I forms the 'League of Armed Neutrality' against Britain.

1801 The Treaty of Lunéville is signed with Austria in February. Nelson wins the battle of Copenhagen (1

April), helping to sink the 'League of Armed Neutrality'. An expedition is despatched to regain control of St Domingue late in the year after Toussaint Louverture had been named governor-general for life.

1802   Toussaint is captured and imprisoned in France. The Treaty of Amiens is signed with Britain in March; the Concordat is officially published in April; the Legion of Honour is founded in May; and Napoleon is proclaimed Consul for life in August. David finishes *Napoleon Crossing the Saint Bernard Pass*; Denon publishes *Voyages dans la Basse et la Haute Egypte* and De Staël publishes *Delphine*.

1803   Peace with Britain ends in May.

1804   The Duke of Enghien is executed and the Civil Code is proclaimed in March. Napoleon is proclaimed hereditary Emperor in May and the coronation is held at Notre Dame in December. Dessalines is crowned Emperor of Haiti in October. Gros paints *Bonaparte Visiting the Victims of the Plague at Jaffa*.

1805   Napoleon is crowned King of Italy in May. The Third Coalition is formed in August and subsequent battles include Ulm (20 October), Trafalgar (21 October) and Austerlitz (2 December). The Treaty of Pressburg is signed with Austria in December.

1806   Creation of the Confederation of the Rhine in July is followed shortly thereafter by formation of the Fourth Coalition. Prussia is badly mauled in the battles of Jena and Auerstadt (both on 14 October). The Berlin Decrees announce the Continental Blockade in November. Ingres paints *Napoleon Enthroned*. Mehemet Ali is recognized as the Pasha of Egypt by the Ottoman Porte.

1807   The battles of Eylau (7 February) and Friedland (14 June) lead to the Treaties of Tilsit with Russia and Prussia in July. The British navy bombards Copenhagen. French occupation of Lisbon commences the Peninsular War in November. Gros paints *Napoleon at Eylau*.

1808   Civil war commences in Spain with the crowning of Joseph as King in July. Napoleon takes personal command of the army in Spain in November.

1809   Napoleon departs Spain after the battle of Corunna (16 January) and the Fifth Coalition is formed in April. Battles include Aspern-Essling (21–22 May) and Wagram (5–6 July). Pius VII excommunicates Napoleon in June and is put in captivity in July. The Treaty of Schönbrunn is signed with Austria in October. The French Senate pronounces the divorce of Napoleon and Josephine in December.

1810   Napoleon marries Marie-Louise of Austria in April. De Staël's *On Germany* is banned from the Empire.

1811   The King of Rome is born in March. Henry Christophe becomes King Henry I and rules northern Haiti.

1812   The Sixth Coalition begins to form in March and the Russian campaign commences in June. After the battle of Borodino (7 September), Napoleon enters Moscow a week later. The retreat from Moscow begins in October and Napoleon returns to Paris on 19 December. David paints *Napoleon in his Study*.

1813   Prussia declares war on France on 16 March and the battles of Lützen (2 May), Bautzen (21 May) and Vitoria (19 June) ensue. Austria declares war on France on 12 August and the 'Battle of Nations' (16–19 October) at Leipzig follows. Wellington begins slow advance into south-west France in October.

1814   The campaign of France begins in January. Constant publishes *On the Spirit of Conquest and Usurpation* and Wordsworth writes 'Ode written during the negotiations with Buonaparte in 1814'. Marmont surrenders Paris on 31 March and Napoleon abdicates on 6 April. The First Restoration commences and Napoleon begins his exile at Elba in May. Chateaubriand publishes *De Bonaparte et des Bourbons*. The First Treaty of Paris is signed on 30 May and the Congress of Vienna assembles in September.

1815   Napoleon's 'Flight of the Eagle' touches down in Paris on 20 March and begins the Hundred Days. Constant collaborates in drawing up the Acte Additionnel and publishes *Principles of Politics* in May. The battle of Waterloo (18 June) is followed by Napoleon's second abdication on 22 June. The Second Restoration begins in June, the White Terror starts in July, and Napoleon departs for Saint Helena in August. The Second Treaty of Paris is signed on 20 November. Géricault finishes painting *Wounded Cuirassier*.

1817   Lamartine publishes 'Ode aux Français'.

1818   De Staël's *Considerations on the Principal Events of the French Revolution* is published posthumously. Débraux publishes 'Ode to the Column'.

1819   Géricault's lithograph *The Swiss Sentry at the Louvre* is produced.

1820   Constant publishes *Mémoires sur les Cent-Jours*.

1821   Napoleon dies on 5 May, leading to Manzoni's 'Il Cinque maggio', Lamartine's 'Bonaparte', and a surge of pamphlet literature. Talma mimics Napoleon in de Jouy's *Sylla*.

1822   O'Meara publishes *Napoleon in Exile*.

1823   Las Cases publishes the *Memorial de Sainte-Hélène*; Hugo publishes 'A mon Père' and Pushkin publishes 'Ode to Napoleon'.

1827   Scott publishes *The Life of Napoleon Buonaparte*. Hugo publishes 'A la Calonne' and 'Lui'.

1828   Béranger publishes *Memories of the People*.

1830   The July Revolution leads to foundation of the July Monarchy with Louis-Philippe as King. Pushkin publishes 'The Hero'; Hazlitt publishes *Life of Napoleon*, and the Pellerin printing firm begins its mass run of wood-block broadsheets depicting the Napoleon of the people.

1831   Stendhal publishes *The Red and the Black* and Pushkin publishes *Eugene Onegin.*

1832   The death of the Duke of Reichstadt (Napoleon's son) makes Louis-Napoleon the Bonapartist pretender. Louis-Napoleon publishes *Political Reflections.*

1833   Seurre's statue of the 'Little Corporal' is placed atop the Vendôme Column. Balzac publishes *The Country Doctor.*

1834   Balzac publishes *Père Goriot* and Pushkin publishes *Queen of Spades.*

1835   Vigny publishes *Servitude and Grandeur of Arms.*

1836   Musset publishes *Confession of a Child of the Century.* Louis-Napoleon attempts to seize power at Strasbourg.

1839   Louis-Napoleon publishes *Napoleonic Ideas* and Stendhal publishes *The Charterhouse of Parma.*

1840   Thiers entangles France in the Egyptian Crisis. Louis-Napoleon again attempts to seize power at Boulogne. Napoleon's remains are returned to Paris and over 200,000 visitors pay their respects at the Invalides on 19 December. General Espartero becomes Prime Minister and Regent for Isabella II of Spain. Lermontov publishes *A History of Our Time.*

1841   Carlyle publishes *On Heroes and Hero-worship* and Lermontov publishes 'The Last Resting Place'. General Santa Anna establishes the first of his quasi-dictatorships in Mexico.

1842   Pellerin production of Napoleonic broadsheets hits a peak with 875,000 prints.

1845   Thiers begins to publish his *History of the Consulate and Empire.*

1846   Headley publishes *Napoleon and his Marshals.*

1847 Rude's *The Awakening of Napoleon* is unveiled at Fixin.

1848 The February Revolution leads to creation of the Second Republic. Publication of Chateaubriand's *Memoirs* begins and Thackeray publishes *Vanity Fair*. Louis-Napoleon is elected President in December.

1849 Faustin Soulouque becomes Emperor Faustin I of Haiti.

1850 Emerson publishes *Representative Men*.

1851 Lamartine begins to publish his *History of the Restoration* and Abbot begins serial publication of *Napoleon Bonaparte* in *Harper's Magazine*. Louis-Napoleon seizes power in December.

1852 Tennyson sounds the alarm with 'The Penny-Wise'; Hugo publishes *The Chastisements*; and Marx publishes 'The Eighteenth Brumaire of Louis Bonaparte'. The Second Empire is established in December.

1853 The second period of quasi-dictatorship under Santa Anna begins in Mexico.

1854 An Imperial Commission is established to publish Napoleon's correspondence. Revolution in Spain brings Espartero back to power.

1855 Berlioz's *L'Impériale* is performed at the Paris Universal Exhibition.

1861 Visconti completes his tomb of the Emperor at the Invalides.

1863 The 'Little Corporal' is transferred from the Vendôme Column to Courbevoie and replaced by Dumont's Imperial Napoleon.

1865 Louis-Napoleon publishes *Histoire de Jules César* and Dostoevsky begins to publish *Crime and Punishment*.

1867 Lanfrey publishes the first volumes of his *History of Napoleon I*.

1869   Tolstoy publishes *War and Peace.*

1870   Defeat by Prussia at Sedan leads to the fall of the Second Empire and proclamation of the Third Republic in September.

1871   The revolt of the Paris Commune leads to destruction of the statue of Napoleon atop the Vendôme Column.

1875   Volumes dealing with Napoleon in Michelet's *Histoire du XIXe Siècle* begin to appear.

1876   Stendhal's *Napoleon* is published posthumously.

1878   Weeks publishes *Getting on in the World.*

1885   General Boulanger is named Minister of War.

1887   Nietzsche publishes *The Gay Science* and Tilley publishes *Masters of the Situation, or some Secrets of Success.*

1894   Conan Doyle publishes *The Final Problem.*

1896   McKinley poses as Napoleon during the American presidential campaign.

1897   Barrès publishes *Les Déracinés.*

1921   The *Revue des etudes napoléoniennes* helps to organize centennial commemorations of Napoleon's death.

1922   The 'March on Rome' brings Mussolini to power in Italy. Barrès publishes *Memoirs of a Napoleonic Officer.*

1923   Atatürk becomes President of Turkey.

1924   Guérard publishes *Reflections on the Napoleonic Legend.*

1925   Vallaux publishes an article in the *Mercure de France* comparing Napoleon to Kaiser Wilhelm II.

1927   Gance's *Napoléon* is released.

1931   Bainville publishes *Napoléon* and Deschamps publishes *Sur la légende de Napoléon.*

1932   Maurras publishes *Napoléon avec la France ou contre la France.*

1933   Hitler becomes German Chancellor. Gershoy publishes *The French Revolution and Napoleon.*

1935   Lefebvre publishes *Napoléon.*

1936   Freud discusses Napoleon's 'Joseph complex' in a letter to Thomas Mann.

1937   Bainville publishes Dictators. Leonard's *The Firefly* is released.

1938   Bruun publishes *Europe and the French Imperium.*

1939   Bainville publishes *L'Empereur*, Daudet publishes *Deux idoles Sanguinaires: La Révolution et son fils Bonaparte*, and Cobban publishes *Dictatorships.*

1941   Korda's *That Hamilton Woman* is released.

1942   Oman publishes *Napoleon at the Channel.*

1944   Geyl publishes *Napoleon: For and Against.*

1945   Jung discusses the 'mana-personality' in *The Relations between the Ego and the Unconscious.*

1955   Guitry's *Napoléon* is released.

1964   Bondarchuk's *War and Peace* is unleashed.

1970   De Laurentiis and Bondarchuk release *Waterloo.*

1982   Gilliam and Palin release *Time Bandits.*

1989   Herek releases *Bill and Ted's Excellent Adventure.*

Select bibliography

General works cited at various points in the text

Alexander, R.S., *Bonapartism and Revolutionary Tradition in France* (Cambridge, 1991).

Blanning, T.C.W., *The French Revolutionary Wars 1787–1802* (London, 1996).

Bluche, Frédéric, *Le Bonapartisme* (Paris, 1980).

Broers, Michael, *Europe under Napoleon 1799–1815* (London, 1996).

Day-Hickman, Barbara-Ann, *Napoleonic Art: Nationalism and the Spirit of Rebellion in France (1815–1848)* (Newark, N.J., 1999).

Deschamps, Jules, *Sur la légende de Napoléon* (Paris, 1931).

Doyle, William, *The Oxford History of the French Revolution* (Oxford, 1989).

Ellis, Geoffrey, *Napoleon* (London, 1997).

Esdaille, Charles J., *The Wars of Napoleon* (London, 1995).

Fisher, H.A.L., *Bonapartism* (Oxford, 1908).

Gates, David, *The Napoleonic Wars 1803–1815* (London, 1997).

Geyl, Pieter, *Napoleon: For and Against* (London, 1986).

Gildea, Robert, *The Past in French History* (New Haven, 1994).

Gonnard, Philippe, *The Exile of St Helena* (London, 1909).

Guérard, Albert, *Reflections on the Napoleonic Legend* (London, 1924).

Holtman, Robert, *Napoleonic Propaganda* (Baton Rouge, La., 1950).

Holtman, Robert, *The Napoleonic Revolution* (Baton Rouge, La., 1978).

Kafker, Frank, and James Laux, eds, *Napoleon and his Times: Selected Interpretations* (Malabar, Fla., 1989).

Las Cases, Comte Emmanuel de, *Memorial de Sainte-Hélène. Journal of the private life and conversations of the Emperor Napoleon at Saint Helena* (London, 1823).

Lucas-Dubreton, Jean, *Le Culte de Napoléon 1815–1848* (Paris, 1960).

Lyons, Martyn, *Napoleon Bonaparte and the Legacy of the French Revolution* (London, 1994).

McLynn, Frank, *Napoleon* (London, 1998).

Ménager, Bernard, *Les Napoléon du Peuple* (Paris, 1988).

Sutherland, D.M.G., *France 1789–1815* (London, 1985).

Thody, Philip, *French Caesarism* (Basingstoke, 1989).

Tombs, Robert, *France 1814–1914* (London, 1996).

Tulard, Jean, *L'Anti-Napoléon* (Paris, 1965).

Tulard, Jean, *Le Mythe de Napoléon* (Paris, 1971).

Tulard, Jean, *Napoleon: The Myth of the Saviour* (London, 1985).

Willner, Ann Ruth, *The Spellbinders: Charismatic Political Leadership* (New Haven, 1984).

Woloch, Isser, *The New Regime* (New York, 1994).

Woolf, Stuart, *Napoleon's Integration of Europe* (London, 1991).

Works specific to particular chapters

Chapter 1: The life and times

See the General Works cited above.

Chapter 2: Heir of the Revolution? Napoleon and the French Left prior to World War One

Alexander, R.S., 'Restoration republicanism reconsidered', *French History*, 8: 4 (1994), pp. 442–69.

Alexander, R.S., 'Napoleon Bonaparte and the French Revolution', in Pamela Pilbeam, ed., *Themes in Modern European History 1780–1830* (London, 1995), pp. 40–64.

Alexander, R.S., 'The hero as Houdini: Napoleon and nineteenth-century Bonapartism', *Modern and Contemporary France*, 8: 4 (2000), pp. 457–67.

Brousse, Paul, and Henri Turot, *Consulat et Empire (1799–1815)* (Paris, 1906).

Bullen, Roger, 'France and Europe, 1815–48: the problem of defeat and recovery', in R. Bullen and A. Sked, eds, *Europe's Balance of Power, 1815–48* (New York, 1979), pp. 122–44.

Bury, J.P.T., and R.P. Tombs, *Thiers* (London, 1986).

Cappadocia, Ezio, 'The Liberals and Madame de Staël in 1818', in R.H. Herr and H.T. Parker, eds, *Ideas in History: Essays Presented to Louis Gottschalk* (Durham, N.C., 1965), pp. 183–95.

Cole, Hubert, *Christophe, King of Haiti* (London, 1967)

Collingham, H.A.C., *The July Monarchy* (London, 1988).

Collins, Irene, *Napoleon and his Parliaments, 1800–1815* (London, 1979).

Constant, Benjamin, *Mémoires sur les Cent-Jours*, ed. O. Pozzo di Borgo (Paris, 1961).

Constant, Benjamin, *Benjamin Constant et Goyet de la Sarthe: Correspondance 1818–1822*, ed. Ephraim Harpaz (Geneva, 1973).

Constant, Benjamin, *Political Writings*, ed. Biancamaria Fontana (Cambridge, 1988).

Coulmann, J.-J., *Réminiscences* (Paris, 1862).

Furet, François, *Marx and the French Revolution* (Chicago, 1988).

Goldberg, Harvey, *The Life of Jean Jaurès* (Madison, 1962).

Gooch, Brison D., ed., *Napoleonic Ideas* (New York, 1967).

Hazareesingh, Sudhir, 'The Société Républicaine and the propagation of civic republicanism in provincial and rural France, 1870–1877', *Journal of Modern History*, 71 (June 1999), pp. 271–307.

Herold, Christopher J., *Mistress to an Age: The Life of Madame de Staël* (New York, 1958).

Howorth, Jolyon, 'French workers and German workers: the impossibility of internationalism, 1900–1914', *European History Quarterly*, 15 (1985), pp. 71–97.

Jaurès, Jean, *Histoire Socialiste de la Révolution française* (Paris, 1910).

Jaurès, Jean, *L'Armée nouvelle* (Paris, 1911).

Jaurès, Jean, *Democracy and Military Service*, ed. G.G. Coulton, (New York, 1972).

Jennings, Lawrence C., *France and Europe in 1848* (New York 1973).

Kamenka, Eugene, ed., *The Portable Karl Marx* (Harmondsworth, 1983).

Kernaghan, Stuart, 'The idealised revolutionary: contemporary French politics and the symbolic importance of Maximilien Robespierre' (M.A. thesis, University of Victoria, 1999), pp. 50–3.

Larkin, Maurice, *Church and State after the Dreyfus Affair: The Separation Issue in France* (London, 1974).

McMillan, James, *Napoleon III* (London, 1991).

Manuel, Frank, *The Prophets of Paris* (New York, 1962).

Mellon, Stanley, *The Political Uses of History* (Stanford, 1958).

Millar, Eileen, *Napoleon in Italian Literature, 1796–1821* (Rome, 1977).

Neely, Sylvia, *Lafayette and the Liberal Ideal, 1814–24* (Carbondale, 1991).

Pilbeam, Pamela, *Republicanism in Nineteenth-Century France, 1814–1871* (London, 1995).

Pinkney, David, *The French Revolution of 1830* (Princeton, N.J., 1972).

Proudhon, Pierre-Joseph, *Du Principe Fédératif* (Paris, 1863).

Proudhon, Pierre-Joseph, *General Idea of the Revolution* (London, 1923).

Rothney, John, *Bonapartism after Sedan* (Ithaca, N.Y., 1969).

Spitzer, Alan B., *Old Hatreds and Young Hopes* (Cambridge, Mass., 1971).

Staël, Baroness de, *Considerations on the Principal Events of the French Revolution* (London, 1821).

Staël, Baroness de, *Ten Years of Exile* (New York, 1972).

Thureau-Dangin, Paul, *Le Parti Libéral sous la Restauration* (Paris, 1876).

Tocqueville, Alexis de, *Selected Letters on Politics and Society,* ed. Roger Boesche (Berkeley, 1985).

Villefosse, Louis de, and Janine Bouissounouse, *The Scourge of the Eagle: Napoleon and the Liberal Opposition* (New York, 1972).

Wood, Dennis, *Benjamin Constant* (London, 1993).

Ziolkowski, Theodore, 'Napoleon's impact on Germany: a rapid survey', *Yale French Studies*, 26 (Fall–Winter 1960–61), pp. 94–105.

Chapter 3: Napoleon and the nineteenth-century Right: the Great Commander and the Man on Horseback

Bertaud, J.-P., 'Napoleon's officers', *Past and Present*, 112 (August 1986), pp. 91–111.

Bertaud, J.-P., *The Army of the French Revolution: From Citizen-soldiers to Instruments of Power* (Princeton, 1988).

Bethell, Leslie, ed., *The Cambridge History of Latin America* (Cambridge, 1985).

Brandt, Joseph, *Toward the New Spain* (Philadelphia, 1933).

Burke, Edmund, *Reflections on the Revolution in France*, ed. T. Mahony (New York, 1955).

Callcott, Wilfred Hardy, *Santa Anna* (Hamden, Conn., 1964).

Carlyle, Thomas, *On Heroes and Hero-worship* (Oxford, 1968).

Carr, Raymond, *Spain 1808–1975* (Oxford, 1982).

Chandler, David G., *The Campaigns of Napoleon* (New York, 1966).

Chateaubriand, René de, *The Memoirs of Chateaubriand*, ed. R. Baldick (Harmondsworth: Penguin edition, 1965).

Childs, Elizabeth, 'Secret agents of satire: Daumier, censorship, and the image of the exotic in political caricature, 1850–1860', *Proceedings of the Annual Meeting of the Western Society for French History*, 17 (1990), pp. 334–46.

Christiansen, E., *The Origins of Military Power in Spain* (Oxford, 1967).

Clausewitz, Karl von, *On War* (New York, 1943).

Cole, Hubert, *Christophe: King of Haiti* (London, 1967).

Connelly, Owen, *Blundering to Glory* (Wilmington, Del., 1987).

Costeloe, Michael, *The Central Republic in Mexico, 1835–1846* (Cambridge, 1993).

Cotner, Thomas Ewing, *The Military and Political Career of José Joaquin De Herrera, 1792–1854* (New York, 1949).

Duffy, Michael, *The Englishman and the Foreigner* (Cambridge, 1986).

Elting, John R., *Swords around a Throne: Napoleon's Grande Armée* (New York, 1988).

Fernández, Gilbert, 'The making of Spain's first *Caudillo*' (Ph.D. dissertation, Florida State University, 1974).

Finer, Samuel E., *The Man on Horseback* (Harmondsworth, 1975).

Frick, Carolyn E., 'Dilemmas of emancipation: from the Saint Domingue insurrections of 1791 to the emerging Haitian state', *History Workshop Journal*, 46 (1998), pp. 1–15.

Fuller, J.F.C., *A Military History of the Western World* (New York, 1955).

George, M. Dorothy, *English Political Caricatures* (Oxford, 1959).

Gibson, Robert, *Best of Enemies* (London, 1995).

Gruening, Ernest, *Mexico and its Heritage* (New York, 1928).

Hanighen, Frank C., *Santa Anna: The Napoleon of the West* (New York, 1934).

Haythornthwaite, Philip J., *et al.*, *Napoleon: The Final Verdict* (London, 1996).

Heinl, Robert and Nancy, *Written in Blood* (Boston, 1978).

Holt, Edgar, *The Carlist Wars in Spain* (London, 1967).

James, C.L.R., *The Black Jacobins* (London, 1980).

Jomini, Baron de, *The Art of War* (Philadelphia, 1862).

Kiernan, V.G., *The Revolution of 1854 in Spanish History* (Oxford, 1966).

Lote, Georges, 'La Contre-Légende Napoléonienne et la mort de Napoléon', *Revue des études napoléoniennes*, 30 (June 1931), pp. 324–49.

Lynn, John, 'Towards an army of honour: the moral evolution of the French Army, 1789–1815', *French Historical Studies*, 16 (Spring 1989), pp. 152–82.

Macaulay, Thomas Babington, *Napoleon and the Restoration of the Bourbons* (London, 1977).

MacCunn, F.J., *The Contemporary English View of Napoleon* (London, 1914).

MacLeod, Murdo J., 'The Souloque regime in Haiti, 1847–1859': a reevaluation', *Caribbean Studies*, 10 (1970), pp. 35–48.

Marichal, Carlos *Spain (1834–1844)* (London, 1977).

Marx, Karl, and Friedrich Engels, *Revolution in Spain* (New York, 1939).

Nicholls, David, *From Dessalines to Duvalier* (Cambridge, 1979).

Ortega Y Gasset, José, *Invertebrate Spain* (New York, 1974).

Payne, Stanley, *Politics and the Military in Modern Spain* (Stanford, Calif., 1967).

Pilbeam, Pamela, 'Revolutionary movements in western Europe', in P. Pilbeam, ed., *Themes in Modern European History 1780–1830* (London, 1995), pp. 125–50.

Porch, Douglas, *Army and Revolution: France 1815–48* (London, 1974).

Raat, W. Dirk, ed., *Mexico* (Lincoln, Nebr., 1982).

Robinson, Fayette, *Mexico and her Military Chieftains* (Glorietta, N.M., 1970).

Rodriguez O, J.E., ed., *The Independence of Mexico* (Irvine, Calif., 1989).

Ros, Martin, *Night of Fire: The Black Napoleon and the Battle for Haiti* (New York, 1994).

Rothenberg, Gunther, *The Art of Warfare in the Age of Napoleon* (Bloomington, Ind., 1978).

Tyson, George F., ed., *Toussaint L'Ouverture* (Englewood Cliffs, N.J., 1973).

Wilson, Robert T., *History of the British Expedition to Egypt* (London, 1803).

Chapter 4: Prototype for Hitler and Mussolini? Napoleon and fascism

Bainville, Jacques, *Napoléon* (Paris, 1931).

Bainville, Jacques, *Dictators* (London, 1937).

Bainville, Jacques, *L'Empereur* (Paris, 1939).

Barrès, Maurice, *Les Déracinés* (Paris, 1897).

Barrès, Maurice, ed., *Memoirs of a Napoleonic Officer, Jean-Baptiste Barrès* (London, 1925).

Blatt, Joel, 'Relatives and rivals: the responses of the Action Française to Italian fascism, 1919–26', *European Studies Review*, 11: 3 (July 1981), pp. 263–92.

Bullock, Alan, *Hitler: A Study in Tyranny* (London, 1952).

Bullock, Alan, *Hitler and Stalin: Parallel Lives* (New York, 1992).

Carr, William, *Hitler: A Study in Personality and Politics* (London, 1978).

Cobban, Alfred, *Dictatorship* (London, 1939).

Daudet, Léon, *Deux idoles sanglantes, la Révolution et son fils Bonaparte* (Paris, 1939).

Doty, C. Stewart, *From Cultural Rebellion to Counterrevolution: The Politics of Maurice Barrès* (Athens, Ohio, 1976).

Fest, Joachim, *Hitler* (New York, 1974).

Friedrich, Carl J., and Zbigniew K. Brzezinski, *Totalitarian Dictatorship and Democracy* (New York, 1956).

Fulton, Bruce, 'The Boulanger Affair revisited: the preservation of the Third Republic, 1889', *French Historical Studies*, 17: 2 (Fall 1991), pp. 310–29.

Gilbert, Martin, *The Roots of Appeasement* (New York, 1966).

Gopnik, Adam, 'The good soldier', *New Yorker*, 24 November 1997, pp. 106–14.

Gregor, A. James, *Italian Fascism and Developmental Dictatorship* (Princeton, N.J., 1979).

Hanna, Martha, 'Iconology and ideology: images of Joan of Arc in the idiom of the Action Française, 1908–24', *French Historical Studies*, 14: 2 (Fall 1985), pp. 215–39.

Hutton, Patrick, 'Popular Boulangism and the advent of mass politics in France, 1886–90', *Journal of Contemporary History*, 11 (1976), pp. 85–106.

Irvine, William, *The Boulanger Affair Reconsidered* (Oxford, 1989).

Irvine, William, 'Fascism in France and the strange case of the Croix de Feu', *Journal of Modern History*, 63 (June 1991), pp. 271–95.

Kershaw, Ian, *Hitler* (London, 1991).

Lee, Stephen J., *The European Dictatorships 1918–1945* (London, 1987).

Leith, James, 'The French Revolution: the origins of modern liberal culture?', *Journal of the Canadian Historical Association*, 2 (1991), pp. 177–93.

Mack Smith, Dennis, *Mussolini's Roman Empire* (London, 1976).

Mack Smith, Dennis, *Mussolini* (London, 1981).

Maurras, Charles, *Jeanne d'Arc, Louis XIV et Napoléon* (Paris, 1938).

Morgan, Philip, *Italian Fascism, 1919–1945* (London, 1995).

Mosse, George L., 'Fascism and the French Revolution', *Journal of Contemporary History*, 24: 1 (1989), pp. 5–25.

Oman, Carola, *Napoleon at the Channel* (Garden City, N.Y., 1942).

Passmore, Kevin, 'The Croix de Feu: Bonapartism, national populism or fascism?', *French History*, 9: 1 (March 1995), pp. 67–92.

Presseisen, Ernst, *Amiens and Munich: Comparisons in Appeasement* (The Hague, 1978).

Rémond, René, *Les Droites en France* (Paris, 1982).

Schom, Alan, *Napoleon Bonaparte* (New York, 1997).

Seager, Frederic, *The Boulanger Affair* (Ithaca, N.Y., 1969).

Seward, Desmond, *Napoleon and Hitler: A Comparative Biography* (London, 1988).

Sibalis, Michael, 'Prisoners by *Mesure de Haute Police* under Napoleon I: reviving the *lettres de cachet*', *Proceedings of the Annual Meeting of the Western Society for French History*, 18 (1991), pp. 261–9.

Soucy, Robert, 'French fascism and the Croix de Feu: a dissenting interpretation', *Journal of Contemporary History*, 26 (1991), pp. 159–88.

Sternhell, Zeev, 'National Socialism and antisemitism: the case of Maurice Barrès', *Journal of Contemporary History*, 8: 4 (1972), pp. 47–66.

Sternhell, Zeev, *Neither Right nor Left* (Berkeley, 1986).

Talmon, J.L., *The Origins of Totalitarian Democracy* (London, 1952).

Taylor, A.J.P., *From Napoleon to Stalin* (London, 1950).

Taylor, A.J.P., *The Trouble Makers* (Bloomington, Ind., 1958).

Wilson, Stephen, 'The "Action Française" in French intellectual life', in J. Cairns, ed., *Contemporary France: Illusion, Conflict and Regeneration* (New York, 1978), pp. 139–67.

Chapter 5: The Great Man: Napoleon in nineteenth-century literature and art

Balzac, Honoré de, *Old Goriot*, trans. Marion Crawford (London, 1951).

Barzun, Jacques, *Classic, Romantic and Modern* (London, 1961).

Bertier de Sauvigny, Guillaume de, *The Restoration* (Philadelphia, 1966).

Boime, Albert, *A Social History of Modern Art II: Art in an Age of Bonapartism 1800–1815* (Chicago, 1990).

Boorsch, Jean, 'Chateaubriand and Napoleon', *Yale French Studies*, 26 (Fall–Winter 1960–61), pp. 55–62.

Burton, June, *Napoleon and Clio: Historical Writing, Teaching and Thinking during the First Empire* (Durham, N.C., 1979).

Byrd, Melanie, 'Denon and the Institute of Egypt', *Consortium on Revolutionary Europe Proceedings* (1989), pp. 438–43.

Calleo, David, 'Coleridge on Napoleon', *Yale French Studies*, 26 (Fall–Winter 1960–61), pp. 83–93.

Charleton, D.G., ed., *The French Romantics*, I (Cambridge, 1984).

Charpentier, John, *Napoléon et les hommes de lettres de son temps* (Paris, 1935).

Comeau, Paul T., *Diehards and Innovators: The French Romantic Struggle: 1800–1830* (New York, 1988).

Connolly, John L., 'The origin of the star and the bee as Napoleonic emblems, and a reflection on the Oedipus of J.A.D. Ingres', *Consortium on Revolutionary Europe Proceedings* (1984), pp. 131–46.

Cornell, Kenneth, 'May 5, 1821 and the poets', *Yale French Studies*, 26 (Fall–Winter 1960–61), pp. 50–4.

Cranston, Maurice, *The Romantic Movement* (Oxford, 1994).

Cro, Stelio, 'Alessandro Manzoni and the French Revolution', *Consortium on Revolutionary Europe Proceedings* (1989), pp. 383–91.

Descotes, Maurice, *La Légende de Napoléon et les écrivains français du XIXe siècle* (Paris, 1967).

Dostoevsky, Feodor, *Crime and Punishment*, Norton critical edition (New York, 1975).

Doyle, Arthur Conan, *The Memoirs of Sherlock Holmes* (Harmondsworth, 1971).

Fortescue, William, *Alphonse de Lamartine* (London, 1983).

Friedlaender, Walter, *David to Delacroix* (Cambridge, Mass., 1952).

Gemie, Sharif, 'Balzac and the moral crisis of the July Monarchy', *European History Quarterly*, 19 (1989), pp. 469–94.

Gerato, Erasmo, 'Manzoni's "Il Cinque maggio" and Lamartine's "Bonaparte"', *Consortium on Revolutionary Europe Proceedings* (1989), pp. 863–8.

Gonzalez-Palacios, Alvar, *The French Empire Style* (London, 1970).

Hegel, Georg W.F., *Philosophy of History*, trans. John Sibree (New York, 1956).

Jackson, Robert, 'Napoleon in Russian literature', *Yale French Studies*, 26 (Fall–Winter 1960–61), pp. 106–18.

Le Bourhis, Katell, ed., *Costume in the Age of Napoleon* (New York, 1990).

Lermontov, Mihail, *A Hero of Our Time*, Anchor Books edition (New York, 1958).

Maras, Raymond, 'Napoleon and levies on the arts and sciences',

Consortium on Revolutionary Europe Proceedings (1987), pp. 433–46.

Marrinan, Michael, *Painting Politics for Louis-Philippe* (New Haven, 1988).

Miller, William, 'Napoleon and Cherubini: a discordant relationship', *Consortium on Revolutionary Europe Proceedings* (1989), pp. 260–9.

Musset, Alfred de, *Confession of a Child of the Century* (Paris, 1905).

Napoleon III, *Histoire de Jules César* (San Francisco, 1865).

Nietzsche, Friedrich, *The Complete Works of Friedrich Nietzsche*, ed. Oscar Levy (New York, 1964).

Nietzsche, Friedrich, *The Will to Power*, ed. Walter Kaufmann (New York, 1968).

Nietzsche, Friedrich, *Thus Spoke Zarathustra*, ed. R.J. Hollingdale (Harmondsworth, 1969).

Peace, R.A., 'The Napoleonic theme in Russian literature', in H.T. Mason and W. Doyle, eds, *The Impact of the French Revolution* (Gloucester, 1989), pp. 47–63.

Polowetzky, Michael, *A Bond Never Broken: The Relations between Napoleon and the Authors of France* (London, 1993).

Pushkin, Alexander, *The Captain's Daughter and Other Short Stories*, Vintage Russian Library edition (New York, 1936).

Pushkin, Alexander, *Eugene Onegin*, Dutton paperback edition (New York, 1963).

Quynn, D.M., 'The art confiscations of the Napoleonic wars', *American Historical Review*, 50: 1 (October, 1944), pp. 437–60.

Ridge, George Ross, *The Hero in French Romantic Literature* (Athens, Ga., 1959).

Scott, Walter, *The Life of Napoleon Buonaparte, Emperor of the French* (Paris, 1827).

Stendhal, *Red and Black*, ed. Robert M. Adams (New York, 1969).

Symons, Julian, *Mortal Consequences* (New York, 1977).

Thackeray, William Makepeace, *Vanity Fair: A Novel without a Hero*, ed. F.E.L. Priestley (Toronto, 1969), and the earlier version edited by Geoffrey and Kathleen Tillotson (Boston, 1963).

Tudesq, André-Jean, *L'élection présidentielle de Louis-Napoléon Bonaparte* (Paris, 1965).

Vigny, Alfred de, *The Military Condition*, a translation of *Servitude et grandeurs militaires* by Marguerite Barnett (London, 1964).

Wilson-Smith, Timothy, *Napoleon and his Artists* (London, 1996).

Chapter 6: The people's choice? Napoleon and popular culture

Athanassoglou-Kallmyer, Nina Marie, 'Sad Cincinnatus: "Le Soldat Laboreur" as an image of the Napoleonic veteran after the Empire', *Arts Magazine*, 60 (May 1986), pp. 65–77.

Balzac, Honoré de, *The Country Doctor* (London, Caxton edition, 1899).

Brininstool, Earl, *Dull Knife (a Cheyenne Napoleon)* (Hollywood, 1935).

Dieck, Herman, *The most complete and authentic history of the life and public services of General Grant, 'The Napoleon of America'* . . . (Cincinnati, 1885).

Driault, Edouard, 'Napoléon, le génie de l'ordre', *Revue des études napoléoniennes*, 30 (1930), pp. 8–25.

Driault, Edouard, 'Après un siècle de légende et d'histoire', *Revue des études napoléoniennes*, 31 (1930), pp. 87–100.

Emerson, Ralph Waldo, *Representative Men*, in *The Collected Works of Ralph Waldo Emerson*, IV, eds. Wallace E. Williams and Douglas Emory Wilson (Cambridge, Mass., 1987), pp. 129–48.

Forrest, A., *Conscripts and Deserters: The Army and French Society during the Revolution and Empire* (Oxford, 1989).

Grand-Carteret, John, 'La Légende Napoléonienne par l'image vue sous un jour nouveau', *Revue des études napoléoniennes* (January–February 1923), pp. 28–46.

Herz, Micheline, 'From the "Little Corporal" to "Mongénéral": a comparison of two myths', *Yale French Studies*, 26 (Fall–Winter 1960–1), pp. 37–44.

Horward, Donald, and Warren Rogers, 'The American press and the death of Napoleon', *Journalism Quarterly*, 2 (Winter 1966), pp. 715–21.

Humm Cormier, Leslie, *et al.*, *All the Banners Wave* (Providence, R.I., 1982).

Kennet, Lee, 'Le Culte de Napoléon aux Etats-Unis jusqu'à la

Guerre de Sécession', *Revue de l'Institut Napoléon*, 124 (1972), pp. 145–56.

Lote, Georges, 'La mort de Napoléon et l'opinion bonapartiste en 1821', *Revue des études napoléoniennes*, 21 (July 1930), pp. 19–58.

Lyons, Martyn 'What did the peasants read? Written and printed culture in rural France, 1815–1914', *European History Quarterly*, 7: 2 (1997), pp. 165–97.

Meynier, Albert, 'Levées et pertes d'hommes sous le Consulat et l'Empire', *Revue des études napoléoniennes*, 30 (1930), pp. 26–51.

Morvan, Jean, *Le Soldat Impérial* (Paris, 1904).

Mumford Jones, Howard, and Daniel Aaron, 'Notes on the Napoleonic legend in America', *Franco-American Review*, 43 (January 1937), pp. 10–26.

Newman, Edgar L., 'What the crowd wanted in the Revolution of 1830', in John Merriman, ed., *1830 in France* (New York, 1975), pp. 17–40.

Reeves, Jesse S., *The Napoleonic Exiles in America* (Baltimore, 1905).

Tulard, Jean, *La vie quotidienne des Français sous Napoléon* (Paris, 1978).

Vallaux, Camille, 'La Légende Napoléonienne aux Etats-Unis', *Mercure de France*, 15 January 1925, pp. 289–307.

Vidalenc, Jean, *Les Demi-Soldes* (Paris, 1955).

Woloch, Isser, *The French Veteran from the Revolution to the Restoration* (Chapel Hill, N.C., 1979).

Woloch, Isser, 'Napoleonic conscription: state power and civil society', *Past and Present*, 111 (May 1986), pp. 101–29.

Zajewski, Wladyslaw, 'Le Culte de Napoléon à Dantzig', *Revue d'histoire moderne et contemporaine*, 23 (1976), pp. 556–72.

Chapter 7: The Great Man meets the twentieth century

Alexander, R.S., '"No minister": French restoration rejection of authoritarianism', in L. Riall and D. Laven, eds, *Napoleon's Legacy* (Berg, 2000), pp. 29–47.

Armstrong, H.C., *Grey Wolf* (London, 1935).

Arnold, Eric A., *Fouché, Napoleon and the General Police* (Washington, 1979).

Bergeron, Louis, *France under Napoleon* (Princeton, N.J., 1981).

Brown, Howard G., 'From organic society to security state: the war on brigandage in France, 1797–1802', *Journal of Modern History*, 69 (December 1997), pp. 661–95.

Bruun, Geoffrey, *Europe and the French Imperium 1799–1814* (New York, 1938).

Carrington, Dorothy, *Napoleon and his Parents: On the Threshold of History* (Harmondsworth, 1984).

Cobban, Alfred, *A History of Modern France*, II (Harmondsworth, 1961).

Corrado Pope, Barbara, 'Revolution and retreat: upper-class French women after 1789', in Carol R. Berkin and Clara M. Lovett, eds, *Women, War, and Revolution* (New York, 1980), pp. 215–36.

Dodwell, Henry, *The Founder of Modern Egypt* (Cambridge, 1931).

Doyle, William, *Origins of the French Revolution* (Oxford, 1999).

Fleming, Katherine E., *The Muslim Bonaparte: Diplomacy and Orientalism in Ali Pasha's Greece* (Princeton, N.J., 1999).

Flower, Raymond, *Napoleon to Nasser* (London, 1972).

Ford, Franklin L., 'The Revolutionary–Napoleonic era: how much of a watershed?', *American Historical Review*, 69: 1 (October 1963), pp. 18–29.

Ford, Franklin L., *Europe 1780–1830* (Longman 1970).

Freud, Sigmund, *Letters of Sigmund Freud*, ed. Ernst L. Freud (New York, 1960).

Freud, Sigmund, *The Standard Edition of the Complete Psychological Works of Sigmund Freud*, ed. James Strachey (London, 1966–74).

Furet, François, *Revolutionary France 1780–1880* (Oxford, 1996).

Gershoy, Leo, *The French Revolution and Napoleon* (New York, 1964).

Goldschmidt, Arthur, *Modern Egypt* (Boulder, Colo., 1988).

Groag Bell, Susan, and Karen M. Offen, *Women, the Family, and Freedom* (Stanford, Calif., 1983).

Hartley, Samantha, 'Not a "women's issue": divorce and the family as a political background for secularizers and Catholics from 1792 to 1816' (M.A. dissertation, University of Victoria, 1999).

Hufton, Olwen, *The Prospect Before Her* (New York, 1996).

Hunt, Lynn, *The Family Romance of the French Revolution* (Berkeley, Calif., 1992).

Johnson, Douglas, *Guizot* (London, 1963).

Jung, Carl G., *The Development of Personality* (Princeton, N.J., 1954).

Jung, Carl G., *Two Essays on Analytical Psychology* (Cleveland, 1967).

Jung, Carl G., *The Symbolic Life* (Princeton, N.J., 1976).

Kazancigal, Ali, and Ergun Ozbudun, eds, *Atatürk: Founder of a Modern State* (London, 1981).

Kinross, Lord, *Atatürk* (London, 1964).

Landau, Jacob M., ed., *Atatürk and the Modernization of Turkey* (Boulder, Colo., 1984).

Landes, Joan B., *Women and the Public Sphere* (Ithaca, N.Y., 1988).

Laven, David, and Lucy Riall, eds, *Napoleon's Legacy* (London, 2000).

Lefebvre, Georges, *Napoleon* (New York, 1969).

Lewis, Bernard, *The Emergence of Modern Turkey* (Oxford, 1968).

Markham, F.M.H., *Napoleon and the Awakening of Europe* (London, 1966).

Michelet, Jules, *The People*, trans. John P. McKay (Chicago, 1973).

Michelet, Jules, *Oeuvres Complètes*, ed. Paul Viallaneix, XXI (Paris, 1982).

Parker, Harold T., 'The formation of Napoleon's personality: an exploratory essay', in Harold T. Parker, ed., *Problems in European History* (Durham, N.C., 1979), pp. 72–88. Also in *French Historical Studies*, 7 (1971), pp. 6–26.

Parker, Harold T., 'Why did Napoleon invade Russia?', *Consortium on Revolutionary Europe 1750–1850, Proceedings 1989* (1990), pp. 80–96.

Parker, Harold T., 'Napoleon and the values of the French army: the early phases', *Proceedings of the Annual Meeting of the Western Society for French History*, 18 (1991), pp. 233–42.

Paterson Jones, Proctor, ed., *Napoleon: An Intimate Account of the Years of Supremacy 1800–1814* (San Francisco, 1992).

Perrot, Jean-Claude, and Stuart Woolf, *State and Statistics in France, 1789–1815* (London, 1984).

Phillips, Roderick, *Putting Asunder* (Cambridge, 1988).

Richardson, Frank, *Napoleon: Bisexual Emperor* (New York, 1973).

Richmond, J.C.B., *Egypt 1798–1952* (London, 1977).

Rose, R.B., 'Feminism, women and the French Revolution', *Historical Reflections*, 21: 1 (1995), pp. 187–205.

Seward, Desmond, *Napoleon's Family* (London, 1986).

Silvera, Alain, 'The first Egyptian student mission to France under Muhammad Ali', in Elie Kedourie and Sylvia G. Haim, eds, *Modern Egypt* (London, 1980), pp. 1–22.

Soboul, Albert, 'Le héros, la légende et l'histoire', *La Pensée*, 143 (1969), pp. 37–61.

Soboul, Albert, *Le Directoire et le Consulat* (Paris, 1972).

Soboul, Albert, *Le Premier Empire* (Paris, 1973).

Tocqueville, Alexis de, *The Old Régime and the French Revolution* (Garden City, N.Y., 1955).

Tocqueville, Alexis de, *Democracy in America* (New York, 1961).

Vatikiotis, P.J., *The Modern History of Egypt* (London, 1969).

Weber, Max, *Economy and Society*, ed. Guenther Ross and Claus Wittich (New York, 1968).

Young, Norman, *The Growth of Napoleon: A Study of Environment* (London, 1910).

Chapter 8: Napoleon and Europe: conqueror or unifier?

Blanning, T.C.W., *The Origins of the French Revolutionary Wars* (London, 1986).

Clark, Christopher, 'The wars of liberation in Prussian memory: reflections on the memorialization of war in early nineteenth-century Germany', *Journal of Modern History*, 68 (September 1996), pp. 550–76.

Connelly, Owen, *Napoleon's Satellite Kingdoms* (New York, 1965).

Ellis, Geoffrey, *Napoleon's Continental Blockade: The Case of Alsace* (New York, 1981).

Ellis, Geoffrey, *The Napoleonic Empire* (Atlantic Highlands, N.J., 1991).

Fregosi, Paul, *Dreams of Empire: Napoleon and the First World War, 1792–1815* (London, 1989).

Harvey, A.D., *Collision of Empire: Britain in Three World Wars, 1793–1945* (London, 1992).

Hobsbawm, E.J., *Nations and Nationalism since 1780* (Cambridge, 1990).

Kennedy, Paul, *The Rise and Fall of the Great Powers* (London, 1989).

McKay, Derek, and H.M. Scott, *The Rise of the Great Powers 1648–1815* (London, 1983).

Schroeder, Paul W., *The Transformation of European Politics 1763–1848* (Oxford, 1994).

Woolf, Stuart, 'French civilization and ethnicity in the Napoleonic Empire', *Past and Present*, 124 (1989), pp. 96–120.

Woolf, Stuart, 'The construction of a European world-view in the Revolutionary–Napoleonic years', *Past and Present*, 137 (1992), pp. 72–101.

Index

Printed in the United States
200811BV00002B/10/A

9 780340 719169